A

Grimms' Bad Girls and Bold Boys

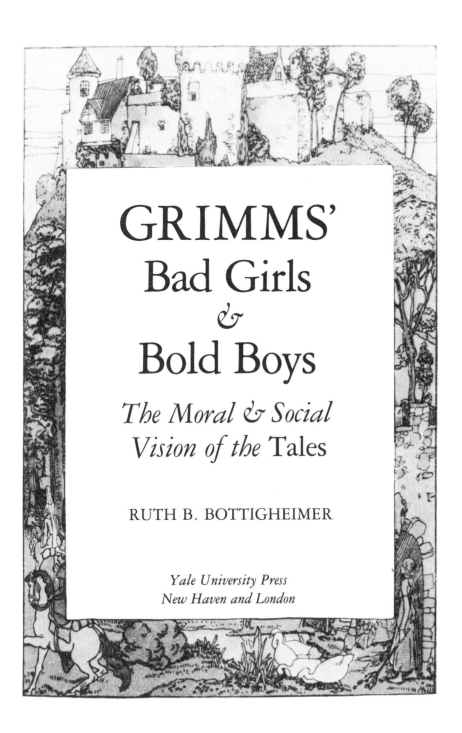

GRIMMS'
Bad Girls
&
Bold Boys

The Moral & Social
Vision of the Tales

RUTH B. BOTTIGHEIMER

Yale University Press
New Haven and London

The decoration on the title page is taken from an illustration of "The Goosegirl" by Heinrich Vogeler-Worpswede, in *Kinder- und Hausmärchen* (Leipzig, 1907).

Designed by Nancy Ovedovitz and set in Garamond No. 3 type by Keystone Typesetting Company, Orwigsburg, Pennsylvania. Printed in the United States of America by Thomson-Shore, Inc., Dexter, Michigan.

Library of Congress Cataloging-in-Publication Data

Bottigheimer, Ruth B.
    Grimms' bad girls and bold boys.
    Bibliography: p. 193
    Includes index.
    1. Kinder- und Hausmärchen.   2. Psychoanalysis and
literature.   3. Sex role in literature.   I. Title.
PT921.B67   1987   398.2'1'0943   87–2219
ISBN 0–300–03908–5 (cloth)
ISBN 0–300–04389–9 (pbk.)

The paper in this book meets the guidelines for permanence and durability of the Committee on Production Guidelines for Book Longevity of the Council on Library Resources.

10   9   8   7   6   5   4   3   2

Dedicated in loving and grateful memory to

Edna Gabell Wiest Ballenger
1911–1981

and

Louis E. Ballenger
1909–1977

Contents

Preface

his is a literary study of a remarkable nineteenth-century text, *Grimms' Tales*, the *Kinder- und Hausmärchen gesammelt durch die Brüder Grimm*. It attempts a content analysis of the *Tales'* 211 discrete units, which consist of a welter of individually inconsequential but collectively significant details comprising plot, motif, image, and dialogue. By focusing on the narrative and textual context in which motifs, themes, and events are set and by correlating and analyzing heretofore unexplored affinities among motifs—rather than their simple occurrence—it is possible to discern coherent patterns and to ascertain the premises on which the collection rests, which are nowhere articulated but everywhere apparent.

As a text, *Grimms' Tales* can be viewed from numerous perspectives, depending on the reader's predisposition and interests. Four perspectives have dominated *Märchen* research in the recent past: Freudian, Jungian, Marxist, and feminist. In general, Freudian interpreters of *Grimms' Tales* interpret motifs as they occur individually, with exegetic efforts centered on sexual and social maturation. Jungian interpreters understand specific motifs as being embedded within broader contexts, and in so doing they scrutinize the cross-cultural significance of motif complexes. Their studies typically relate literary data to classic texts, as well as to exotic cultural patterns. Marxist critics assert and assess the socializing uses to which literary texts can be and have been put; and feminist interpreters bring a special sensitivity to gender associations to their readings of the *Tales*.

My own focus was undoubtedly set by what I had read about *Grimms' Tales* before I began this study, for I am certain that the questions I raised shaped themselves as part of a continuing though unspoken dialogue with commentators and interpreters who precede me. Several readings of *Grimms' Tales* gave me a sense of the issues that pervade the collection, and I began to ask questions for which the available literature provided no satisfactory answers.

One's interests exert both an inclusive and an exclusive influence, and I do not note every theoretically possible category in *Grimms' Tales*. For example, I largely ignore horticultural, architectural, musical, or zoological references. I also read past questions of color, shape, and texture, which have been treated extensively by Max Lüthi. Whenever I perceived a jarring inconsistency between my reading of a tale and that offered in received scholarship, I set up a category for further examination, as, for instance, when I began to notice patterns in discourse that didn't tally with what I had been led to expect by previous analyses of Wilhelm Grimm's literary style. It is principally though not exclusively my sense of inadequate, incomplete, or misleading treatments of specific material that determines the subject matter of this study.

My basic premise is that *Grimms' Tales* is a historical document with its roots firmly in nineteenth-century Germany, an assumption that both Freudians and Jungians would dispute to a greater or lesser degree. I reject Freudian interpretations insofar as they assert the ahistoricity of the text; and while I do not subscribe to the Great Mother thesis of Jungian provenance, I value and sometimes utilize the painstakingly assembled collections and collations of data on which Jungian interpretations are based.

Methodology and perspective have quite different significance. Methodology involves the way in which one goes about gathering, sorting, and analyzing information, and to this end I employ a variety of techniques, borrowing freely from relevant disciplines. This releases me from the constraints imposed by a single approach to many different kinds of evidence, since certain methodologies enable the scholar to pursue avenues of inquiry that others do not. In this effort I have benefited immeasurably from careful readings by colleagues in several disciplines: anthropology, linguistics, history, folklore, and literature. Methodologically, rudimentary quantification coexists with close reading in this study, and both keep company with sociohistorical and linguistic approaches.

Although my goal is to provide a content analysis of *Grimms' Tales*, I have not excluded an interpretive component. The motifs of the tales are, with some reservations, identifiable from Thompson's *Motif Index;* yet without a clear understanding of the literary context in which these motifs function, such listings remain empty bits of information. Furthermore, it seems necessary to treat motifs and themes not as isolated units but as part of an entire structure. Therefore I deal with motifs and themes collectively rather than individually as manifestations of a catalogue of transcendent folk and fairy tale motifs and tale types. For instance, by putting together the information about work and its reward in many tales it is possible to arrive at new conclusions about how work is viewed in *Grimms' Tales*. My study rarely refers either to the Aarne-Thompson *Index of Tale Types* or to the Thompson *Motif Index of Folk-Literature* and only occasionally draws on the notes of Bolte-Polívka, although variants are considered insofar as they illuminate Wilhelm Grimm's intentions or editorial actions. I also want to understand the implications of apparently contradictory inferences that can be made about women's association with nature. Sometimes dominating natural forces, at other times dominated by them, women appear in problematic conjunction with nature throughout the collection, a puzzle, which yields some answers to aggregate analysis.

In a few cases I include illustration histories because of the peculiarly powerful transforming effect illustrations have on readers' comprehension of texts. This represents an area of inquiry that I hope to be able to pursue in greater detail at a later date. I also occasionally incorporate material from the editorial development of *Grimms' Tales,* because the steady movement toward a specific resolution often throws the end result into high relief, and in several chapters I discuss a tale's cultural origins or surroundings to illuminate its content. The scholar must proceed very cautiously with the material in *Grimms' Tales.* Virtually any point of view, from serious to outrageous, can be—and has been—proven with isolated examples from the collection, because its thematic breadth and parabolic style allow the text to be construed to corroborate nearly any theoretical construct. It is for precisely this reason that I adopted a methodology that requires multiple confirmation. Its conclusions consist, in part, of composite images arrived at additively, not from a single tale but from many tales within the collection.

In this study I am interested in the motivations underlying the use of individual motifs. I take up where Stith Thompson left off in *The Motif Index of Folk-Literature* and implement Vladimir Propp's suggestions in *The Morphology of the Folktale.* Thompson himself acknowledged that "no attempt has been made to determine the psychological basis of various motifs or their structural value in narrative art."[1]

Readers familiar with the debate about which of the two brothers was responsible for editing the collection may well be curious about my preference for the plural form *Grimms' Tales.* Certainly the German title page has credited both brothers from the First Edition (1812) onward with its bulky title: *Kinder- und Hausmärchen gesammelt durch die Brüder Grimm* (Nursery and Household tales Collected by the Brothers Grimm). Both Jacob and Wilhelm contributed to this volume, but as correspondents sent tales to the brothers in response to Jacob's circular calling for legends, tales, and proverbs, it was Wilhelm who undertook their sorting, collation, and final preparation for publication, and in succeeding years as Jacob's and Wilhelm's scholarly interests diverged, it was Wilhelm who shepherded the tales through subsequent revisions, enlarging the collection until it finally reached the total of two hundred for which he seemed to have been aiming—even though he had to have two no. 151s to keep to the limit. Jacob asserted, however, that he had done as much as Wilhelm had in developing the collection, and there is good

---

1. *Folklore Fellows Communications* 106 (Helsinki: Suomalainen Tiedeakatemia, 1932), 3. (Hereafter FFC.) This statement disappears from the revised edition of the *Motif Index of Folk-Literature* (1955), but the fact remains.

reason to infer his active participation in later years. My working assumption is that Wilhelm Grimm is solely responsible for the style of this collection, but that Jacob Grimm continued to funnel material to his brother as he unearthed it in his own archival work. This assumption underlies an inquiry that I hope to develop in a subsequent study, which will trace, analyze, and account for shifts in style and content from the earliest notations to the final Large Edition of 1857, the edition that has served as the source for nearly every subsequent reprinting of *Grimms' Tales*.[2]

What the 1857 edition contains is of the utmost importance, for it is the locus classicus commonly acknowledged to have been one of the most powerful formative influences on generations of German, European, and American children in the nineteenth and early twentieth centuries as well as a clear reflection of children's (or adults') psyches. These twin assumptions appear to be mutually contradictory, and for a variety of reasons, which I discuss in chapter 2, I conclude that the premise about the tales' mirroring psychic development is substantially flawed.

The more closely one reads the literature of fairy tale scholarship, the more one realizes that, although it has long been hinted at or approached by social historians, feminists, Marxists, and teaching professionals, a systematic revisionist inquiry about the moral and social values and vision inhering in *Grimms' Tales* has yet to be undertaken.[3] Assertions abound, recriminations are tossed about, and one approach or another is either enthusiastically embraced or curtly dismissed. Numerous scholars have addressed the question of stylistic development in the *Tales,* have counted conjunctions, numbered paragraphs, and evaluated the folk quality of discourse. Others have tabulated shifts from indirect to direct speech but have never asked who speaks or how much. Generalizations about the content and meaning of the *Tales* often serve up a summation of the author's convictions based on a confirmatory sampling. Yet *Grimms' Tales* consists in its entirety of more than two hundred tales to which are appended ten religious legends: a proper analysis of content must consider the entire document. This is the task I have set myself. I try to read *Grimms' Tales* with as few preconceptions as possible although, like all scholars, I cannot escape all the assumptions of my place and time. My conclusions about gender distinctions with reference to isolation, eroticism,

2. *Grimms' Tales* appeared both in the so-called Large Edition (Grosse Ausgabe), intended for a scholarly audience, and in a Small Edition (Kleine Ausgabe) for a youthful readership between 1812 and 1858.

3. See, for instance, Rudolf Schenda, "Prinzipien einer sozialgeschichtlichen Einordnung von Volkserzählungen": "Trotz dieser Schwierigkeiten plädiere ich für eine verstärkte sozialhistorische Interpretation von Volkserzählungsinhalten . . . im Rahmen eines multidimensionalen Forschungsansatzes . . ." (190). ("Despite these difficulties, I plead for increased social-historical interpretation of folk tale content . . . within the framework of interdisciplinary research efforts.")

Christianity, laying spells, speech, and the transformation of power arise from the patterns that emerge from piecing together overlapping motifs and themes, the same method I use in conjunction with other categories, such as work, money, and anti-Semitism.

Because the issues discussed belong to the study of German language and literature, as well as to history, anthropology, folklore, and women's studies, this book is addressed to readers in several disciplines. To make the primary material as accessible as possible both to English-speaking and to German-speaking readers, quotations from *Grimms' Tales* appear in both languages in the text. There are currently two easily available translations of the complete collection. What Ralph Manheim's translation offers by way of grace, the Margaret Hunt/James Stern translation (*Grimm's Fairy Tales,* New York: Pantheon, 1944, 1972) makes up for in word-for-word translation. Therefore (with the kind permission of the publishers) I have used the Hunt/Stern translation for the sake of non-German readers, since it places the English-speaking reader as close as possible to the German original. Where it falls short, I have altered the text and signal the change with my bracketed initials. All English renderings of the 1857 Final Edition come from this translation; all other translations, from Grimm or other sources, I undertook myself.

Why read *Grimms' Tales* at all, if the content is as gloomy in terms of gender and social antagonisms as I depict it? The individual tales are good yarns, which also open doors to other national traditions, for as a country with few natural boundaries to the east, north, or west, Germany shares in an international storytelling repertoire that is richly represented in the collection. And finally, to the extent that the nineteenth century is still our intellectual and emotional homeland, the tales tell many of us where we have come from.

I hope that this book will contribute new ways of looking at *Grimms' Tales* to *Märchen* research: aggregate analysis of motifs and themes and close scrutiny of the language in which the tales are told. The five-person dramatis personae discussed in the appendix also offers a different means of probing the tales, as does the interdisciplinary approach of the study as a whole.

I did not have the good fortune to have at my disposal the *Enzyklopädie des Märchens* (*EM*), a magnificently comprehensive reference work, when I was writing this study, but I include references to articles therein that illuminate and/or extend material I analyze here. As additional volumes appear, the *EM* will offer greater opportunities for quick and efficient review of existing research on specific topics.

Acknowledgments

The research on which this book rests began in 1979 as an attempt to account for the characteristics and associations of witches and witchlike figures in

Grimms' Tales. Subsequent research was based on library and archival work that owes much to the willing helpfulness of many people whom I should like to thank here: Margaret Coughlin of the Library of Congress; the staff of the Fondation Bodmer in Geneva; the staff of the Inter-Library Loan Services at Firestone Library, Princeton University, and at Melville Library, the State University of New York at Stony Brook; Klaus Doderer and Ingeborg Wernicke of the Institut für Jugendbuchforschung in Frankfurt am Main; Dr. Willi Stubenvoll of the Verwaltung der staatlichen Schlösser und Gärten Hessen, Bad Homburg vor der Höhe; the staff of the Manuscript Collection of the Preussischer Kulturbesitz in Berlin; Dr. Hans-Heino Ewers, Bonn; Dr. Dieter Hennig and Ursula Lange-Lieberknecht at the Brüder Grimm-Archiv, Cassel; and Dr. Vera Leuschner, an independent scholar at the Grimm-Gesellschaft, Cassel. The staff of the software company The Mark of the Unicorn were uniformly helpful and gracious in illuminating the workings of The Final Word, the word processing program I used.

The painstaking textual publications by Heinz Rölleke of the Bergische University in Wuppertal immeasurably ease the process of research for Grimm scholars who live beyond easy reach of German and Swiss archives. He is owed a great debt of gratitude for his past and continuing publication of editions of *Grimms' Tales* that are either unique, like the Ölenberg MS and the First Edition with its marginalia; no longer widely available, like the Second Edition of 1819, which marks the beginning of the familiar textual tradition for many of the tales; or difficult to locate, like the Large Edition of 1837.

I am greatly indebted to friends and colleagues who have read individual chapters of the manuscript in early or final form: Ruth K. Angress, University of California, Irvine; Shirley Ardener, Center for Cross-Cultural Research on Women, Oxford; Karl S. Bottigheimer and Ann Geneva, Department of History, and Barbara Elling, Department of Germanic and Slavic Languages and Literatures, State University of New York at Stony Brook; Linda M. Dégh, Folklore Institute, Indiana University; James W. Fernandez, Department of Anthropology, University of Chicago; Cheris Kramarae, Department of Speech Communication, University of Illinois at Urbana; Elfriede Moser-Rath, Göttingen University; Maria M. Tatar, Harvard University; and Jack Zipes, University of Florida; Gainesville. Lutz Röhrich, University of Freiburg, and Rudolf Schenda, University of Zurich, each made bibliographical suggestions that I found extremely helpful. I would like to express my particular gratitude to Hans-Jörg Uther, Project *Enzyklopädie des Märchens,* Göttingen University, who read the entire manuscript, offered learned and valuable suggestions and criticism, and guided me to critical material not readily—or at all—available in the United States. I would also like to thank Jean Aroeste of Firestone Library, Princeton University, whose boundless bibliographic erudition made it possible to track down elusive publications and information.

One chapter of this study has appeared in published form: "Tale Spinners: Submerged Voices in Grimms' 'Fairy Tales'" in the *New German Critique;* and part of another, "Natural Powers and Elemental Differences," will appear in *Cahiers de littérature orale.* Some of the material found in chapters 4–7 appeared in much abbreviated form as "Silenced Women in the Grimms' *Tales:* The 'Fit' between Fairy Tales and Society in Their Historical Context" in my *Fairy Tales and Society: Illusion, Allusion, and Paradigm* (Philadelphia: University of Pennsylvania, 1986) and in a revised, translated version in the *Akten des VII. Internationalen Germanisten-Kongresses der IVG* (Göttingen: Niemeyer, 1986). Portions of this study were presented at conferences or symposia at Princeton University, the University of Illinois, Wayne State University, the University of Minnesota, the State University of New York at Stony Brook, the Modern Language Association, Women in German, the Internationale Vereinigung für germanische Sprach- und Literaturwissenschaft, the Delaware Humanities Forum, and the Secondes Journées d'Etude en Litterature Orale (Paris). Each of these occasions engendered a vigorous dialogue from which I profited as I thought through the questions raised by the material. I am grateful to the Department of Comparative Literature at the State University of New York at Stony Brook in the person of its chairmen, Harvey Gross and Sandy Petrey, and its departmental secretary, Lee Peters, who graciously offered scholarly hospitality during the year in which this book was written. I am indebted to the Department of Germanic Languages and Literatures at Princeton University for a summer travel grant to continue research in German libraries and archives and to the German Academic Exchange Service (DAAD) for supporting travel and research in West Germany.

I would like to thank Ellen Graham and Stephanie Jones of Yale University Press, whose attention to detail has helpfully and sensitively implemented my intentions and improved the book. I would also like to acknowledge the incisive analysis by the Press's anonymous outside reader, who provoked basic rethinking on and reformulation of several issues.

It gives me special pleasure to record my profound gratitude here for the longstanding and affectionate interest in this project demonstrated by my immediate family—Hannah, Nat, and Karl Bottigheimer. Unlike the Grimms' heroines, I have been blessed by a lovingly supportive mother-in-law, Katherine H. Bottigheimer, whom I also thank.

Grimms' Bad Girls and Bold Boys

I

Grimms' Tales and the Three-Thousand-Year Tradition

eople tell tales: peasants and artisans, lords and ladies, mothers and fathers, priests and preachers, girls and boys. The literate read aloud, the gifted recount. Over and over people tell tales whose content seems to remain the same from generation to generation but that nonetheless differs in profound ways. Tales can be coaxed out by the cultural equivalent of the modern tale initiator, "That reminds me of a story . . ."; they may coalesce around a character, for example, Krishna, Ariadne, or Jim Bowie; they may be slotted into a carefully constructed situational context, such as Chaucer's *Canterbury Tales*. These three possibilities begin with a single simple oral tale and move toward a complex highly structured written tradition.

From individual stories tale cycles develop. The *Panchatantra,* recorded approximately two thousand years ago when many of its tales were already ancient, is perhaps the oldest collection available to modern readers. Many of these stories entered the expanding tale tradition of medieval and early modern Europe along trade and war routes from the tenth century onward, enriching the narrative and literary repertoire of European entertainers. The *Panchatantra*'s spread exemplifies the mutual influence of oral and written traditions. In written form a traditional fable collection like the *Panchatantra* can overleap the boundaries of its native culture and penetrate an alien culture, whose literate members may read and recount the tales to an entirely new audience, which then reshapes the tales to fit its own cultural norms, requirements, and clichés.

The collections of Ovid and Apuleius, with their tales of magical transformations, link the ancient Mediterranean world to medieval Europe. Perhaps to redirect the reading public's devotion to Ovid's pagan tales, early Christian commentators glossed them within a Christian tradition; the opening lines of the *Metamorphoses* indicate, they held, that even a pagan believed in a single god who had created the world. Copied and recopied in the Middle Ages, both in Latin and in the vernacular, Ovid's *Metamorphoses* provided basic material for pupils' exercises and courtly romances as well as for frame tale collections.

Entering the European tradition slightly later, *Alf Leila Waleila* or *The Thousand and One Nights* was the next major and enduring collection of tales to expand and nourish European storytelling. Brilliantly crafted and conceived of as a single entity uniting the imaginative variety of its individual tales, it epitomizes the frame tale form. Although individual plots and motifs from the collection entered the European storytelling tradition in the Middle Ages, it was not until Galland's early eighteenth-century French translation that its full range of plots and narrative devices became familiar to European readers of the fantastic.

In the meantime, however, Europeans had raised their own collective narrative genre to a highly organized and internally consistent form, of which the best-known early example, Boccaccio's *Decameron,* appeared in the mid-fourteenth century, followed a few decades later by Chaucer's *Canterbury Tales.* Straparola's mid-sixteenth-century tales, *Tredici Piacevoli Notti,* were immediately disseminated in translation, particularly in France, where an eager reading public had recently devoured Marguerite de Navarre's work, *The Heptameron,* published posthumously in 1558. Basile's *Pentamerone* appeared in the mid-1630s, but its Neapolitan dialect isolated it from the northern European tradition for more than two centuries.[1] The European collections share a similar structure that expresses a common literary theme: a group of men and women thrown together by chance or design who decide to pass the time pleasantly by telling stories.

At the close of the seventeenth century, Perrault's tiny collection, *Contes du temps passé* (1697), set a radically new direction by presenting a group of tales independent of a justificatory frame setting. In strictly formal terms, it cannot truly be said that Perrault offered the tales for their own sake, for in his flattering dedicatory letter to "Mademoiselle" he justifies recounting the fairy tales that follow by claiming that they simply provide a vehicle for the explicit *moralité* appended to each.

Perrault's tales were the simplest representative of a lively French literary tradition.[2] Dozens of volumes of *contes de fées* at the court of Louis XIV originated among the précieuses (literary women of early seventeenth-century French salons), quickly traveled beyond France's borders, and were taken up

1. Wilhelm Grimm had originally intended to include Basile's *Pentamerone* as an integral part of the *Kinder- und Hausmärchen*, but he ultimately decided against it, and Basile's collection was not translated into German until 1846, when Felix Liebrecht published the volume together with a foreword by Jacob Grimm. Jacob's review of this volume is reprinted in his *Kleinere Schriften*, 8:191–201.

2. See Grätz, "Das Märchen in der deutschen Aufklärung."

with alacrity by court and bourgeois circles all over the Germanies, first in French and later in German translation. The *Cabinet des fées,* for example, was published in German in 1761, 1764, and 1770, and Perrault's *Contes du temps passé* in 1780; the Blaue Bibliothek aller Nationen began its series in 1790. Against this backdrop of sophisticated tales of intrigue among fantastic creatures, good and bad fairies, princes and princesses, Johann Gottfried Herder's German call for "a pure collection of children's tales in the right spirit for children's minds and hearts, with all the wealth of magical scenes, gifted as well with the innocence of a youthful spirit," represented a fresh perception of fairy tales as literature for children, which Herder further characterized as a Christmas present for future generations of children.[3] But the adult reading public in Germany had not yet exhausted its own appetite for fairy tales, and the next decades saw the publication of volume after volume of tales whose titles pretended to a national folk character clearly foreign to their actual contents. Johann Karl August Musäus' *Volksmärchen der Deutschen* (1782–86) appeared; Christian Wilhelm Guenther published *Kindermärchen aus mündlichen Erzählungen;* Benedikte Naubert produced *Neue Volksmärchen der Deutschen* (1789–93); the little book *Ammenmärchen* (1791–92) appeared and was attributed to Christian August Vulpius, Goethe's brother-in-law. The long procession of fairy tale books continued with Johann Gottlob Muench's *Märleinbuch für meine lieben Nachbarsleute* (1799), an anonymously produced *Feenmährchen* of 1801, Ludwig Tieck's *Volksmärchen,* and Albert Ludwig Grimm's *Kindermärchen* (1809). Each of these collections consisted of literary fairy tales, often substantially reworked, but always based on long and convoluted plots developed around magical themes and recurrent motifs.

Jacob and Wilhelm Grimm nowhere speak of tales remembered from their own youth, and it is unlikely that any of the collections of fairy tales popular in eighteenth-century Germany entered their comfortable but strictly religious and closely governed home. The Grimms, despite their privileged childhood, were exposed directly to the major political traumas of the day. The French Revolution of 1789, which was followed by grisly reports of the executions of Thermidor, affected Wilhelm's young imagination. His earliest extant watercolor drawing depicts a bloody scene from Louis XVI's execution, as his head is held aloft before the gathered mob.[4] Nor could the thick stone walls surrounding the Grimms' official residence in Steinau protect the children from the frightening sight of marauding French troops on the Frankfurt–Leipzig highway.

When Jacob and Wilhelm were eleven and almost ten respectively, their father's sudden death declassed the entire family in one stroke. Poverty replaced position, and they had to exchange their commodious official resi-

---

3. *Adrastea,* II, 6, in Herder's *Werke,* 14:235.
4. Schloßarchiv, Bad Homburg v.d.H., Watercolor 1.3.131.

dence for humble quarters in Steinau. First Jacob and then Wilhelm was sent off to school in Cassel where they boarded, sharing a bed, at the home of the court cook. As students in Marburg, still sharing a room but with their own beds, they were only slightly more comfortable but were free to pursue their developing interest in German medieval literature alongside their legal studies and to form attachments to friends and mentors.

Their return to Cassel at the conclusion of their studies plunged them back into the world of French–German conflict. Napoleon's brother, Jerome, took up residence in Cassel as the King of Westphalia, forcing Jacob's tightfisted patron, Elector Wilhelm I of Hesse-Cassel, into exile. Between 1806 and 1813 both brothers chafed under the constraints of immediate and inescapable French rule, and during this period they began to collect the tales that formed the basis of their pioneering volume, *Kinder- und Hausmärchen*, known variously to subsequent English-speaking readers as *Grimm's Fairy Tales*, *The Household Tales*, *Nursery and Household Tales*, even as *Grimms' Tales for Young and Old* and *Gammer Grethel's Tales*.

In the beginning the Grimms were neither first nor foremost among their German contemporaries in their concern for collecting German oral narratives. In 1806 Karl Teuthold Heinze had placed an article in a German newspaper, a "suggestion for gathering German folktales . . . completely without any romantic prettifications or additions . . . to be collected and written down." Further, "all foreign admixture and embellishment [was] to be removed."[5] The Grimms' own collecting activity seems to have begun the following year, 1807, and it both coincided with and was further stimulated by Clemens Brentano's and Achim von Arnim's publication of folk material in their *Zeitung für Einsiedler*. From then until publication of their volume a little more than five years later, their circle of friends in Cassel added to the growing collection of tales. Both in plot and vocabulary this volume (1812) reflects early nineteenth-century Central German bourgeois experience and values. In their introduction the Grimms themselves called this cheaply printed little book a childrearing manual (*Erziehungsbuch*), an early hint that it offered paradigms for appropriate behavior. At this point Jacob viewed the tales simplistically as part of a stable and continuous oral tradition that had brachiated through millennia and had preserved in variant forms the disparate components of a once coherent mythology,[6] and he prided himself on the

---

5. Newspaper clipping in envelope inside front cover of volume 2 of the Grimms' personal copy of *Deutsche Sagen* in the Nachlaß Grimm, Preußischer Kulturbesitz, Berlin. It reads as follows: "Vorschlag, die Deutschen Volkssagen zu sammeln. Ganz ohne alle romantische Verschönerung und Zuthat müssen diese Deutschen Volkssagen . . . gesammelt und aufgeschrieben werden . . . alle fremdartige Beimischung und Ausschmückung [ist] davon abzuscheiden . . . " It should be noted here that the Grimms used the terms *Märchen* and *Sage* interchangeably in their earliest work.

6. "Ich bin fest überzeugt, daß alle Märchen unserer Sammlung ohne Ausnahme mit allen

faithful simplicity with which the tales had been set down, contrasting them somewhat self-righteously with Clemens Brentano's improvements to the folk songs of *Des Knaben Wunderhorn:*

> He can arrange and decorate everything [as much as he likes], our simple and faithfully collected story will surely shame his every time.

> Er mag das alles stellen und zieren, so wird unsere einfache, treugesammelte Erzählung die seine jedesmal gewißlich beschämen.[7]

The years between 1812 and 1815 brought tremendous alterations in the Grimms' scholarly and personal lives. They had originally intended to translate Basile's *Pentamerone* as the second part of their collection, but with the appearance of their little volume in 1812 people began to send the Grimms stories they had heard or read. And the brothers themselves recorded numerous tales told by Dorothea Viehmann, a market woman from Zwehrn who often stopped at their apartment on the way home from selling her goods in Cassel. In addition, Napoleon's defeat and Jerome's hasty removal from Cassel in 1813 spurred a general outpouring of loyalist and nationalist sentiment, shared by the Grimms, surrounding the return of the Hessian monarch. Jacob was sent off first in the train of Hessian troops pursuing Napoleon's retreating army and later to the Congress of Vienna, while Wilhelm was left alone to edit volume 2 of the *Kinder- und Hausmärchen.*

The Grimms' editorial method expressed their basic belief about folk narratives. They shared in the emerging positivistic credo of an unbroken chain of events, although in their view a constantly branching tradition replaced the image of a single chain. Each branch or twig of tradition preserved a fragment of original myth, which one could approach ever more closely by piecing together variants of a single tale, a method in which the Grimms were well practiced from their painstaking work collating and editing medieval manuscripts. Each slip of paper, each letter from an informant, each fragment from early printed books and sermons provided a piece of the puzzle. It is significant for the editorial development of the tales in the collection that the

---

ihren Umständen schon vor Jahrhunderten erzählt worden sind. Nur nach und nach ist manches Schöne ausgelassen worden." Quoted in Bolte-Polívka, *Anmerkungen zu den "Kinder- und Hausmärchen,"* 4:427. Wilhelm, too, firmly believed that the tales as he recorded them grew out of an oral tradition, specifically, a *German* oral tradition. For instance, Wilhelm lists seven tales from the *Kinder- und Hausmärchen* in an essay with the revealing title, "Übersicht der Märchen, die im *Pentamerone* und in der deutschen Sammlung im Ganzen übereinstimmen" (*Kleinere Schriften,* 2: 221–25). Later he modified this position, adumbrating the concept that certain medieval poetry might derive from oral tradition with a written source to assist the performer's memory. This position no doubt made it easier for him to include numerous tales from published sources in later editions. Wilhelm Grimm develops this idea in his notes to *Der Rosengarten,* published in *Zeitschrift für deutsches Alterthum,* 11:28.

7. Quoted in Steig, *Clemens Brentano und die Brüder Grimm,* 187.

Grimms only considered quantifiable material as relevant, that is, they worked with motifs and never with motivations.

As Wilhelm, in Cassel, was editing volume 2 for publication, Jacob, now in Vienna, was forming the Wollzeilergesellschaft, a small society (comprising thirteen members) of enthusiasts for German folk culture. Its recently discovered constitution, dated December 1814, lists the oral forms to be sought out and recorded and is itself the forerunner of the famous circular letter of 1815 calling for the preservation of folk songs and rhymes, folk tales and fairy tales, jests, puppet theater, customs, superstitions and proverbs.[8] These concerns proved crucial in the final formulation of many of the tales in the collection, for the Grimms essentially redefined German folk culture as emanating from the people rather than filtering outward from their own bourgeois and educated acquaintances. However, they jettisoned only part of the collection's bourgeois beginnings, retaining motifs but shifting motivations and speech patterns in ways that made sense to them. They were not alone in this manner of dealing with folk narrative. Moritz Haupt, submitting a contribution to the collection, wrote, "It would please me greatly if you accepted the Lausitz tales for your new edition. And I anticipate that you will have to improve much in the formulation. Only when I rewrote this tale into a human form from the unbearably jokey version in which I got it, did I come to appreciate your unparalleled narrative mastery."[9]

Thus the tales took shape. They first appeared as a group in 1810, when Wilhelm sent them off to his friends, Achim von Arnim and Clemens Brentano, who were preparing their own collection. Written in brown ink on small sheets of paper, with a wide margin left for notes, comments, and additions, each tale occupies its own piece of paper, the shorter ones on one or both sides of a single sheet, the longer ones taking up both sides of a double folded sheet. Jacob's script is open, Wilhelm's cramped and small.[10]

Georg Reimer published volume 1 of the first edition of 1812, followed by volume 2 in 1815. The two-volume Second Edition (1819) incorporated many changes, particularly in the tales of volume 1. When Edgar Taylor published an illustrated translation of a selection of these tales in England, its commercial success induced Wilhelm to undertake a Small Edition of fifty tales illustrated by his younger brother, Ludwig Emil Grimm. With alterations and additions, the *Kinder- und Hausmärchen* appeared in seventeen editions,

8. See Volker Schupp, "'Wollzeilergesellschaft' und 'Kette.'" The circular letter is reprinted in Jacob Grimm, *Kleinere Schriften*, 7: 593–94; it was also reproduced in facsimile, ed. Ludwig Denecke.

9. Undated letter (probably from the 1840s) from Moritz Haupt to Wilhelm Grimm, Nachlaß Grimm 819, Preußischer Kulturbesitz, Berlin.

10. The original of the Ölenberg Manuscript is in the Bodmer Library in Cologny-Genève outside Geneva; it is transcribed in Rölleke, *Die älteste Märchensammlung der Brüder Grimm*.

large and small, between 1812 and 1858, gaining popularity and increasing in sales through the years.

One of the first attempts to assess the relationship between the Brothers Grimm and their tales grew out of a lawsuit that was brought after Wilhelm's death, when pirated versions threatened to erode the income to Wilhelm's heirs deriving from sales of the *Kinder- und Hausmärchen*. The lawsuit was brought against the publisher of one such edition, Hirzl and Schmidt, by Jacob Grimm and Wilhelm's sons, Hermann and Rudolf Grimm, and the draft of a letter contains the following assessment:

> The recognition of the first instance rests incomprehensibly on two false assumptions: (1) that the plaintiffs are not the authors but only the collectors of the household and nursery tales; and (2) that the assertion of their authorship was not brought in the writ, but only in the counter-plea.
>
> It is acknowledged and recognized throughout Germany that the Brothers Gr. were first intent on the collection, consideration, and publication of legends and tales circulating from time immemorial among the folk and thereby created a completely new branch of our literature which has since grown considerably. Over a number of years they gathered the material for it laboriously and with considerable expenditure, compared countless versions with each other, judged and chose critically, but did not compose. Their collection became the mother of all subsequent collections and continues to claim pride of place among them; in it lies the distinct individuality which authors manifest, [and] if any claim to authorship may be asserted, it rests with them. Not in the sense that they composed and invented an uncomposable, uninventable material, but far more in the higher [sense] that they understood how to save this material from degeneration and how to breathe new life into it. . . . The truth and fidelity of their published material establishes its value and it stands as their complete and well-earned possession.[11]

This letter is meant to define the tales legally, not literarily, but it nonetheless clearly sets forth the terms in which Jacob Grimm understood their, and particularly Wilhelm's, effort. The letter states that this collection legally belongs to them because of the formative effect they had upon it, an evaluation that provides the basic premise of my study, namely, that any consideration of the content of the *Kinder- und Hausmärchen* must include an appreciation of the extent and nature of Wilhelm Grimm's reformulation of the text.[12]

Genre and Terminology

This brief account of tale collections raises a number of questions, the first of which involves the question of genre and appropriate terminology. In the

---

11. Draft of a letter, Nachlaß Grimm 1763, Preußischer Kulturbesitz, Berlin.

12. This subject has been brought to the fore in several recent studies, most notably in Ellis, *One Fairy Story Too Many*.

simplest terms, *Märchen* simply denotes a brief narrative. Before the nineteenth century the many forms of brief narrative were not regularly distinguished from one another terminologically, and *Märchen* was interchangeable with *Sage, Historie,* and *Geschichte* in German criticism and description.[13]

After 1815 Jacob and Wilhelm both understood legends (*Sagen*) as historically or geographically linked narratives, and tales that conformed to their definition of legend were published as *Deutsche Sagen* in 1816–18, immediately after the second volume of the First Edition of the *Kinder- und Hausmärchen* appeared (1815). The Grimms' criteria for including any given tale in *Kinder- und Hausmärchen* were grounded in their years of experience transcribing and publishing medieval German manuscripts. Their operational concept was *maerlin,* the Middle High German designation for a brief narrative of any sort, which they subsequently differentiated into the two categories *Sage and Märchen:* "The fairy or folk tale stands aside from the world in a peaceful undisturbed place, beyond which it does not wander. Therefore it knows neither name nor location nor a particular region, and it is something common to the entire fatherland."[14] From an early point both Wilhelm and Jacob Grimm understood the fairy or folk tale, the Märchen, as isolated from time and place. In Wilhelm's eyes the quality of isolation set it apart from the legend, Sage, and as the decades passed, he wrote this quality into the Märchen, refining them, until—in Max Lüthi's words—the folk tales that made up the Grimms' collection were sufficiently emptied of real world content that they could be referred to as "sublimated."[15]

The Grimms defined the Märchen with reference to its content and its provenance. Beyond the subject of content, which principally occupies me in this study, contemporary folk narrative research has followed many avenues of exploration: style, form and structure, and the narrative situation. The Grimms subscribed to a set of definitions quite different from those of subsequent scholars; their traditional definitions do not overlap neatly with those advanced by critics in Russia, France, Hungary, or the United States, or even with those of later German critics. The contemporary designation, Märchen, comprises many subcategories: anecdotes, etiological tales, animal tales, jests, burlesques, and fairy tales, both folk tales (*Volksmärchen*) and literary fairy tales (*Kunstmärchen*), local legends (*Sagen*) and religious legends (*Legenden*). Most of these subgenres appear in *Grimms' Tales,* with the notable exception of anecdotes and local legends.

Within each national tradition, scholarly and popular treatments of fairy tales divide roughly into three groups: attempts to define the genre, confirma-

13. Rudolf Schenda, "Telling Tales—Spreading Tales: Change in the Communicative Forms of a Popular Genre," in Bottigheimer, ed., *Fairy Tales and Society.* See also Herder's discussion of the Märchen in *Adrastea,* pt. 6.

14. Wilhelm Grimm, "Über das Wesen der Märchen," *Kleinere Schriften,* 1:333.

15. "Sublimation and All-Inclusiveness," in *The European Folktale,* 66–80.

tory criticism of this genre, and interpretations of specific tales in the canon, in particular those that comprise *Grimms' Tales*.[16]

Other characteristics set the fairy and folk tale apart from its fellow minor genres. Magic is often introduced to bring about what can be understood as wish fulfillment: sudden riches, an advantageous marriage for an impoverished heroine or hero, or unlimited food. Folk tales with no magical component generally mock the world as we can imagine it being experienced by the characters within the tales. Religious legends (*Legenden*), as stated above, exhibit a relentlessly teleological focus on death with its heavenly or hellish consequences.

Structurally, fairy and folk tales (*Märchen*) are distinct from legends (*Sagen*). With their adherence to triplet trials, fairy and folk tales require elaborated narrative development, while the emphasis on the uniqueness of an event, which defines legends, necessitates a simpler narrative structure. All of the distinctions made between fairy and folk tales on the one hand and legends on the other assume a supracultural theoretical purity in the genres that does not, in fact, exist—but these distinctions make useful starting points.[17]

More important to this study, however, is the distinction between fairy or folk tales on the one hand (*Märchen*) and the religious legends (*Kinderlegenden*) appended to the collection. These "legends" are not the same as the Sagen so often contrasted with the Märchen.[18] In religious legends, characters typical of fairy tales, such as a mother and her three daughters and a prince, appear along with extremely atypical figures—a holy idiot, an old woman living alone, or a hermit, for example.

What principally separates the ten religious legends from the Märchen that precede them in the Grimms' collection is their teleological thrust. Whereas the folk and fairy tales press on to encounter the next narrative hurdle—marriage, killing a giant, locating a treasure—the religious legends attend to the final questions of death and the afterlife.

Beyond thematic characterizations, a second requirement for the tales in the collection was based on the German language itself. This emphasis emerged from the chaotic years of national humiliation under Napoleon during which the Grimms began to collect their tales. They developed at that time the conviction that a common language defined national identity, and that these tales were, themselves, linguistic monuments of a common culture.

16. In discussing Märchen as a genre, national scholarly vocabularies often do not translate at all well, either figuratively or actually. As a group, Russian *skazki* cannot be superimposed onto *Märchen*, which in turn are hardly identical with *fairy tales* or *contes de fées*.

17. See Ranke, "Kategorienprobleme der Volksprosa"; Ben-Amos, ed., *Folklore Genres*, esp. "Analytical Categories and Ethnic Genres"; Hand, "Status of European and American Legend Study"; Dégh, "Folk Narrative"; Dégh and Vazsonyi, "The Dialectics of the Legend"; Jolles, *Einfache Formen;* Lüthi, *The European Folktale.*

18. For a pithy discussion, see Lüthi, "Aspects of the Märchen and the Legend," in Ben-Amos, ed, *Folklore Genres.*

The persona of the narrator has long occupied fairy and folk tale scholars and buffs, because language, whatever it is taken to signify, requires and presupposes a speaker, and because tales presume a real or fictive narrator. A virtual mythology has grown up around the notion that women have a special inborn capacity to tell stories. Even though deprived of her tongue, Philomela literally weaves her tale of seduction and mutilation in Ovid's *Metamorphoses,* [19] and Boccaccio portrays the archetypal storyteller as "a maundering old woman, sitting with others late of a winter's night at the home fireside making up tales of Hell, the fates, ghosts, and the like."[20] Certainly two of the Grimms' most prolific contributors were women, Marie Hassenpflug and Dorothea Viehmann. Yet the role of narrator has been shared by men and women in the long history of storytelling. Fictive male narrative voices formulate and tell the stories of the *Panchatantra;* a fictive female narrator recounts those of *The Thousand and One Nights.* Male and female figures together recount the *Canterbury Tales,* the *Decameron,* and the *Heptameron,* while real men and women actually composed these compendia. Male priests and preachers of the Counter-Reformation incorporated jests, burlesques, and folk tales into their sermons; female spinners, midwives, and nursemaids were supposed to have provided the voice behind subsequent tales, including the Grimms'. The history of fictive and real storytelling is clearly of mixed gender.

Grimms' Tales inherits earlier assumptions about the female provenance of its stories, though many of them derive individually from male informants. This, like many other aspects of the collection, represents a national belief not uniformly shared by Germany's western or eastern neighbors in contemporary publications. The frontispieces of Edgar Taylor's 1823 and 1826 translations of the tales depict a man reading aloud in volume 1 and a woman recounting in volume 2.[21] In some tales the question of narrative voice is relatively inconsequential, even though the tales traveled a complex narrative route before publication. For instance, male draymen told tales that the young Dorothea Viehmann heard and later recounted to Wilhelm Grimm, who tidied them up for his readership. Identifying the real narrative voice in the spinning tales is crucial, however, because mixed and often contradictory messages emerge from different narrative levels within these tales, and because narrators seem to favor heroic figures of their own sex.[22]

19. Karen E. Rowe, "To Spin a Yarn: The Female Voice in Folklore and Fairy Tale," in Bottigheimer, ed., *Fairy Tales and Society.*

20. *Boccaccio on Poetry,* 54.

21. In "The Tale Occasions," *Folktales and Society* (91), Linda Dégh states that "older and newer collections show that the role of women in storytelling is less significant than that of men."

22. Satu Apo discusses the narrator and the gender of heroic figures in connection with the repertoire of the storyteller, Marina Takalo, in "The Structural Analysis of Marina Takalo's Fairy Tales Using Propp's Model," 156.

The Grimms' scholarly methods set them apart from their many predecessors who created fairy and folk tale compendia. I shall skip over the avowed purpose adumbrated by the authors of tale collections, since more often than not it simply expresses a literary conceit, true to a certain extent even in the case of *Grimms' Tales*. If we take Chaucer as an example, we immediately see that his most apparent creative contribution was the "Prologue," which provides both the frame tale for the collection and individual portraits of the narrators and their accompanying host. His fictive narrators, the company of pilgrims, with their smudged tunics, gap teeth, and ruddy complexions, seem far readier to step off the page into our world than does Dorothea Viehmann, the celebrated source of many of the tales in volume 2 of the Grimms' First Edition. Her real portrait typifies laboring womanhood but does not articulate her individuality, as Chaucer's verbal portraits do. By clearly outlining highly individual narrators, Chaucer provides the rationale for infusing his tales—most of which were culled from an international narrative repertoire—with a psychological piquancy expressing their fictive narrators' style.

Chaucer's method, then, individualizes tales that were already well-known and presents them as they would be told by a specific narrator, who is, in turn, also Chaucer's literary creation. Wilhelm Grimm worked in the opposite direction: he collated individual versions of stories to return to what he imagined to be the tale's core. In terms of their interest in the narrator's effect on the narrative, twentieth-century narrator studies are far closer to Chaucer's six-hundred-year-old concerns than they are to Wilhelm Grimm's.

Grimms' Tales is unique among modern collections of tales, for unlike the other collections discussed, half a century of continuous editing by Wilhelm Grimm produced a collection whose values became ever more internally consistent. The rest of this book investigates the precise nature of those values as they emerge from the 210 tales of the Grimms' *Kinder- und Hausmärchen*.

2

Fairy Tales, Society, and Scholarship

etween fairy tales and society there exists a complex relationship, the nature of which is understood in radically different ways from one discipline to another and from one investigator to the next. Furthermore, the apparent relationship of fairy tales to society shifts according to whether one regards the fairy tale as a record and reflection of society, as a normative influence on its reader or listener, or as a combination of both. Within the context of fairy tales as social records, the existence of specific themes informs us that a given society recognized and addressed these topics, but not how a particular individual regarded them. Too many layers interpose themselves between us and the tale in its oral phase to allow us to infer reliably past individual or group attitudes toward these themes, though it is certainly possible to draw some rough conclusions.

The hallowed iconography of the provenance of *Grimms' Tales* is summed up in (and was perhaps further formed by) L. Katzenstein's group portrait of the Grimms listening intently to Dorothea Viehmann, who sits facing them, telling a tale as she sews. Surrounding her are a mother and infant and a small girl and boy amongst chickens, apples, and sturdy country furniture in the main room of a simple peasant dwelling. Lithographed by the thousands and hung in countless German parlors, the print depicts an event which never took place. Dorothea Viehmann, that prolific source of tales for volume 2 of the *Kinder- und Hausmärchen*, actually recounted them one or two at a time to Jacob and Wilhelm Grimm in the living room of their Cassell home, stopping there after she had sold her goods at the town market and before she returned to her village, Zwehrn, a few miles to the south. But this lithograph does capture the spirit of the Grimms' repeated assertions that these tales welled up from the people and represented a "natural poetry" (*Naturpoesie*). Wilhelm Grimm anticipated the broad variety of interpretive modes that would be addressed to his collection when he stated, "All genuine poetry . . . is capable of the most varied analysis, for since it has emerged from life, it returns to life again and again."[1]

Grimm, as always, here expresses his thoughts in terms of origins. Subsequent literary critics postulate a correlation between literature and life, asserting that literature coordinates its public, uniting the concepts of literature as both a record of and an influence on society. The Grimms' contemporary, Ludwig Bechstein, discusses the ethical value of traditional oral narrative, calling it "holy," "immortal," and "pure" and defining it as a "moral philosophy for the people."[2] A nineteenth-century critic, Edmund Wengraf (1889), discusses the effect of popular literature on its reading public, asserting that it purveys a falsified image of reality to them, and especially to its female readership; while yet a third perspective, that of the readers themselves, emerges from Rudolf Schenda's penetrating analysis of the characteristics of popular literature, which he defines as highly conservative because of its readers' preference for familiar material with which they can easily identify.[3]

The complexity of the relationship between fairy tales and society clearly vitiates a simple equation of fairy tale content with any single cultural entity, whether individual, institutional, or national. Yet fairy tales have frequently been assessed uncritically and sometimes mistakenly as a reliable source of evidence for intrafamilial and social relationships, daily habits, nutritional levels, and psychological realities.[4] The tendency to elevate tales of the common people to a paramount position was evident as early as the eighteenth century, when J. K. A. Musäus wrote (1773) that "they belong to national taste, which never completely degenerates."[5]

Researchers wishing to investigate fairy tales as sources for legal history, social history, or psychology have typically turned to *Grimms' Tales,* despite the fact that it is only one of scores of regional and national fairy tale collections published in the nineteenth and twentieth centuries.[6] This choice, rarely recognized either by authors or by their readers as a conscious decision, derives

---

1. "Über das Wesen der Märchen," *Kleinere Schriften,* 1:335.

2. *Über den ethischen Wert der deutschen Volkssagen* 6–7.

3. The material in this paragraph is drawn from Schenda, *Volk ohne Buch,* especially the Introduction and chap. 5.

4. In "Hessian Peasant Women, Their Families and the Draft," Hermann Rebel and Peter Taylor attempt to investigate peasant mentality from peasant narrative. Their effort falters on the questionable attribution of three of the four tales analyzed. The "Old Marie" they accept as a blacksmith's daughter has been persuasively presented by Heinz Rölleke as an older sister in the bourgeois Hassenpflug family. See Rölleke, "Alte Marie," "The 'utterly Hessian' Fairy Tales by 'Old Marie.'"

5. Quoted in Bolte and Polívka, *Anmerkungen,* 4:80–81.

6. Isolated archaicisms do not provide persuasive evidence for a tale's suitability as a historical, legal, or anthropological source, since archaizing material has all too often been introduced by later narrators or editors. See Moser, "Altersbestimmung des Märchens."

from a cultural designation of the Grimms' enormously popular book as the collection of choice. Positive readership response to *Grimms' Tales* had established the primacy of this collection by the last third of the nineteenth century. Myriad regional and national collections were excluded or ignored, and in the mind of the general reading public in Europe and North America nearly every other published collection was displaced by *Grimms' Tales*.

The glorification and canonization of the Grimms' work began even before its publication, when Clemens Brentano called the growing collection a "treasure" (1807). Eduard Mörike referred to it as a "golden treasure of genuine poetry" in 1842.[7] In the introduction to his anthology of tales, J. W. Wolf speaks (1851) of "the circulation that the *Tales* have found and continue to find, the success that they have enjoyed as a childrearing manual."

In a key that sets the tone for generations of fairy tale interpretation, Wolf continues: "Most fairy tales are documents in hieroglyph, whose enigmatic characteristics we have hardly begun to investigate."[8] With such support, it is hardly surprising that scholars and commentators who have inherited this tradition (and who are sometimes the product of it), automatically turn to *Grimms' Tales* as an unimpeachable source.

Johannes von Mueller, in his *Historische Critik* of 1811, states that fairy tales should be included in the "wisdom of the peoples by which one lives."[9] The very fact that such a statement appeared in a volume published by Cotta, at that time the most prestigious German publishing house and one to which the Grimms themselves unsuccessfully aspired, suggests the position fairy tales occupied in the general intellectual climate of the early nineteenth century.

When Eugen Labes addressed a Gymnasium convocation in the 1880s in ringing nationalistic tones about the abiding importance of the Brothers Grimm for the education of German youth, he claimed that the Grimms were revered because they revealed the German nation's true identity to itself. Carried away by his own rhetoric, Labes compares Jacob and Wilhelm to another famous fraternal pair, the Dioscuri, Castor and Pollux, a horse tamer and master boxer respectively: "In a sweep of victory in the last few decades our German people have regained lost ground; even more, their unity represents a conclusion long yearned for in the establishment of the German empire. . . . Hail to us, that we see such Dioscuri light the way."

Labes incorporates Georg Curtius' designation of the Grimms as "those heroes in the realm of art and scholarship" who knew how to mine pure treasures from the depths of the German folk spirit.[10]

---

7. Quoted in Gerstner, Die *Brüder Grimm*, 138.

8. *Deutsche Hausmärchen* (1851), x, xi.

9. Quoted in Bolte and Polívka, 4:85. (Orig. Tübingen: J. G. Cotta, 1811.)

10. Later published as *Die bleibende Bedeutung der Brüder Grimm für die Bildung der deutschen Jugend*, 1, 26, 28.

Hermann Hesse, among many others, continued this rhapsody in 1915: "Grimms' fairy tales. We may surely inscribe the noble fidelity with which [the tales] are edited into the Germans' album of honor. It is obvious that specific German national characteristics are to be gathered from the content of the tales, but that is not the concern here. The literature of the tales and the legends refers us, often with frightening agreement, to something transcendent, to the very concept of the human race."[11]

The canonization of everything associated with *Grimms' Tales* is a process that continues well into the twentieth century. For example, Georg Textor constructed a family tree in 1965 to prove that the Grimms' chief informant for volume 2, Dorothea Viehmann, was distantly related to none other than Johann Wolfgang von Goethe![12]

Once *Grimms' Tales* had come to be understood in these nationalistically archetypal terms, the collection could easily be understood or misunderstood as an independent source complete in itself, rather than as a collection assembled by human agency. Significantly, this perception developed after Wilhelm Grimm's death, when the collection had been solidified at its canonical two hundred tales with ten appended religious legends, and when his editorial revisions were no longer before the public eye. The collection came to be perceived as a unique source enabling individuals to understand themselves psychologically. Until recently most nonscholarly and some scholarly Western European and American interpretations of *Grimms' Tales* shared one basic premise, sometimes expressed, but usually assumed: namely, that fairy tales exist independently of the variables introduced by individual narrators, the narrative situation, the recorder of the tales, the relationship between narrator and recorder, and/or the participatory effect of the audience.[13] Each of these interpreters bases his or her thought on the certainty of fairy tales' independent existence, thus building an elaborate theoretical edifice on a foundation that ignores their essential historicity. Thus, many researchers have selectively overlooked the nineteenth-century origins and editing of *Grimms' Tales*. For instance, Max Lüthi wrote in 1969 that prince or princess figures represented the prince or princess in each of us that can be developed or revealed.[14] Latter-day Jungian interpreters, exemplified by Marie-Louise von Franz, find that "fairy tales are the purest and simplest expression of collective unconscious psychic processes. Therefore their value

11. Quoted from "Deutsche Erzähler," Gerstner, 138.

12. "Die Ahnen der Märchenfrau."

13. Linda Dégh discusses many of these issues in *Folktales and Society*. With reference to the relationship between them she writes: "The folktale arises from a need experienced at a certain stage of development in human society. It is the circumstances which generate a folktale, which form its conception, its shape, and its narrative style; as long as these circumstances prevail, the folktale will endure" (63).

14. *So leben sie noch heute*, 10.

for the scientific investigation of the unconscious exceeds that of all other material. They represent the archetypes in their simplest, barest, and most concise form. . . . [Fairy tales] mirror the basic patterns of the psyche more clearly [than myths]."[15] This basic premise provides the starting point for numerous Jungian interpretations. Freudian psychologists have also turned to *Grimms' Tales* to illustrate or substantiate their theories of human behavior. Foremost in this group is Bruno Bettelheim's *Uses of Enchantment,* which has deeply influenced subsequent readings of fairy tales.

A lone early voice urging perspective and caution came from Russia, where Isidor Levin wrote in 1963, "Seen in human terms, it is obvious that even the Grimms themselves were socially conditioned by community and tradition."[16] Levin's perspective presupposes generational and regional differentiation in *Grimms' Tales* that sanctions their exploitation as sources for describing society and its institutions. He basically believes that fairy tales reflect the particular community (*Gemeinschaft*) from which they emerge. Among scholars who subscribe to this view, two groups exist. The first holds that individual tales developed at specific moments and passed unchanged through subsequent eras. August Nitschke's *Soziale Ordnungen im Spiegel der Märchen* bases its entire discussion on the premise that certain tales represent ritual behavior specific to particular types of culture, such as herding and agricultural societies. His position in turn rests on the unlikely assumption that ritual from any part of the world may surface in folk narrative thousands of miles distant and that ritual or the memory of ritual within a culture may survive unchanged through centuries or even millennia. Both of these assumptions deny the historicity of important aspects of oral narrative. Nitschke joins Friedrich von der Leyen in this approach although von der Leyen did not assume that fairy tales were impermeable to cultural influence. Even before von der Leyen's work, George Lawrence Gomme had expressed his "profound belief in the value of folklore as perhaps the only means of discovering the earliest stages of the psychological, religious, social, and political history of modern man," a stance which also assumes that fairy tales remained unchanged through vast stretches of time.[17] Freudian and Jungian interpreters also maintain an ahistorical position by positing a transcendent psychological reality which merely expresses itself in the idiom of an age or culture.

All of the approaches discussed above owe their credibility to the primacy of motif cataloguing and research. As long as a tale retained building blocks recognizable as part of a similar tale, the tale was considered to have remained unchanged. The most dramatic example of the blinders that this approach sets on its adherents occurs with reference to Wilhelm Grimm's reformulation of

---

15. *An Introduction to the Interpretation of Fairy Tales,* 1.
16. "Das russische Grimmbild," 399.
17. *Folklore as an Historical Science,* xiv.

"Rumpelstiltskin" (no. 55). In the 1810 version, the heroine's vexing problem grows out of her only being able to produce gold when she spins, whereas in the revised version (1812), her quandary has become the necessity to spin straw to gold—or die. Radically different stories, but since they both concern a girl spinning something to gold, they have represented variants of the same tale to Wilhelm and to generations of subsequent scholars. Although the motifs remain the same, however, motivations reverse, and the tale no longer tells the same story.

In recent scholarship, fairy tales have been analyzed as the speech of everyday reality, showing ambivalence toward official culture, or revealing patterns of culture of which the narrators themselves might not have been consciously aware.[18] Important and sometimes unanswerable questions have to be addressed before one can approach fairy tales knowledgeably. Who tells the tales? That is, whose voice do we actually hear? Gretchen Wild may be the nominal informant for "Our Lady's Child" (no. 3), but fifty years of editing infused the tale with much that was more characteristic of Wilhelm Grimm than of Gretchen Wild and her circle. How much of that editing represented Wilhelm Grimm's personal bias, moral stance, and social concern, and how much simply passed on his society's values? When we say "his society" do we mean his bourgeois circle in Cassel, Göttingen, and Berlin? Or does "his society" include the landless swineherd as well as the rural householder? Whoever the narrator, his or her possible use of ironic distance as a narrative device hangs yet another veil between the scholar and the source.

Ironic distance functions in quite another context when a narrator reformulates text. To produce an ironic effect, the narrator must be certain that the audience is familiar with the text from which he or she deviates. For instance, the mid-nineteenth-century Münchener Bilderbogen no. 122 depicts "Frieder mit der Geige," essentially the same tale told in the Grimms' "The Jew among Thorns" (no. 110). Given the fact that many editions of both the Large and Small Editions had appeared in Germany by then, this poster with its non-Jewish victim represents a tacit commentary on the overt anti-Semitism of the Grimms' version. A different mechanism is probably at work in the post-World War II reformulation (1947) of the same tale in *Grimms Märchen* published under the department of Military Government Information Control in Nuremberg as "The Old Man in the Thornbush."[19] And irony bordering on sarcasm informs Anne Sexton's narrative voice when she calls Snow White a "dumb bunny." Here, the humor resides in the listener's knowing the generally sedate language of the original tale, which makes Sexton's ironic distancing quite apparent to the twentieth-century reader. Identification of

18. See Darnton, "Peasants Tell Tales"; Le Roy Ladurie, *Love, Death and Money in the Pays d'Oc;* Thelander, "Mother Goose and her Goslings"; and Weber, "Fairies and Hard Facts."
19. (Ludwig Liebel, 1947), 86–88.

such distancing in tales told in the past, however, is only possible through exhaustive analysis of publishing history, readership response, and extant variant forms. These limitations inhere in the study of oral narrative in its published forms and attenuate the usefulness of such study for describing and analyzing the societies from which the tales arise.

A very different situation emerges when one looks at *Grimms' Tales* in the context of children's literature. Before fairy tales could leave the realm of adult entertainment, of which they formed a part until the late eighteenth century, and enter the domain of children's literature, childhood itself had to be demarcated as a discrete and identifiable span of time within an individual life.[20] Reading matter in seventeenth-century England, such as John Bunyan's *Pilgrim's Progress,* served young and old alike. Goethe writes at length about his early reading in book 1 of his autobiography, *Dichtung und Wahrheit.* Of the books he perused as a child, only Comenius' *Orbis Pictus* was designed specifically for children, and the multilingual vocabulary listings on its tiny pages were meant to instruct, not to amuse. For literate bourgeois youngsters, Christian Felix Weisse published songs (1765) originally composed for his own children. Ten years later, he launched a newspaper, *Der Kinderfreund,* and in 1784 he published the illustrated, highly moralistic *Briefwechsel der Familie des Kinderfreundes.*[21] Such books and periodicals enjoyed a painfully limited circulation among perhaps as little as 1 percent of the juvenile population of Germany in 1800.

Following the widespread introduction of elementary schooling, with its consequent rise in literacy rates, a veritable explosion of publications for children became available by mid-century; and by the last quarter of the nineteenth century, periodicals and books for children were streaming off Germany's presses in vast numbers. In 1883–87, 2,000 periodicals and 500 illustrated books, of which 200 were fairy tale books, were published. In 1893–97 there were published 2,700 periodicals and 700 illustrated books, of which 400 were fairy tale books.[22] Singly or in series, fairy tales had saturated the market in Germany once *Die blaue Bibliothek* was established in imitation of the *Bibliothèque Bleue* in France. First as *Die blaue Bibliothek aller Nationen oder Teutsche Volksmährchen* and later bearing the formidable title *Die blaue Bibliothek des Feenreichs, der Kobolde, Zwerge und Gnomen oder Deutschlands Zaubermärchen, Hexengeschichten und Schwänke zur ergötzlichen bildenden Erhaltung für die Jugend und Erwachsene,* it distributed fairy tales throughout Germany as far as its pied powder colporters could carry them.[23]

Within children's literature in the nineteenth century, *Grimms' Tales* oc-

---

20. For more on this subject, see Ariès, *Centuries of Childhood.*
21. Hazard, *Books, Children and Men,* 38–41.
22. Schenda, *Volk ohne Buch,* 74–84.
23. Ibid., 303.

cupies a pivotal position. The Grimms appeared to share the contemporary intention that children's literature should improve its readers religiously, morally, and socially (though not necessarily educationally, as in *Orbis Pictus*). Eighteenth- and early nineteenth-century stories generally concluded with a moralistic summation or at the very least a pointed reminder about correct behavior. In contrast to these homiletic appendages, Grimm's endings offer no such overt moralizing. Rather than appearing as discrete behavioral prompts, the precepts in *Grimms' Tales* inhere in the texts themselves. In this sense many of the tales are far more closely related to paradigmatic adolescent *Mädchen-literatur* like the *Trotzkopf* series or *Heidi,* whose heroines' young lives are crowned with marriage, than to *Max und Moritz* or *Struwwelpeter,* whose misdeeds contravene the stern ethic of absolute obedience and lead directly to unrealistically grisly retribution.

From the beginning, the Grimms seemed to anticipate the profound effect their collection would exert on German youth. Their serious purpose apparently led them to object to the spirit of amusement which informed Edgar Taylor's English translation of their tales. When Taylor respectfully posted a copy of his little volume, *Popular German Stories,* to the Grimms in June 1823, he enclosed a letter which referred to his translation as "a small tribute of gratitude for the information and amusement afforded by your entertaining work," adding that he and his assistant had "had the amusement of some young friends principally in view, and were therefore compelled to conciliate local feelings and deviate a little from strict translation."[24] The stiffness of the Grimms' reply may be inferred from the more formal and defensive posture Taylor adopted in his letter accompanying the second volume: "I am afraid you will still think me sacrificing too much to the public taste, but in truth I began the work less as an antiquarian than as one who meant to amuse."[25] Twenty-five years later Mr. Taylor was still apologizing for his mirthful translations: "I hope that you may have seen in my book the evidence of care and thoughtfulness, and have been satisfied with the *general spirit* of the translation. . . . But I am trespassing too long on your patience and indulgence."[26] One can only imagine the blistering replies that transformed Taylor's ingenuous enthusiasm of 1823 into the somber hat-in-hand approach of 1848 and that suggest the seriousness of social purpose that the Grimms attributed to their work.

Wilhelm Grimm's social purpose emerges from the additions and substitutions made in the collection as it grew toward the canonical two hundred tales. Diligent work, gender-specific roles, a generally punitive stance toward girls and women, and a coherent world view conducing to stability in the social fabric take shape over his years of editing and expanding the collection. In one

24. Nachlaß Grimm 1700, Preußischer Kulturbesitz, Staatsbibliothek, Berlin.
25. Ibid.
26. Ibid.

of his rare alterations to the final Large Edition of 1857, Wilhelm substituted "The Moon" (no. 175) for "The Misfortune." "The Moon" provides an excellent example of Grimm's attempt to install morality privately at a time when government was removing it publicly.[27] This tale, similar to many of the Christian morality tales added to the collection in his last years of editorial work, involves the restoration of natural and moral order to a world gone awry. It is typical of Grimm that order is returned to the world by an arch-Christian male figure:

> [St. Peter] reduced the dead to subjection, bade them lie in their graves again, took the moon away with him, and hung it up in heaven.

> [Der heil. (sic) Petrus] brachte die Toten zur Ruhe, hieß sie sich wieder in ihre Gräber legen, und nahm den Mond mit fort, den er oben am Himmel aufhing.

As soon as he learned of the commercial success of Edgar Taylor's 1823 translation of his tales, Wilhelm Grimm approached his Berlin publisher, George Reimer, suggesting a similar illustrated selection. Such a book, Wilhelm was certain, would sell better than did the two-volume sets published in 1812–15 and 1819. The tales Grimm chose to set before young people are especially good examples of what he considered socially desirable and safe for their eyes. In general, the Small Edition includes tales particularly suited to maintaining the status quo, with stories of girls—sweet, marriageable and often suffering—preponderant. Tales of female rascality are notable principally for their absence; the hint of scatology in "Thumbling" (no. 37) is quickly followed by an exclamation about what constitutes proper behavior, while male rascality and its rewards—exhibited for example, in "Brother Lustig" (no. 81)—remain safely out of sight of young eyes in the Large Edition. The roster for the Small Edition is completed by a few overtly Christian tales, two anti-Semitic tales (of the three in the Large Edition), and all the tales most familiar then and now—"The Frog-King" (no. 1), "Hansel and Gretel" (no. 15), "Cinderella," (no. 21), "Snow-White" (no. 53), "Little Red Riding Hood" (no. 26), "The Musicians of Bremen" (no. 27), "Little Briar-Rose (no. 50), and "Rumpelstiltskin" (no. 55). Tales of rebellion and tricksters also remained out of children's hands during Wilhelm's lifetime.

It was generally held in Wilhelm's time that social stability rested on a stable family structure, which the various censorship offices of the German states wished to be presented respectfully, as examples put before impressionable minds might be perceived as exerting a formative influence. True to these beliefs, fairy tales consistently depict role constraints in the relationship between the sexes and they offer the growing child behavioral models[28]

27. For example, the government of Hesse, an area always close to Wilhelm Grimm's heart, had just deleted phrases describing itself as a Christian state in its constitution.
28. This point is developed in Röhrich, *Sage und Märchen,* 22ff.

including a regularly encoded gender antagonism. Typical of scholarship which concludes that the ethic incorporated in *Grimms' Tales* was somehow inevitable is Friedrich Panzer's glorification of male gratification, which was undoubtedly solidly founded in popular perception: "The conclusion and goal of the fairy tale is always marriage, though only in the sense of a happy, soothing situation for the hero, in which his labors find their well-earned reward."[29]

Remarkably little research has addressed the question of the actual effect of fairy tales on children. A tiny move in that direction confirms what common sense would suggest, namely, that fairy tale plot and content rather than the person or medium of narration determine children's perception of the tales.[30]

Familiar and readable, *Grimms' Tales* has been put to use in the home and in school much as the Bible had been formerly, as a familiar text whose exegesis clarified or anchored social values. The tales were an admirably simple instrument for socialization, which could easily be turned to psychosocial, economic, and political purposes.[31] As early as 1850 *Grimms' Tales* appeared on Prussian elementary school syllabi. Tending to avoid tales that incorporated fantasy, such as "Cinderella," "Little Briar-Rose," "Snow-White," and "Rumpelstiltskin," school editions concentrated on those that could serve as a basis for discussions of family life, comradely relationships, and the relationship between master and servant or host and guest.[32] In 1888 Wilhelm Eick's *Das Märchen und seine Stellung im Volksschulunterricht* discussed the value of fairy tales for "moral, religious [education] and ultimately for rearing [children] for the fatherland."[33]

Tome after tome glorified fairy tales as an effective medium for instruction, while in the classroom *Grimms' Tales,* officially chosen over the Bechstein versions, was expounded in minute and dreary detail. A model for the teacher's script was prepared word for word. For instance, "The Star Money" (no. 153) was to be taught as follows:

> *Goal:* (Read or spoken aloud to the assembled class) We are going to discuss a story about a little girl who is richly rewarded.
> 1. *Preparation.* What's your name? Where do you live? Who's with you at home?

29. *Märchen, Sage und Dichtung,* 12. Note particularly the gender specificity of the male hero and his labors, which ignores the existence of those tales in which a female's quest is similarly rewarded.

30. Michael Sahr discusses children's perception of two versions of "Old Sultan" (no. 48), one printed and one televised, concluding that the changes edited into the text, rather than the medium of narration, primarily determines how children perceive the tale. See "Zur Wirkung von Märchen," 351–65. See also Richter and Vogt, eds., *Die heimlichen Erzieher.*

31. This process is discussed at length in Dahrendorf, *Das Mädchenbuch und seine Leserin;* and Zipes, *Breaking the Magic Spell* and *Fairy Tales and the Art of Subversion.*

32. Bastian, *Die "Kinder- und Hausmärchen" der Brüder Grimm* 69.

33. Ibid., 66–67.

Father, mother, brother. What do you receive from your father and your mother? Food, clothing, shelter. (To be determined by additional questions!)

2. *Presentation.* What would you like to know first about the little girl? Her name. I know your name. But I don't know the little girl's name. . . . Now what would you like to know about the little girl? Where she lived. . . . ?

But soon the little girl was in distress. How did that come about? Her father died. She cried a lot. Then things got even worse. What happened? Her mother died too. Why was that so bad for the girl? Her parents gave her everything, a room, a little bed for sleeping, food. . . .

What do you like about the little girl? I like the way *she loved her parents.* What would she have said to her mother, when she was given a new dress, a piece of cake, an apple, and so on? Thank you, dear mother. That's how the little girl showed herself grateful. What do you like about the little girl?—that she was grateful. . . .

What did God like most about her?

That she trusted in God.

That she was compassionate.

All children should be like that. . . .

. . . But how can you show your parents that you love them? Help at home, be tractable [*folgsam*], don't make noise when father wants to rest, don't get your clothes dirty, and so on. . . . [34]

This approach, though perhaps one of the most oppressive, was only one of scores of discussions about *how* to use fairy tales in the classroom. *Whether* to incorporate them into the elementary school curriculum had been decided long before. Their use continued through World War II, when their exegesis took a sinister turn. *Rassenpolitische Unterrichtspraxis* (The Application of Racial-Political Teaching) contained an almost hysterical call to the teaching of fairy tales: "No German childhood without fairy tales; no folk-specific and racial education without them!"[35]

The German pedagogical academy itself published Nazi interpretations of *Grimms' Tales* that included a reading of "Cinderella" in which the prince recognizes and desires Cinderella's purity of blood, whereas her racially alien (*rassenfremd*) stepmother and sisters are justifiably punished.[36]

Although specific goals have changed, contemporary German pedagogy has preserved these methods, and *Grimms' Tales* continues as a text of choice in many German schools. Carefully formulated questions based on fairy tale texts are still used as a device to lead German pupils toward a desired conclusion.[37]

Educators attribute great importance to children's reading material, be-

34. Troll, *Der Märchenunterricht in der Elementarklasse,* 18–21. Quoted in Bastian, 70–71.

35. Published in Leipzig in 1938; quoted in Bastian, 161ff.

36. Schott, *Weissagung und Erfüllung im deutschen Volksmärchen* (1936), 40. See also Zipes, "Grimms in Farbe, Bild und Ton."

37. Kaiser and Pilz, *Erzähl mir doch /k/ein Märchen!* For an implicitly more flexible approach, see Dahrendorf, *Kinder- und Jugendliteratur im bürgerlichen Zeitalter.*

cause of their basic assumption that young minds are open to influence and instruction through what they experience and read. In this context, the content of children's literature is of supreme importance and it has often occasioned trenchant criticism, especially in Germany in the 1970s. Liberal German educators were likely to turn to demystifying and debunking works with titles like *Die heimlichen Erzieher: Kinderbücher und politisches Lernen* (The Secret Educators: Children's Books and Political Learning) or *Böses kommt aus Kinderbüchern* (Bad Things Come Out of Children's Books).[38] In the United States many teachers shunned *Grimms' Tales* in the classroom, but at the same time numerous Freudian and Jungian analysts consulted fairy tales, and in particular Grimms' collection, for paradigms and archetypal situations related to human development.[39]

Scholars have investigated the overall structure of fairy tales, and they have elaborated in detail on the social, historical, and psychological significance of their beginnings and conclusions. But what lies in between—the content of fairy tales—has been largely ignored. In the following chapters, I attempt to provide a thorough content analysis of the entire corpus of *Grimms' Tales*. In my readings of the *Tales* certain themes have emerged recurrently. By analyzing them both in their own context and in relationship to one another, I hope to be able to provide a clear view of the social and moral vision which *Grimms' Tales* presents to all its readers, youthful and mature.

38. Richter and Vogt, eds., *Die heimlichen Erzieher;* Gmelin, *Böses kommt aus Kinderbüchern.*
39. The popularity of their conclusions is reflected in publishing data for Bruno Bettelheim's Freudian analysis, which concludes that children need fairy tales. Between 1976 and 1985 *The Uses of Enchantment* was translated into fourteen languages, including Japanese, Turkish, Swedish, Serbo-Croatian, and Polish.

3

Natural Powers and Elemental Differences

n the prefaces to volumes 1 and 2 of the First Edition (1812, 1815), amalgamated and retained in subsequent editions, Wilhelm Grimm uses a complex metaphor drawn from the natural world to discuss the *Tales*.[1] They were, he said, like ears of grain growing unnoticed by the wayside that the poor peasant harvests for his winter nourishment and for spring seed; they were as pure and natural as rain and dew. Those who worried that material in the tales might be unsuitable for children were told that the collection was "nature poetry" (*Naturdichtung*), and Grimm maintained:

> Nothing can protect us better than Nature itself, which has grown these flowers and foliage in such color and form; whoever because of special requirements finds them noxious can't insist that they should be colored otherwise and snipped. Or again, rain and dew fall as a benefaction for everything on earth, and whoever doesn't risk putting his plants out, because they are too sensitive and might be injured, but rather sprinkles them indoors with lukewarm water, can't demand that rain and dew should therefore absent themselves. Everything natural can be beneficial, and we should focus on that.

> Nichts besser kann uns verteidigen als die Natur selber, welche diese Blumen und Blätter in solcher Farbe und Gestalt hat wachsen lassen; wem sie nicht zuträglich sind nach besonderen Bedürfnissen, der kann nicht fordern, daß sie deshalb anders gefärbt und geschnitten werden sollen. Oder auch, Regen und Tau fällt für alles herab, was auf der Erde steht, wer seine Pflanzen nicht hineinzustellen getraut, weil sie zu empfindlich sind und Schaden nehmen könnten, sondern sie lieber in der Stube mit abgeschreckten Wasser begießt, wird doch nicht verlangen, daß Regen und Tau darum ausbleiben sollen. Gedeihlich aber kann alles werden, was natürlich ist, und danach sollen wir trachten.

Commentators have often noted Grimm's use of natural and elemental imagery in his prefaces and its repeated occurrence within the collection, but a

---

1. These appear in translation in Tatar, *The Hard Facts of the Grimms' Fairy Tales*.

consistent analysis of this imagery in relation to the general ethic and value system of the tales has not yet been undertaken.

Nature flourishes in the tales: birds flutter through the pages, prophesying, assisting, guiding, and suffering; animals speak and are understood; winds respond and trees bend to incantations. The sun, moon, and stars sparkle above, fires crackle and waters of all kinds flow below on earth. In this context the latter two images, fire and water, attract special interest; Wilhelm Grimm alludes repeatedly to water—well water, raindrops, and dew—in his prefaces but never once mentions fire. Because water has itself been so extensively investigated, and so frequently labelled as a quintessentially feminine attribute; because water is basic to life and also to the cosmogonies of so many peoples, it merits close analysis in *Grimms' Tales* together with its antagonistic companion, fire, which has been ignored as a subject for analysis.

Fire can exist as an image of Promethean progress or domestic comfort, as well as a Satanic symbol. Water likewise has both positive and negative connotations as life sustainer and life destroyer, as the Water of Life and as a means of executing criminals (by drowning). Neither fire nor water is a unitary phenomenon in *Grimms' Tales*. Instances of fire range from a flickering candle to the blaze of conflagration. A little boy's unquiet spirit wanders about holding a candle; a guttering candle signifies imminent death both in symbolic space and in the real space of a church.[2] The glowing hearth is where the witch sits and also where she meets her end, as well as where Cinderella (no. 21) and Allerleirauh (no. 65) serve their apprenticeship of woe.[3] The pyre threatens Marienkind in "Our Lady's Child" (no. 3) and the youngest sister in three homologous tales; a conflagration claims the life of a barn owl as well as a wicked wizard and his crew; and incendiary destruction wipes out the realm of Maid Maleen's father.[4]

In Western cultural history fire is viewed with circumspect ambivalence, for the gratifying benefits it brings to humankind are balanced by excruciating punishment for the demigod who carried it hither: the gods of Olympus decreed that Prometheus' bold theft should be punished by unending evisceration, and Zeus arranged that mankind in general should suffer by the creation of woman.[5] *Grimms' Tales* offer no parallel tale about the origins of fire and its consequences for humankind, but the composite image of fire which emerges from an analysis of the tales shows that in their collection it belongs peculiarly to male figures and is closely associated with gender antagonism.

The principal male figure associated with fire in *Grimms' Tales* is the devil. In plot and in metaphor hellish powers are regularly accompanied by the

2. "The Shroud" (no. 109); "Godfather Death" (no. 44); "The Aged Mother" (leg. 8).

3. "Frau Trude" (no. 43); "Hansel and Gretel" (no. 15).

4. "The Twelve Brothers" (no. 9), "The Seven Ravens" (no. 25), and "The Six Swans" (no. 49); "The Owl" (no. 174), "Fitcher's Bird" (no. 46), "Maid Maleen" (no. 198).

5. See Donald Ward, "Feuer."

flickering flames associated with the underworld. One sees the devil sitting on a pile of live coals in a field, and sparks flying from the wheels of his swiftly passing coach; he hires a discharged soldier to tend his fires, and, later, appears as a fiery dragon.[6] In all these cases, fire is devilishly male. Even when the text offers us Frau Trude, womanly both in image and in syntax ("And when she got to her . . ."; "Und als es zu ihr kam . . ."), our eyes and the little heroine's are strangely deceived and see Old Nick instead:

> "Ah, Frau Trude, I was terrified; I looked through the window and saw not you, but, as I verily believe, the Devil himself with a head of fire." "Oho!" said she, "then you have seen the witch in her proper costume."

> "Ach, Frau Trude, mir grauste, ich sah durchs Fenster und sah Euch nicht, wohl aber den Teufel mit feurigem Kopf." "Oho", sagte sie, "so hast du die Hexe in ihrem rechten Schmuck gesehen."

By apparent extension fire also belongs to other male divinities, whether greater or lesser, in *Grimms' Tales*. It emblazons the Trinity in "Our Lady's Child," illuminates God and St. Peter in "The Old Man Made Young Again" (no. 147), and serves St. Peter medicinally in "Brother Lustig" (no. 81). Even among mortals in *Grimms' Tales* fire is a differentially male element. Male characters use fire for their own and others' benefit. It warms the poor boy of "The Golden Key" (no. 200), a tale that Wilhelm Grimm was especially devoted to, and serves as a talisman for the youth who went forth to learn what fear was (no. 4). Stressing the positive attributes of fire, the tales show men using fire to consume evil and to remove enchantments from people and objects. For example, when his royal master returns home with his bride, Faithful John (no. 6) recognizes "a wrought bridal garment" (ein gemachtes Brauthemd) not as the cloth of gold and silver it appears to be, but as a sinister robe made of sulfur and pitch. If his master puts it on, Faithful John knows he will be burned to a crisp, and so the loyal servant pits fire against fire and saves his master by incinerating the enchanted robe.

Burning the skin of his enchantment and thereby breaking a spell is something even a hedgehog can bring about, if he is male: Hans the Hedgehog (no. 108) tells his royal father-in-law to have four men light a fire and throw into it the skin he lays aside each night when he retires. A similar storyline informs "The Little Donkey" [RBB] (no. 144), where the concept of fire as a male domain is accentuated by bypassing women's participation in its use. The king himself lights a fire to burn his son-in-law's enchanted skin to ashes, not when his daughter speaks with him about it, but when the (male) servant does.

Men also sustain themselves by lighting a fire to provide light or to prepare food, a function traditionally in the care of women.[7] Whether by lighting a fire

6. "The Peasant and the Devil" (no. 189); "The Three Apprentices" (no. 120); "The Devil's Sooty Brother" (no. 100); "The Devil and His Grandmother" (no. 125).

7. "The Two Brothers" (no. 60).

to get at honey in a beehive or by using it to boil meat in the kettle, men can use fire to satisfy their hunger.[8]

The fire that nourishes fairy tale heroes can be employed against fairy tale malefactors, and in extreme situations men turn to fire to summarily punish wrongdoers. For example, princes in "The Two Brothers" (no. 60) and "The Pink" (no. 76) each use fire to vanquish their evil opponents. In the first tale, the two "seized the witch, bound her and laid her on the fire" (griffen . . . die Hexe, banden sie und legten sie ins Feuer), and in the second, the prince feeds live coals to the evil cook who has brought about his mother's downfall.

In all the examples cited above, fire's associations with male fairy tale characters are anchored in the plot, but fire also serves metaphorical and symbolic functions in *Grimms' Tales*. In "The Goose-Girl at the Well," (no. 179) a wise old woman characterizes the count's love for the goose-girl as fire onto which one must not pour oil, while in "The Juniper Tree" (no. 47), an elaborately intricate and beautiful symbol links classical allusions to immortality with Germanic and Biblical ones and narrates the first stage of the murdered boy's return to life:

> Then the juniper tree began to stir itself, and the branches parted asunder, and moved together again, just as if someone were rejoicing and clapping his hands. At the same time a mist seemed to arise from the tree, and in the centre of this mist it burned like a fire, and a beautiful bird flew out of the fire singing magnificently, and he flew high up in the air, and when he was gone, the juniper tree was just as it had been before, and the handkerchief with the bones was no longer there.

> Do füng de Machandelboom an, sik to bewegen, un de Twyge deden sik jümmer so recht von eenenner, un denn wedder tohoop, so recht as wenn sik eener so recht freut un mit de Händ so dait. Mit des so güng dar so 'n Newel dar brennd dat as Führ, un uut dem Führ dar flöög so 'n schönen Vagel heruut, de süng so herrlich und flöög hoog in de Luft, un as he wech wöör, do wöör de Machandelboom, as he vörhen west wöör, un de Dook mit de Knakens wöör wech.

In this image, fire both mediates and *is* the male soul, the soul of the murdered stepson. In his incarnation as the red-, green-, and gold-feathered phoenix the boy drops a mill stone onto his terrified stepmother's head, whose hair stands out "like flames of fire" (as Führsflammen). *Her* flames manifest the immanence of the Evil One (de Böse), who had entered into her, filled her mind, and prompted her to carry out her misbegotten plan to murder her husband's child. In this literary fairy tale the image of fire operates as a sign of male identity (the boy's soul), as a symbol of the devil, and as the mythic means of the murdered child's return to life.

In "The Juniper Tree" the flameborn phoenix can execute the flamehaired stepmother, which neatly illustrates the fact that with rare exceptions, men in *Grimms' Tales* are themselves uniquely exempt from death by fire. Indeed, one

---

8. "The Queen Bee" (no. 62); "Brother Lustig."

character in "The Six Servants" (no. 134), the Frosty One, has the odd ability to lie down in the midst of a fire, bear it "for three days until all the wood was consumed" (drei Tage, bis alles Holz verzehrt war) and yet be utterly unaffected by it. The drummer (no. 193) repeats this feat when he "sprang into the midst of the flames, but they did not hurt him, and could not even singe a hair of his head" (sprang mitten in die Flammen, aber sie taten ihm nichts, nicht einmal die Haare konnten sie ihm versengen). Reversals and contradictions of all sorts form part and parcel of the fairy tale tradition, so we should not be surprised at the existence of fire that does not consume in *Grimms' Tales*. What surprises the reader is fire's gender specificity. Not a single woman enjoys a similar immunity to flame. On the contrary, the same man whose hair remains wholly unsinged in the flames moments later

> seized the old woman with both his hands, raised her up on high, and threw her into the jaws of the fire, which closed over her as if it were delighted that an old witch was to be burnt.

> da packte er die Alte mit beiden Händen, hob sie in die Höhe und warf sie den Flammen in den Rachen, die über ihr zusammenschlugen, als freuten sie sich, daß sie eine Hexe verzehren sollten.

The text's implicit explanation and justification for the woman's fiery end lies in the revelation that she is a witch.

It is easy to attribute witch-burnings in *Grimms' Tales* to a surviving memory of historical events, but that does not sufficiently account for why the vocabulary of the tales habitually avoids letting good girls and women manipulate fire, even in the form of the apparently innocent flames of the domestic hearth.[9] The good little girl who is sent out to hunt strawberries in the snow warms herself not by the fire, but "on the bench by the stove" (auf die Bank am Ofen).[10] It is therefore not surprising that the domestic hearth, which we should otherwise look to for nourishing sustenance and homely warmth, appears in an ambiguous light. The youngest sister in "The Twelve Brothers" "sought for the wood for cooking and herbs for vegetables, and put the pans *on the fire* so that the dinner was always ready when the eleven came" (suchte das Holz zum Kochen und die Kräuter zum Gemüs und stellte die Töpfe *ans Feuer*, also daß die Mahlzeit immer fertig war, wenn die elfe kamen) (emphasis mine). This phrase is repeated in the very different tale, "The Poor Man and the Rich Man" (no. 87): "Then she put the potatoes on the fire" (Dann setzte sie Kartoffeln ans Feuer). The heroine may cook *at* the fire (ans Feuer), but it is the peasant himself who sits and pokes the fire in "Thumbling" (no. 37), or Herr Korbes who comes into the kitchen, about to light the fire (no. 41).

---

9. Gerhard O. W. Mueller, "The Criminological Significance of the Grimms' Fairy Tales," in Bottigheimer, ed., *Fairy Tales and Society*.

10. "The Three Little Men in the Wood" (no. 13).

Woman and fire stand separate from one another. Fire is something that she may approach but cannot ignite or control. It is presumably the smallest brother, Benjamin, who lights the fire in "The Twelve Brothers," and we are left to infer that a woman who does the same is somehow bad, an inference that "The Lazy Spinner" (no. 128) corroborates. Editorially castigated as "an odious woman" (eine garstige Frau), she is also the only female who lights a fire in *Grimms' Tales,* and she does so with the deliberate intention of deceiving her husband:

> Early in the morning she got up, lighted a fire, and put the kettle on, only instead of the yarn, she put in a lump of tow, and let it boil.

> Frühmorgens stand sie auf, machte Feuer an und stellte den Kessel bei, allein statt des Garns legte sie einen Klumpen Werg hinein und ließ es immerzu kochen.

The only positively portrayed female figure who controls fire, albeit at one remove, is the white bride, who—not in human form but as a white duck— orders the kitchen boy to light a fire so that she may warm her feathers. [11] Far more characteristic of the apparently illicit relationship between women and fire is the old woman sitting by the fire in "The Old Woman in the Wood" (no. 123). Not an old wise woman like Mother Holle (no. 24), she is instead the heroine's arch antagonist.

It is theoretically conceivable that the positive association of men with fire and the domestic hearth may simply reflect household practice in the Germanies of an earlier day, although I have no evidence for this. In literary terms, however, the imagery of men, women, and fire exist as part of a larger symbolic matrix in *Grimms' Tales* that bears close examination. Narratively, fire and its attendant ashes are useless for a girl. This is particularly evident in "The Robber-Bridegroom" (no. 40), where the wind blows away the ashes a hapless maiden has strewn as a marker in the woods. In addition, ashes from hearth fires provide the mark and metaphor of degradation for two fairy tale heroines, Allerleirauh and Cinderella. They also provide her abasing name, Aschenputtel, not only in *Grimms' Tales,* but in most other traditions, for example, Ashpet (Appalachian), Cinderella (English), Cendrillon (French), and La Gatta Cenerentola (Italian).

In this dualistic world fire belongs to men, and its opposite, water (or at least certain kinds of water), appertains exclusively to women. Wells, springs, brooks, and streams seem peculiarly under feminine sway. [12] The stream that is so often a boon to female characters is a bane to males, as Little Brother discovers when thirst drives him to drink from the bewitched brook, and he is transformed into a roebuck. [13]

---

11. "The White Bride and the Black Bride" (no. 135).

12. Both *well* and *spring* are rendered by the same German word, *Brunnen,* in *Grimms' Tales.*

13. "Brother and Sister" (no. 11).

Water, like fire, has its own literary and folk history. As an integral component of the history of creation, water initiates the theogonies and cosmogonies of the Western world. In the Judeo-Christian tradition, water is mentioned even before light in the opening verses of the Bible:

> In the beginning God created the heavens and the earth. The earth was without form and void, and darkness was upon the face of the deep; and the Spirit of God was moving over the face of the waters. (Gen. 1:1–2)

Correspondingly, Oceanus represents primal matter in the Greek tradition. Water also maintained its primacy over fire in late eighteenth- and early nineteenth-century German doctrines about the formation of the earth's crust. In general German geologists were Neptunists, who left it to the Vulcanists of France and Italy to defend the notion that fire had been responsible for certain rock formations. Although the Grimms themselves may not have participated in this controversy, a great fire-water controversy was in the air and other leading Romantics, like Friedrich von Hardenberg (Novalis) did become involved.

Some forms of water, such as wells and brooks, have been thought to be particularly holy and to have purifying capacities; others are supposed to have special attributes, like mantic springs. The widespread distribution of some of these attributes has led many serious scholars to posit a universal association of water imagery with female generativity.[14] There is much to corroborate this viewpoint in *Grimms' Tales,* but there is also a gender specificity about springs, wells, and brooks that not only favors women but at the same time threatens men.

In *Grimms' Tales* water performs diverse functions, many of which appear in an archetypal fairy tale, "The Three Little Men in the Wood" (no. 13). Its narrative consists of familiar components: a widower who remarries; a wicked stepmother who favors her own, wicked daughter over the stepfather's good

14. In his first edition of the *Tales,* Wilhelm Grimm wrote in the appended notes that when children ask where their little brother or sister came from their parents reply: "One fetches them out of the well" (Aus dem Brunnen da hole man sie heraus), and when the child looks into the well, he or she can see a child's face, which strengthens the belief. Another answer is "an angel brings them" (Ein Engel bringe sie), or "the stork fishes for them in the water and brings them in his red beak" (Der Storch fische die Kinder im Wasser und bringe sie in seinem rothen Schnabel getragen). See also Erich Neumann's lengthy discussion of groundwater symbolism in *The Great Mother,* where he writes: "To the realm of the earth water belong not only the pond and lake but also the spring. While in the well the elementary character of the Feminine is still evident—it is no accident that in fairy tales a well is often the gate to the underworld and specifically to the domain of the earth mother" (48). Springs and wells represent the entrance to the underworld in many cultures without reference to feminine principles, so that Neumann's "universal" may here represent a phenomenon specific to a more limited geographical area. Mircea Eliade also sees a close association between water and female generative properties in all European religions.

daughter; a forest; three dwarfish men; a hut; gold; toads; marriage to a king; a murder and subsequent spell; and a grisly execution. In most of the plot segments water figures prominently. Its divining powers in the opening paragraph decide an essentially male–female relationship, namely, whether a widowed father should remarry. Characteristically, it is the widower's daughter who carries out the divination. Water identifies the good girl, but in a confusing ambiguity, it both signals her deprivation and marks her moral superiority: she is given water for washing and for drinking, while her sinful sister receives milk for washing and wine for drinking. Water tests the two girls, for the snow under which the girls must seek strawberries blankets an earth "frozen as hard as a stone" (steinhart gefroren) and stands as a metaphor of an impossible task as well as a striking image of intense cold. Naturally the good girl succeeds at her impossible task and is blessed by the three little men in the wood, whereas her indulged sister earns only curses from them. Despite her success, or perhaps because of it, the good girl's trials continue as her wicked stepmother tries to do her in. Rinsing yarn through a hole in the ice on the river results, however, not in her death, but in meeting and marrying the king. Water thus functions as a locus of reversal and transformation: the poor harried stepdaughter becomes queen of the realm. Water mediates a second transformation when the wicked stepsister and her mother subsequently throw the queen from a palace window into a stream in order to drown her. When the queen rises from the waters as a duck, she goes on to pose pithy and ultimately self-revelatory questions to palace servants and succeeds in telling the scullion how to break the spell. Finally, water becomes a method of execution when the king poses the question, "What does a person deserve who drags another out of bed and throws him in the water?" (Was gehört einem Menschen, der den andern aus dem Bett trägt und ins Wasser wirft?). The stepmother answers, "The wretch deserves nothing better . . . than to be taken and put in a barrel stuck full of nails, and rolled down hill into the water" (Nichts Besseres . . . als daß man den Bösewicht in ein Faß steckt, das mit Nägeln ausgeschlagen ist, und den Berg hinab ins Wasser rollt). The king then pronounces the sentence, and the water of execution, until this point unspecified, is clarified as a river:[15] "And then the top was hammered on, and the barrel rolled down hill until it went into the river" (dann ward der Boden zusammengehämmert und das Faß bergab gekullert, bis es in den Fluß rollte).[16]

The good girl who washes herself in "The Three Little Men in the Wood" keeps company with other female bathers: Briar-Rose's mother bathes (no. 50)

15. It is apparently impossible to execute a woman by drowning her in a well within the Grimm tradition, although other narrative traditions carry out executions of women in wells. See Uther, "Brunnen."

16. Larger bodies of water—ponds, lakes, rivers, and the ocean—offer no clearly delineated gender association in *Grimms' Tales*.

and so does the queen in "The Pink" (no. 76), but that filthiest of all fairy tale characters, "Bearskin" (no. 101), does not wash himself at the end of a seven years' renunciation of bathing, hair-cutting, and nail-cutting, but makes the Devil himself clean him up (reinigen). Humbling Old Nick at the parting of their ways makes a good narrative, and it also underlines the fact that men do not fetch water or bathe in *Grimms' Tales*. Concluding the seven years' pact by making the Devil do women's work ends the tale in a manner particularly humiliating to him:

> Whether the Devil liked it or not, he was forced to fetch water, and wash Bearskin, comb his hair, and cut his nails.

> Der Teufel mochte wollen oder nicht, er mußte Wasser holen, den Bärenhäuter abwaschen, ihm die Haare kämmen und die Nägel schneiden.

Water specified as generative or curative remains unambiguously within a female domain. The frog who creeps out of the water and confronts the queen in "Little Briar-Rose" announces that she will bear a daughter, not a son, before a year goes by. The curative water of life is given out or administered exclusively by women and girls, whether it is in "The King of the Golden Mountain" (no. 92), "The Three Little Birds" (no. 96), or "The King's Son Who Feared Nothing" (no. 121). A man may seek the water of life, but he can't lay hands on it without female intervention. Impossible tasks involving water are consistently carried out by female helpers, whether young and beautiful or old and haglike. If a hero or a heroine needs to empty a pond with a thimble or a perforated spoon, a woman must assist.

But all these special associations of water and women pale before that of women and wells.[17] In "Mother Holle" a diligent daughter arrives in an eternally vernal world by falling into a well. Once inside Mother Holle's subterranean realm, she discharges tasks socially defined as feminine—baking, plumping up bedding, keeping house, energetically affirming fruitful plenty and domestic order—for all of which Mother Holle returns a shower of gold, the ultimate reward in so many fairy tales. The highly Christianized "Bearskin" provides a rare exception. One of the proud sisters drowns herself in a well in angry frustration.

In striking contrast, wells confront men with a broad range of dangers. Lucky Hans (no. 83) provides a clear example of the antipathy between men and wells, for when he sits down by the edge of the well, he loses the last remnant of his pay for seven years' labor: "he made a slip, pushed against the

---

17. One should not be misled by the Grendel-like Iron Hans, whose "naked arm stretches itself out of the water" (ein nackter Arm streckte sich aus dem Wasser). This water is not the female-dominated clear, potable, potentially curative water of a well, but that of a *Pfuhl,* a slough or pit, whose water is the color of Iron Hans himself, "brown like rusty iron" (braun . . . wie rostiges Eisen).

stones, and both of them fell into the water" (versah er's, stieß ein klein wenig an, und beide Steine plumpten hinab). Likewise, what links the Frog King (no. 1) to many other unfortunates in *Grimms' Tales* is not his frogginess, but the fact that the well is the unlucky location of his enchantment. A wicked witch bewitched him, the ugly frog tells the princess at the end of the tale. He does not tell us why he was changed into a well-dwelling frog rather than into any other creature or object. It is simply a given of this tale. But in "The Seven Ravens" a well functions more explicitly as the source of the seven brothers' misfortune. Instead of fetching baptismal water for their sister from the well, they accidentally drop the jug into it. Frightened of returning home empty-handed, they tarry and their angry father wishes them all into ravens:

> Hardly was the word spoken before he heard a whirring of wings over his head, looked up and saw seven coal-black ravens flying away.

> Kaum war das Wort ausgeredet, so hörte er ein Geschwirr über seinem Haupt in der Luft, blickte in die Höhe und sah sieben kohlschwarze Raben auf und davon fliegen.

Wells and well water are as dangerous for boys as fire is for girls, a hypothesis that can be tested by comparing "Our Lady's Child" and "Iron Hans" (no. 136), where fire and water occupy analogous positions. The Trinity's fire and splendor in the forbidden room gilds Marienkind's finger and exposes her guilt; it is water in the forbidden well that performs the same function for the prince in "Iron Hans." In both cases, the gilded finger leads directly to the child's expulsion from his or her protected place into the dangers and hardships of the world.[18]

It is highly dangerous for a man to so much as approach a well, a fact that can appear explicitly or implicitly in the tale. In "The Golden Bird" (no. 57) the prince's magic helper, a little fox, expressly warns him against wells: "Be careful about two things. Buy no gallows'-flesh, and do not sit at the edge of any well" (Vor zwei Stücken hüte dich, kauf kein Galgenfleisch und setze dich an keinen Brunnenrand).[19] The prince marvels at the fox's strange whims, but subsequently forgets himself on a hot day, and at his wicked brothers' suggestion sits down on the edge of a well, into which they promptly throw him. He survives the fall, but gets out again only with great difficulty.[20]

In like manner, a witch sends a poor discharged soldier into her old dry well to fetch out her magic blue light, but she will not draw him out again. He

18. The dangers themselves are treated differently, however: see chap. 10.

19. This tale is a German form of the Russian firebird tale, in which the prince's animal helper, a gray wolf, warns the prince—equally fruitlessly—against taking the golden cage and bridle.

20. Women are warned away from wells in other narrative traditions, but not in *Grimms' Tales.* See Uther, "Brunnen."

avoids injury when he falls onto the moist ground of the well, and with the aid of the blue light the soldier finds his way through an underground passage to the witch's treasure houses. Unlike the good daughter in "Mother Holle," the soldier requires overt magical assistance to escape from the well into the everyday world.

Even giants can be endangered by wells in *Grimms' Tales,* a notion that leads a perfidious bailiff to send a young giant into a well to clean it. He believes he will be able to drop a mill stone onto the giant's head and kill him, but naturally the plan fails, because the giant's supernatural strength makes him perceive the crushing weight of the mill stone as a trivial encumbrance. The significance of the incident lies in the fact that the narrator chooses a well as the potentially hazardous tight spot for the giant, rather than any other place, such as the hole in a fence (in the Reynard cycle of tales), or a manmade aperture familiar from tight spot anecdotes in the Western tradition.[21] Even in animal tales wells bode ill for male characters. The wolf in "The Wolf and the Seven Little Kids" (no. 5) drowns miserably when the heavy stones in his stomach drag him to the bottom of the well (Brunnen).

When pieced together, the many bits and pieces of fire and well imagery produce a bifurcating pattern of gender segregation and conflict in *Grimms' Tales.*[22] This is hardly unique in the history of Western literature, as the gender antagonisms following humanity's acquisition of fire in Greek mythology clearly indicate. When Zeus undertook to punish man in general for Prometheus' theft, he created the first woman, Pandora, ostensibly to accompany but principally to plague him. In his omniscience, Zeus apparently knew that Pandora, married to Prometheus' brother, would unleash evil upon the world when curiosity overcame her. What is significant is that the opposition associated with elemental forces, fire and water, seems to stand for gender

21. A single counterexample exists in "The Giant and the Tailor" (no. 183), where the boastful tailor actually fetches a pitcher of water from the well on the giant's command. He turns the well and the spring into a source of terror for the giant, however, by suggesting that instead of fetching just a pitcher of water he bring the well and the spring back as well, whereupon the giant becomes still more terrified of him. Like the Schwank in general, "The Giant and the Tailor" inverts conventions, in this case, a fairy tale convention.

22. As though to underline the gender antagonisms of *Grimms' Tales,* a male is powerless and stupefied in an ideal female landscape. For example, the count in "The Goose-Girl at the Well" (no. 179) lies down in a landscape reminiscent of that in the tale of Mother Holle (no. 24) "It is quite delightful here," said he, "but I am so tired that I cannot keep my eyes open; I will sleep a little. If only a gust of wind does not come and blow my legs off my body, for they are as rotten as tinder" ("Es ist recht lieblich hier," sagte er, "aber ich bin so müde, daß ich die Augen nicht aufbehalten mag: ich will ein wenig schlafen. Wenn nur kein Windstoß kommt und bläst mir meine Beine vom Leib weg, denn sie sind mürb und wie Zunder"). The water, a brook, which here forms part of an enervating landscape, also provides a male metaphor for disaster. The poor man who begs for help in "The Grave-Mound" (no. 195) explains his situation by saying: "I stand here like one who feels the water rising above his head" (ich stehe da wie einer, dem das Wasser bis an den Kopf geht).

antipathies considered natural in *Grimms' Tales*. Despite the royal wedding that unites hero and heroine in so many of the narratives, underlying images and metaphors connote an antagonistic division between man and woman that informs many of the analytic categories in this study. Wilhelm Grimm, who himself associated water with the tales of the collection, seems to have been unaware of the presence or significance of fire in conjunction with water.

The possibility that men and women in *Grimms' Tales* might inhabit radically different worlds as indicated by their associations with fire and water is nowhere overtly stated in the collection. The chief scholarly problem in this connection thus involves the "retrieval of latent content."[23] Within *Grimms' Tales* the meaning implicit in image and motif frequently contradicts plot and editorial commentary. The reader, left with an apparent message that differs from the declared message, does well to pause and consider the significance of this disjunction.[24]

One Plot, Three Tales, and Three Different Stories

The preceding section draws together what seem initially to be randomly distributed and unrelated references to fire and water. Considered as a group, they reveal a pattern of associations that none of the individual pieces contains. Aggregate analysis of content produces a comprehensible and consistent set of images associated with the motifs of fire and wells, even though the individual motifs and images have been drawn from genres as different as literary fairy tales, animal tales, and traditional fairy tales, whose plots differ radically from one another.

One can begin at the other end, so to speak, with a group of tales whose plots are similar, to see how the same plot can be made to tell different stories. Different social or geographical environments harbor vastly different social views and tend to amend popular tales in accordance with familiar social codes. Basile's *Pentamerone* and Perrault's *Contes* both retain the same or very similar constituents to tell a Cinderella story, but motivations and outcomes differ profoundly from the Grimms' version, illustrating quite neatly how contemporary mores, audience expectations, narrative voice, and authorial intentions color tale elements. In "La Gatta Cenerentola," Basile's Cinderella figure, Zezolla, participates actively in the construction of her own fate, scheming to kill her stepmother at the instigation of her ambitious governess, who then becomes a hated stepmother herself. Plunged from favor to the fireside embers of the tale's title, Zezolla begs her father to commend her to the love of the

23. Alicia Ostriker uses this phrase with reference to Ann Sexton's *Transformations*, a cycle of poems that grew directly from *Grimms' Tales*, in "The Thieves of Language," 73.

24. Barbara Johnson ponders these questions in her "Opening Remarks" in *The Critical Difference*.

fairies. The tale follows the same broad outlines as Perrault's and the Grimms', ending, however, with the disconsolate stepsisters espousing an astrological fatalism: "He is mad who would oppose the stars." Basile thus manipulates traditional motifs to tell his own tale.

In Perrault's *Contes,* it is Cendrillon's goodness and patience, virtues absent from Zezolla's criminously pragmatic character, that attract the aid of her fairy godmother. Despite the stepsisters' taunting and teasing, the tale's conclusion curtsies toward courtly convention as Cendrillon provides them with rich husbands. Thus, despite Perrault's admonition about "la bonne grâce" in his *moralité,* he embeds an anti-moral within the plot itself: biting mockery can lead to brilliant matches.

The Grimms' Cinderella (Aschenputtel) has no fairy godmother, at least from the Second Edition onward. Instead, she forms her attachments and derives her strength from her biological parents, by planting a hazel twig her father brings her on her mother's grave and watering it with her tears. From its branches a dove casts down ball gowns of extraordinary beauty. This tale, however, differs radically from Basile's or Perrault's Cinderella tales, ending on a ghastly punitive note. As Cinderella and her prince go to the church to be married, the doves who act as supernatural benefactresses peck out her sisters'eyes to punish them for their malice and treachery, even though the girls' mutilation of their own toes and heels to make them fit into Cinderella's tiny slipper would seem punishment enough.

In Walt Disney's mid-twentieth-century film version of Perrault's "Cendrillon," a cloyingly pretty and passive heroine contrasts with old and ugly female schemers. This corresponds to the desired image of women in the 1940s and 1950s but is certainly antipodal to Basile's Zezolla, who takes matters into her own hands in an effort to improve her lot.[25]

Despite these four tales' underlying plot similarities, each implies a radically different pattern of female behavior. Given their origins in four different cultures at intervals of 60–125 years, this is hardly surprising. Traditionally, tales with overlapping plot elements like these have been compared historico-geographically in the manner of the Finnish school to demonstrate the widespread existence of similar motifs and tale types.[26] But tale comparison can be taken a step further to show how broader literary themes—for instance, the heroine's position in fairy tales—vary according to the place occupied by standard motifs in a set of closely related tales.

There are several groups of recurrent tale types in *Grimms' Tales,* but many of them are embedded in elaborated plots, so that unambiguous shifts in the

25. Kay Stone discusses Disney's transformation of the traditional tales in "Things Walt Disney Never Told Us."

26. In the Finnish school of scholarship the existence of a motif, rather than its function, is stressed. Alan Dundes takes a different approach in "The Symbolic Equivalence of Allomotifs."

story's meaning are obscured by the tale within which it appears. One set of tales, however, provides narratives that are homologous from beginning to end: "The Twelve Brothers," "The Seven Ravens," and "The Six Swans." By looking closely at this group, we can focus clearly on shifting functions and associational patterns of motifs within a narrative. A close reading of the tales illuminates the mechanics of alternate tellings of a single plot. Each variant offers a similar constellation of motifs yet produces a significantly different narrative, because the placement and function of motifs within the tale, carefully calibrated to correspond to the kind of story being told, alters images and thus the story that the images produce.[27]

"The Twelve Brothers," "The Seven Ravens," and "The Six Swans" share a common core plot: the birth of a daughter directly or indirectly causes her brothers' departure from home; and the brothers turn into birds, an enchantment from which their sister's efforts directly or indirectly release them. Despite the similarity of the underlying plot, the three tales offer a wide range of views of women and power, and the narrative association of motifs in each suggests a consistent ordering of symbols congruent with assessments of women ranging from inherently powerful to utterly enfeebled.

It is difficult if not impossible to reconstruct the narrative milieu in which Jacob or Wilhelm collected these tales. Jacob Grimm seems to have noted down "The Twelve Brothers," the principal constituents of which come from the Ramus family, although a second version may derive from Dorothea Viehmann.[28] Jacob was also responsible for "The Seven Ravens." The Hassenpflug family was probably the source of his story, to which was added an introductory section from an informant in Vienna. Wilhelm Grimm took down the third tale, "The Six Swans," from Dortchen Wild in a version which owes much to "Die sieben Schwäne" in the 1801 collection, *Feenmährchen*. Despite the crucial importance of the narrative situation for understanding a tale's coloration, it is difficult if not impossible to relate the values inherent in each of these tales to the narrative situation itself in the absence of more detailed information about them.[29]

The underlying narrative assumes that one girl is worth twelve, seven, or six brothers respectively. In each of the tales, a sister redeems her transformed brothers. Their narrative similarity notwithstanding, the three tales differ in that they progressively weaken the figure of the sister in the numerically ordered sequence "The Twelve Brothers," "The Seven Ravens" and "The Six

---

27. In this context I use *tale* to mean the text in *Grimms' Tales*, and *story* to mean the narrative together with its meaning and implications.

28. The following discussion of attributions is based on the 1856 notes to the *Tales* together with Heinz Rölleke's conclusions, both of which appear in his critical edition of the 1857 *Kinder- und Hausmärchen*, 3: 32, 56–59, 93–97, 445–46, 453–54, 463.

29. See Max Lüthi's discussion of Kollektivdichtung in "Urform und Zielform in Sage und Märchen," in *Volksliteratur und Hochliteratur*, 198–210.

Swans." Although a core of similar motif vocabulary exists in each tale, the motifs have been shifted about in a manner that affects motivation, especially with reference to the power and independence evident in the sister. The father's responsibility for his sons' transformation into birds in each tale reveals in particular the daughter's shifting value. In "The Twelve Brothers" the father intends to kill his twelve sons "in order that [his daughter's] possessions may be great, and that the kingdom may fall to her alone" (damit [seiner Tochter] Reichtum groß wird und das Königreich ihm allein zufällt). In "The Seven Ravens," however, the father merely curses his sons out of pique at what he believes to be their carelessness. In "The Six Swans," the stepmother bewitches the king's sons in order to be rid of them. This motivation depends entirely on the tradition of a wicked stepmother figure, for the stepmother in this tale has been rid of the children from the beginning, the king having hidden them away from her in the woods.

In like manner, shirts perform different functions with reference to the sister. In "The Twelve Brothers," shirts provide the first clue to her brother's existence when the princess sees them and asks whose they are, thus displaying an initiative that characterizes her throughout the tale. Shirts do not appear in the second tale, "The Seven Ravens"; but in the third, "The Six Swans," shirts appear first as the means by which the wicked stepmother turns the boys into swans, and second as the instrument of redemption, six shirts sewn out of the tiny fragile flower, starwort.

A star appears in each of the tales, but with progressively attenuated import. In the first, a golden star shines forth from the sister's forehead, an integral part of her body and appearance.[30] In the second, the sister journeys to the sun, moon, and stars to learn how to redeem her brothers, while in the third, the star resides in the ephemeral image of the starwort, from whose delicate gauzy substance the sister must sew the redemptive shirts. Thus the astral image consistently retreats from intimate association with the sister figure, changing from an integral part of her body to the material of a task she fails to complete. The manner in which each sister sets off on a quest to save her brothers similarly corroborates the general tenor of each tale: in the first she sets off openly, and in the second and third she resorts to subterfuge, departing secretly.

The basic premise of "The Twelve Brothers" is that disposing of the brothers will allow for a greater accretion of wealth and power to the sister. Therefore, it is surprising that once this statement has set the whole tale moving, no more is heard about the father's (and mother's?) kingdom, which the princess is to inherit. The theme of female inheritance is entirely absent from the second and third tales.

The mother's role likewise diminishes from tale to tale. In "The Twelve

---

30. Sun, moon, and stars traditionally signal beauty. See Uther, "Schönheit im Märchen."

Brothers" she is an active queen, whose timely intervention saves her sons and assists her daughter; in "The Seven Ravens" she is a passive nonroyal mother; in "The Six Swans," the narrative slot is occupied by a witch's daughter, the wicked stepmother. Indeed, "The Six Swans" offers a full complement of familiar nineteenth-century fairy tale characters and motifs: innocent, powerless, and good princess, wicked stepmother, treachery, threat of death by fire, and redemption at the last minute by a male figure.

In the three variants of the bewitched brothers plot, the motifs remain more or less constant (shirts, birds, years of silence, wicked stepmother, star[s], sitting in the tree, a king hunting in the forest), but their altered relationships to each other modulate the motivation for actions in the tales. The clearest example appears in the motif of the hunting king.[31] In "The Twelve Brothers," where the princess evinces much more innate power—in her narrative independence as well as in the way motifs function in the tale—it is significant that the king himself discovers her and asks her to marry him, to which she assents by nodding her head. The motif of the king in the woods appears twice in "The Six Swans": it both introduces the tale, providing the king with his wicked wife, and recurs later when a different king's hunting expedition occasions his discovery of the princess in the tree. Not the king, however, but his huntsmen discover the princess, who strips off her clothes one piece at a time in a vain attempt to drive them off.

The process of recasting positive images of female power continues in the illustration tradition accompanying the text. A 1922 edition of "The Twelve Brothers," illustrated with rich but foreboding hues of purple, gold, and black, displaces the star from the princess' forehead to the crown she wears, denying her inborn powers and transferring them to an artifact of kingdoms and kingship.[32]

Telling a story of weak or strong womanhood is not just a matter of plot, as in the Cinderella variants, but also of conscious manipulation of the motifs and images of which the tales are composed. This seems so self-evident as to be unnecessary to state. Yet the "meaning" of fairy tales has too often been seen as wholly natural and unpremeditated. The many modifications of the figure of the independent princess as she appears in "The Twelve Brothers" result in the personally ineffectual little sister in "The Six Swans." Abandoned in the forest, treed, silenced, pursued by a malevolent witch, married to a king, accused of cannibalism, and tied to the stake, the little sister's plight summarizes and introduces many of the subjects that the following chapters treat in detail.

31. Introductory phrases underwent much alteration under Wilhelm Grimm's editing. The Ölenberg MS (1810) records the queen in the tale initiator: "Es war einmal ein König und eine Königin, die hatten zwölf Kinder zusammen . . . ." while the 1812 version has displaced the queen from her initial position: "Es war einmal ein König, der hatte zwölf Kinder, das waren lauter Buben, er wollte auch kein Mädchen haben und sagte zur Königin . . . ."

32. Hamburg: A. Blencke, 1922.

4

Witches, Maidens, and Spells

sk any three people about *Grimms' Tales* and two of them will respond, "Witches, ogres, wolves . . ." Ask again what witches do, and the questioner will hear that witches lay spells and enchant young heroes and heroines. All of this is correct, and yet these answers obscure some rather surprising facts. Of the many supposed spell-laying verses in *Grimms' Tales,* only a few represent true conjuring.[1] Not a simple act, conjuring in the German tradition accomplishes something by invoking or commanding a spirit, a natural being, or a natural power by means of a spell or a sacred name. Of the successful spells actually laid in *Grimms' Tales,* the overwhelming majority, if not all, are performed by young, beautiful, and usually nubile girls. Furthermore, the girls' effectiveness in laying spells seems related to an inborn connection to nature itself. It takes close and careful reading to come to this conclusion, because the text often imputes fearsome powers to old women and young men. For example, Rapunzel's godmother (no. 12) was an "enchantress, who had great power and was dreaded by all the world" (Zauberin, die große Macht hatte und von aller Welt gefürchtet ward).

We also hear about witches who lay spells with dire consequences:

> But the wicked step-mother was a witch, and had seen how the two children had gone away, and had crept after them secretly, as witches creep, and had bewitched all the brooks in the forest. ("Brother and Sister," no. 11)

> Die böse Stiefmutter aber war eine Hexe und hatte wohl gesehen, wie die beiden Kinder fortgegangen waren, war ihnen nachgeschlichen, heimlich, wie die Hexen schleichen, und hatte alle Brunnen im Walde verwünscht.

But on closer examination we see that the only magical voice heard in this text does not belong to the witch: it belongs to the brook that warns Little Sister away from its witch-enchanted waters that will turn Little Brother into a tiger

---

1. Throughout this chapter, *conjuring* is used interchangeably with *spell-laying* in a verbal sense, rather than with the connotation of manual legerdemain.

or a wolf. The same is true of the witchlike enchantress in the perennial German favorite, "Jorinda and Joringel" (no. 69). We do not hear a single one of her seven thousand bewitchings that change virgins into caged birds, not even the one that entraps Jorinda.[2] To judge from his notes to the tales as well as from the list of verbal forms to be gathered that was included in the constitution of the Wollzeilergesellschaft,[3] spell-laying generally escaped both Grimms' editorial sifting, though on at least one occasion Wilhelm added an invocation to a fairy tale.[4]

Spell-laying is a quite specific act that has to satisfy several formal requirements to fit the traditional Germanic model. First, the conjurer must be human. Second, the spell itself should consist of three parts: naming the deity or natural force invoked, describing a past act that proves the effectiveness of the power invoked, and finally requesting in the imperative form. Since none of the spells laid in *Grimms' Tales* includes a description of a past act, the requirements here are reduced: the invocation of a natural force followed by a command.

Some apparent spells do not fulfill the principal criterion that the conjurer be human, as in the toad's verses in "The Iron Stove" (no. 127).[5] The spell itself must incorporate a command. Pure wishing does not constitute conjuring, though wishes accompanied by unintended results appear often in *Grimms' Tales*.[6] They usually reflect character deficiency—greed or short

2. Upon her return, the enchantress "said in a hollow voice: 'Greet you, Zachiel. If the moon shines on the cage, Zachiel, let him loose at once' " (sagte mit dumpfer Stimme: "Grüß dich, Zachiel, wenn's Möndel ins Körbel scheint, bind los, Zachiel, zu guter Stund"): a rare, perhaps unique, example of an old woman actually using words magically. She is, perhaps significantly, disenchanting Joringel with her words rather than laying a spell.

3. Founded by Jacob Grimm while he attended the Vienna Congress in 1815 as a member of the Hessian legation.

4. In both the 1810 and 1812 versions of "Hansel and Gretel," the children return home on their own, but in the 1819 edition, Wilhelm added the white duck, whom Gretel summons by calling: "Oh, dear duckling, take us on your back" ("Ach, liebes Entchen nimm uns auf deinen Rücken"). Grimm later elaborated this brief command into a quasi spell, perhaps unwittingly but correctly putting it in a young girl's mouth. That this spell is an invention becomes clear from a comparison with true conjurings, which are always part of a link with nature mediated by a wise woman.

5. She addresses a "little green waiting maid, Waiting-maid with the limping leg, little dog of the limping leg" (Jungfer grün und klein, Hutzelbein, Hutzelbeins Hündchen), telling her to "Hop hither and thither, / And bring me the great box." (hutzel hin und her, / bring mir die große Schachtel her.) The conjuring form remains, perhaps because a female, even though a toad, is speaking.

6. It is not sufficient for an impatient mother to cry out, curselike, to her naughty little daughter, "I wish you were a raven and would fly away, and then I would have some rest" ("Ich wollte, du wärest eine Rabe und flögst fort, so hätt ich Ruhe") (no. 93, "The Raven"), nor for an impatient father to cry angrily about his seven sons, "I wish the boys were all turned into ravens" ("Ich wollte, daß die Jungen alle zu Raben würden") (no. 25: "The Seven Ravens"). See also Belgrader, "Fluch, Fluchen, Flucher."

temper—and comically undermine the character's true desires.[7] The fact that a wish leads to the desired result should not obscure the more important fact that basic conditions for laying a spell have not been met.

Although wishing itself does not meet the formal requirements for laying a spell, conjuring can apparently develop out of a wish. In "The Knapsack, the Hat, and the Horn" (no. 54), the youngest of three brothers astonishes himself with the effectiveness of simply wishing for food. Climbing down a tree, tormented by hunger, he thinks to himself: "If I could but eat my fill once more" (Wenn ich nur noch einmal meinen Leib ersättigen könnte). Immediately he finds a richly spread table beneath the tree. Keeping the tablecloth when he has finished, he later tests its powers, saying: "I wish you to be covered with good cheer again" (So wünsche ich, daß du abermals mit guten Speisen besetzt wärest). His wish works, and the third time he settles into the imperative spell-laying form, though he does not address it to a natural power, saying only: "Little cloth, set {RBB} yourself" (Tüchlein, deck dich).

Traditional German spells require the imperative, not the interrogative form. The stepmother's questions to the mirror in "Snow-White" (no. 53) do not constitute conjuring or spell-laying on two counts: the object addressed is neither a natural force nor a deity and the mood is not imperative. Nonetheless she addresses her mirror formulaically seven separate times:

Looking-glass, Looking-glass, on the wall,
Who in this land is the fairest of all?

Spieglein, Spieglein an der Wand,
wer ist die Schönste im ganzen Land?

More remarkably, it responds seven times, varying its reply to suit the circumstances.

Three modalities characterize a genuine spell in *Grimms' Tales,* when it makes one of its rare appearances. At its most powerful, conjuring power resides within the conjurer, who generates her own incantation rather than having it prescribed for her. At a slight remove is conjuring that depends on specific incantations passed on to the conjurer by a knowledgeable individual. These incantations lose their efficacy if the conjurer deviates even slightly from the prescribed form. And finally there are spells whose efficacy derives from a magical object presented to the conjurer.

Good examples of the three types of conjuring surface in "The Goose-Girl" (no. 89), "The Two King's Children" (no. 113), "Cinderella" (no. 21), "One-Eye, Two-Eyes, and Three-Eyes" (no. 130), and "Sweet Porridge" (no. 103). Each of the spells in these tales conforms to the requirements that a sacred

7. A good example occurs in "The Poor Man and the Rich Man" (no. 87), when the greedy, irascible rich man uses up his three wishes apoplectically and fruitlessly, first responding to his horse's capering about by wishing it would break its neck, then wishing his wife to be stuck to the saddle he is carrying, and finally having to use his third wish to unstick her again.

name or the spirit of a natural force or being be invoked together with a command to perform a specific act, followed in the text by the result requested or commanded. Furthermore, each of these spells proceeds from a woman and links the conjurer to basic natural processes: chthonic, physical, or biological.

The characteristics of the Grimms' spells join them to the oldest preserved German literature, the pre-Christian Merseburg Spells (Merseburger Zauber-sprüche), which bear witness to an early and perhaps continuous belief—or at least continuous reference to—a peculiarly female ability to control, direct or affect natural powers. In one, warrior women, the Idise, are invoked to help release prisoners taken in battle, and in the other, two pairs of sisters, Sintgunt and Sunna, Frija and Volla, whose past help has cured Baldur's steed, are invoked to effect a present cure.

The simple act of commanding may be understood within many different contexts. In his elaboration of speech act theory, John L. Austin suggests that "a necessary part of [a command] is that . . . the person to be the object of the verb 'I order to . . . ' must, by some previous procedure, tacit or verbal, have first constituted the person who is to do the ordering an authority, e.g. by saying 'I promise to do what you order me to do.' "[8] The intimate link between women and natural powers may be viewed as part of a tacit pact between ancient Germanic society and women, that natural processes be understood to be under feminine control, while acts of aggression and governing fall to the male sphere.[9] Clearly, neither wind, birds, nor pots can enter a pact with women and agree to perform responsively. Nonetheless, Austin's sugges-tion—even though made in an entirely different context—evokes the pos-sibility both in the Germanic past and in Grimm's day of a relationship between women and natural forces understood as reciprocal by women and their society.[10] By uttering the right words, a girl causes birds to peck ("Cinderella"), winds to blow ("The Goose-Girl"), and trees to bend down ("One-Eye, Two-Eyes, and Three-Eyes").

The most dramatic spell in *Grimms' Tales* appears in "The Goose-Girl," where a princess made to take her maidservant's place nonetheless retains her abilities to converse with her horse, Falada, and to conjure the winds to blow. Its alliterative verses, internal rhyme, and archaic vocabulary betray its ancient origins:

Blow, blow, thou gentle wind, I say,
Blow Conrad's little hat away,

8. *How to Do Things with Words*, 28–29. The separate chapters constituted the William James lectures of 1955 at Harvard University.

9. In *Das Recht in den Kinder- und Hausmärchen der Brüder Grimm*, Jens Christian Jessen understands the word-immanent power of magic in different terms, as an aspect of promising (*Versprechen*) (27).

10. According to Tacitus (*Germania*, 10), natural forces were believed to confer mantic powers on women by informing them of future events.

And make him chase it here and there,
Until I have braided all my hair,
And bound it up again.

Weh, weh, Windchen,
nimm Kürdchen sein Hütchen,
und laß 'n sich mit jagen,
bis ich mich geflochten und geschnatzt
und wieder aufgesatzt.

This spell, like all others in *Grimms' Tales,* lacks an integral component of the Merseburg Spells, namely, the initial description of a former and successful conjuration. Instead, it opens directly with an address to the force to be activated together with a command. In its first published appearance in volume 2 of the *Kinder- und Hausmärchen* (1815), Wilhelm emphasized that the line "Weh, weh, Windchen" was a command, not an exclamation, apparently wanting his readers to understand the precise nature and importance of this construction.[11] The goose-girl needs no magical object to enable her to conjure; nor does her loss of marital queenship affect her abilities. Her power inheres in her queenship over nature, which one may consider a legacy from her mother, the old queen, who opens this tale:

There was once upon a time an old queen whose husband had been dead for many years, and she had a beautiful daughter.

Es lebte einmal eine alte Königin, der war ihr Gemahl schon lange Jahre gestorben, und sie hatte eine schöne Tochter.

Cinderella similarly derives her power from her mother. Though long dead, she transmits magic capabilities to the upper world through the tree sprig her daughter planted on her grave. Watered with Cinderella's tears, it grows into a beautiful tree from whose boughs a little white bird flutters to her assistance or casts down whatever she wishes for. Twice Cinderella calls on the entire avian kingdom to pick lentils from the ashes where her stepmother, intending to set an impossible task, has scattered them. And twice the birds heed her call:[12]

11. In the First Edition Wilhelm routinely placed notes on the tales in an appendix, but in this case he asterisked the line to a footnote appearing on the same page: "D.h. Windchen wehe! nicht die Ausrufung eher!"

12. The 1810 version of this tale is assumed to have been lost when the Grimms sent their collection to Clemens Brentano, but in the 1812 version this verse appears, requesting beautiful clothes ("wirf schöne Kleider herab für mich"). The spell took its present form in the 1819 edition, possibly to bring it into conformity with the gold- and silver-bearing tree of "One-Eye, Two-Eyes, and Three-Eyes" (no. 130). In the 1856 volume of notes to the collection, Wilhelm mentions a variant, "Hohe Weide, thu dich auf, / gib mir dein schön Geschmeide raus," which evokes precious metals without mentioning them. At this remove it is impossible to know whether the alteration to the spell resulted from his own invention or from a variant form, since the volume of notes that appeared in 1822, i.e., after the 1819 revision, does not mention the

You tame pigeons, you turtle-doves, and all you birds beneath the sky, come and help me to pick
> The good into the pot,
> The bad into the crop.

Ihr zahmen Täubchen, ihr Turteltäubchen, all ihr Vöglein unter dem Himmel, kommt und helft mir lesen,
> die guten ins Töpfchen,
> die schlechten ins Kröpfchen.

Cinderella also conjures the tree itself:

> Shiver and quiver, little tree,
> Silver and gold throw down over me.

> Bäumchen, rüttel dich und schüttel dich,
> wirf Gold und Silber über mich.

The third verse in the Grimms' "Cinderella" is not a spell but a message from the birds to the prince, twice informing him that he has chosen the wrong bride, and finally confirming his choice:

> Turn and peep, turn and peep,
> No blood is in the shoe,
> The shoe is not too small for her,
> The true bride rides with you.

> Rucke di guck, rucke di guck,
> kein Blut im Schuck:
> der Schuck ist nicht zu klein,
> die rechte Braut, die führt er heim.

The preponderance of trees in spells reiterates their special importance in conjunction with women, while the trees' connection with gold and silver unites them to an ancient Western tradition. [13] In the three tales "The Goose-Girl," "Cinderella," and "One-Eye, Two-Eyes, and Three-Eyes," the power of the conjurer over the tree appears in progressively attenuated form. [14] In the first tale, we are left to infer that the goose-girl's magic powers over the wind that blows Conrad's hat and bends the trees derive from her femaleness, while this notion is further developed in "Cinderella" by the image of the tree growing out of the mother's grave (for which "out of the mother's body" may be read), while in "One-Eye, Two-Eyes, and Three-Eyes" a real woman

---

verses. The verses addressed to the tree and the one spoken by the birds remain unchanged through all editions from 1812 to 1858.

13. See a more detailed discussion of this subject in Bottigheimer, "The Transformed Queen."

14. As magic power is attenuated, expressions of grief increase. The goosegirl invokes the wind matter-of-factly; Cinderella waters the grave with her tears; and Two-Eyes weeps "so bitterly that two streams ran down from her eyes."

appears on the scene to instruct Two-Eyes in how to address her goat to obtain food. [15]

> Then the wise woman says: "Wipe away your tears, Two-Eyes, and I will tell you something to stop your ever suffering from hunger again; just say to your goat:
>> Bleat, my little goat, bleat,
>> Cover the table with something to eat,
>
> and then a clean well-spread little table will stand before you, with the most delicious food upon it of which you may eat as much as you are inclined for, and when you have had enough, and have no more need of the little table, just say,
>> Bleat, bleat, my little goat, I pray,
>> And take the table quite away."

> Sprach die weise Frau: "Zweiäuglein, trockne dir dein Angesicht, ich will dir etwas sagen, daß du nicht mehr hungern sollst. Sprich nur zu deiner Ziege:
>> Zicklein, meck,
>> Tischlein, deck,
>
> so wird ein sauber gedecktes Tischlein vor dir stehen und das schönste Essen darauf, daß du essen kannst, soviel du Lust hast. Und wenn du satt bist und das Tischlein nicht mehr brauchst, so sprich nur:
>> Zicklein, meck,
>> Tischlein, weg."

Whatever power the girl displays must first be communicated by the real holder of the power, the wise woman, and can only be potentiated in the presence of a second being, a goat. But Two-Eyes has not become a simple conduit for power from natural sources, for she seems to possess magic powers of her own formulation. Later in the tale, she introduces an original incantation to send her sister off to sleep, although the second time she tries to lay this spell it fails her, an indication within the plot of an attenuated connection between women and natural powers. This failure leads her jealous sisters to kill Two-Eyes' goat, but the wise woman appears once more and directs Two-Eyes to request the goat's innards. Buried in front of the threshold, they produce a magical tree with silver leaves and golden apples, inaccessible to anyone but Two-Eyes, before whom the tree bends to yield its precious fruit.

The image of the tree is more socialized in "One-Eye, Two-Eyes, and Three-Eyes" than in "The Goose-Girl." In the former, the tree provides the heroine with a treasure trove. Thus its story emphasizes the achievement of high social status conferred by possessions rather than the immanent personal power evident in "The Goose-Girl." In these three stories there is a clear pattern: the

---

15. In "The Goose-Girl," trees have no textual association with the goosegirl's conjuring, but the illustration tradition accompanying this tale, begun by Ludwig Emil Grimm, displays trees prominently in the pictorial rendering of her conjuring. See Bottigheimer, "Iconographic Continuity in Illustrations of 'The Goosegirl.'"

heroine's immanent power bears an inverse relationship to the presence of Christian elements. Just as there are no tears in "The Goose-Girl," there also is not a single Christian element. In the second tale, the reader is told that Cinderella cried and prayed three times a day at her mother's grave, while in "One-Eye, Two-Eyes, and Three-Eyes" the reader is not only told that Two-Eyes, the weakest of the spell-layers in these tales, says a prayer before eating, but is also given the text of the prayer: "Lord God, be our Guest forever, Amen" (Herr Gott, sei unser Gast zu aller Zeit, Amen). Since female conjuring and Christianity seem to be in some way incompatible in *Grimms' Tales*, it is consistent that when a prayer appears in a tale about a girl who can lay spells, it should be the shortest one Two-Eyes knows, even though the text credits its brevity to her extreme hunger.

The primacy of possessions evident in "One-Eye, Two-Eyes, and Three-Eyes" may account for a transitional form of conjuring, which requires a magical object rather than a creature from the natural world to potentiate a command. Such an object appears in "Sweet Porridge," where an aged woman meets a starving girl (poor but good) and gives her a magic pot, which will produce sweet porridge when she says: "Cook, little pot, cook" (Töpfchen, koche), until she stops it with the words "Stop, little pot" (Töpfchen, steh). The tale's humor grows out of the inexhaustible store of porridge that fills the village up to the last house, because the girl's mother, who starts the pot, doesn't know how to stop it. The girl, with her knowledge of the correct words, comes home just in time to stop the pot, but we are told that "whosoever wished to return to the town had to eat his way back" (wer wieder in die Stadt wollte, der mußte sich durchessen). Such tales can be found in many cultures throughout the world and over great periods of time, but here its significance lies in the fact that the girl, though the inheritor of the aged woman's knowledge, nonetheless requires an object to perform her magic, while the real magical powers lie not in her, or in her mother, but in the correct words themselves. Without them, the conjurer is powerless. This represents a marked change from the conjurings in "The Goose-Girl," "Cinderella," or "One-Eye, Two-Eyes, and Three-Eyes," for whom no such exactitude is required.

A different object, a magic knotted handkerchief analogous to the magic wand in French and English tradition, potentiates the invocation in the Low German tale "The Two King's Children." Confusingly composite, it unites familiar motifs from disparate traditions in a meandering literary fairy tale (*Kunstmärchen*). Three princesses live in a world populated by men: their father's masculine height is emphasized when he is described as a great tall man on his first appearance; the sisters' bedroom doors are guarded by statues of Saint Christopher; and the youngest sister has sway over numbers of little earth-men, whom she calls forth by taking her handkerchief, tying a knot in it, and striking it three times on the ground while saying; "Earthworkers, come forth" (Arweggers, herut!), and whom she dismisses with the words, "Earthworkers, go home" (Arweggers, to Hus!).

The earthworkers perform the stock impossible tasks for the hapless prince to help him win the youngest daughter as his bride. The king's wife, who materializes quite suddenly in midtale, pursues the fleeing couple and thus occupies the same position that witch figures do in analogous tales. But in an abrupt character reversal she later becomes a helpful maternal figure and provides her daughter with three walnuts, within each of which a beautiful gown is hidden. With them, the mother explains, her daughter can help herself when she is in greatest need. In the meantime, the prince returns home and announces his engagement, but his mother's kiss erases all memory of his betrothed, and he takes another bride. However, with her gowns, the young princess regains her betrothed's love; the prince's mother is declared to be false and must go away together with the false bride; and the two lovers have a merry wedding.

A highly confused picture of the two queens emerges from this tale. The narrator appears to have dimly remembered that old queens pass on magical powers and injects that motif in a timely manner in conjunction with the princess' mother. On the other hand, the prince's mother is made to waffle between an intentionally witchlike mother-in-lawdom and an unwittingly untoward influence on her son. Despite this confusion one element remains in its familiar channel: the earthworkers called forth by the young girl conform to the requirement that effective female conjuring grow out of an ultimate association or connection with the earth.

Men and magic coexist comfortably in *Grimms' Tales.* On occasion a man in a forest encounters an old woman who turns out to be a witch or who passes on important information in her incarnation as a wise woman. In "Donkey Salad" (RBB) (no. 122), for instance, an ugly woman meets a jolly hunter one day and tells him that if he eats the heart of a certain bird he will find a gold piece under his pillow every morning. It becomes clear from the tale, however, that whoever has the heart has the gold, and that the old woman has passed on no magic power to the hunter. All magic remains in the heart, which mindlessly enriches whoever has eaten it.

Men occasionally appear to share in women's spell-laying powers in the tales, but a close examination of these powers suggests that such tales derive from earlier forms with female protagonists or else are modern inventions. Male conjurations with a character distinctly their own exist in three of the tales. The incantation that produces food in "One-Eye, Two-Eyes, and Three-Eyes" reappears in "The Wishing-Table, the Gold-Ass, and the Cudgel in the Sack" (no. 36), but it represents a derivative form. It offers, first of all, a shortened form of the incantation. Second, the magic clearly resides completely in the object rather than in the person. Third, two elements joined in

"One-Eye"—the goat and the incantation—appear logically separated in "The Wishing-Table." And fourth, two elements—the goat and gold—remain linked but in altered form. In "The Wishing-Table" the narrator rather than a mysterious figure describes how one lays a spell:

> His master presented him with a little table which was not particularly beautiful, and was made of common wood, but which had one good property; if anyone set it out, and said: "Little table, spread yourself," the good little table was at once covered with a clean little cloth, and a plate was there, and a knife and fork beside it, and dishes with boiled meats and roasted meats, as many as there was room for, and a great glass of red wine shone so that it made the heart glad.

> [Der Meister] schenkte ihm ein Tischchen, das gar kein besonderes Ansehen hatte und von gewöhnlichem Holz war; aber es hatte eine gute Eigenschaft. Wenn man es hinstellte und sprach: "Tischchen, deck dich," so war das gute Tischchen auf einmal mit einem saubern Tüchlein bedeckt und stand da ein Teller und Messer und Gabel daneben und Schüsseln mit Gesottenem und Gebratenem, soviel Platz hatten, und ein großes Glas mit rotem Wein leuchtete, daß einem das Herz lachte.

The text hints at no particular link between the eldest son and chthonic powers; it is the table that possesses unmediated powers, like the lamps and rugs in the tales of *Thousand and One Nights*.

At first glance "Ferdinand the Faithful and Ferdinand the Unfaithful" (no. 126) seems to offer a clear example of successful male conjuring. Yet the natural creature, the talking white horse, represents an attenuated link with nature, for as the last sentence reveals, the horse is in reality a prince. Nonetheless, in his equine state, the horse tells Ferdinand how to calm dangerous giants and large birds, which he will encounter on his travels:

> When the giants come say:
> "Peace, peace, my dear little giants,
> I have had thought of ye,
> Something I have brought for ye."

> And when the birds come, you shall again say:
> 'Peace, peace, my dear little birds,
> I have had thought of ye,
> Something I have brought for ye."

> Wenn dann de Riesen kümmet, so segg:
> Still, still, meine lieben Riesechen,
> ich habe euch wohl bedacht,
> ich hab euch was mitgebracht.

> Un wenn de Vüggel kümmet, so seggst du wier:
> Still, still, meine lieben Vögelchen,
> ich hab euch wohl bedacht,
> ich hab euch was mitgebracht.

Ferdinand himself, however, never utters these words in the text of the tale, neither in the First Edition nor in any subsequent edition. If he had, then one could cite at least one example of a male who successfully lays a spell, which grows out of a male association with an apparently natural being, for the form of the spell fits the requirements if one allows for an implied imperative form, "Be" (Sei) before the word "peace" (still).

The final spells laid by men occur in "Brother Lustig" (no. 81) and suggest that men's verbal efficacy derives from different sources than women's. Here a soldier watches Saint Peter resurrect a dead princess by dismembering the corpse, boiling the bones, rearranging them properly, and saying three times: "In the name of the holy Trinity, dead woman, arise" (Im Namen der allerheiligsten Dreifaltigkeit, Tote, steh auf). However, when Brother Lustig tries to revive another dead princess in a separate episode, he fails dismally, because he cannot put the bones in the proper order. His flawed knowledge of nature thus prevents the formula from working.

First impressions deceive. It would seem that *Grimms' Tales* is sprinkled with conjuring witches, but instead it is young and beautiful women who call forth and direct powerful natural forces. Each of these young females is also unmarried, and within the terms of these tales, presumably virgin. The forms spells take and the conjurers apparently regarded as licit in the Grimms' collection point toward a latent belief in the natural powers of women, especially of virgins. Unlike the more familiar and thoroughly Christianized French medieval image of the virgin with her inherent ability to attract the magical mythical unicorn, German tradition as it appears in *Grimms' Tales* defines a sharp boundary between female spell-laying powers and Christian belief. [16]

16. This is all the more fascinating, since the Church had attempted, often successfully, to Christianize incantations used in daily life in Germany. For a recent discussion of this subject, see Robert Scribner, "Cosmic Order and Daily Life."

5

Patterns of Speech

s significant as tales of conjuring, the subject of the last chapter, are for offering a paradigm for who can use words to control natural forces, they nonetheless represent a vanishingly small proportion of speech use among the 210 tales of the Grimms' collection. General patterns of direct speech in *Grimms' Tales,* that is, who speaks and in what manner, comprise an essential component of content analysis, for they involve the very language in which the tales are told.[1] The most recent summations of scholarship on this subject call for a systematic categorization of folk narrative dialogue as well as a quantifying comparison in tales of different cultures, which chapters 5–7 address.[2]

A scholarly treatise is not needed to document centuries of male impatience with and irritation at women talking. Titles like *Language and Sex* (1975), *Language, Gender and Society* (1983), *Les Mots et Les Femmes* (1979), *Man Made Language* (1980, 1985), *Gewalt durch Sprache* (1984), and *Sex Differences in Human Speech* (1978) all betray an eager curiosity about and compelling concern with the question of who speaks in given situations, because discourse can be understood as a form of domination, and speech use as an index of social values and the distribution of power within a society.[3] Discourse in canonical

---

1. This chapter examines two aspects of speech in *Grimms' Tales:* frequency of direct and indirect speech and the nature of the verbs that introduce direct speech. Many additional questions can be asked of this material. Other researchers may wish, for example, to characterize utterances according to John Searle's or John Austin's systems (see chap. 4, n. 5). For the questions I pursue in this chapter, I continue to take linguistics as a guide, principally sociolinguistics (and in particular, those studies relevant to gender-specific language use), rather than structural or generative linguistic theory (see n. 3). In the Appendix, I touch on such seemingly transparent questions as the relationship of tale length to the gender of the protagonist. The extent, as distinct from the frequency, of discourse is another area for possible investigation. Responsive discourse and discourse that initiates action are further categories requiring examination.

2. Lüthi, "Dialog"; see also Moser-Rath, "Frau," and Köhler, "Die geschwätzige Frau."

3. The material in this chapter represents an extension into literary history of the lively discussion in linguistic circles about the relationship between gender, language, and social

literary texts, which preserve carefully and consciously crafted speech use and language, offers implicit evidence as well as explicit information about an author's or editor's disposition toward speech use in general and that of specific characters in particular.

Both speech and silencing can be analyzed on at least five levels in a literary text: historical, narrative, textual, lexical, and editorial. (1) At the historical level, the reader discerns whose pen may write. If women regularly use a male pseudonym as a literary subterfuge or if they have no voice in literary gatherings, the reader can infer a historical silencing. (2) The character who is condemned or cursed to a period of silence experiences narrative silencing in the plot. (3) The distribution of direct and indirect or reported speech offers the potential for silencing a character at a third—textual—level, one that is rarely, if ever, investigated in folk or canonical literature. (4) Silencing may also grow out of the verbs used to introduce direct or indirect speech. Certain verbs in *Grimms' Tales* validate the speech that follows, while other introductory verbs mark subsequent speech as illicit. (5) Finally, the author or editor may comment on the text within the text.

In *Grimms' Tales* the language of narration is particularly important in connection with direct and indirect speech. A century of criticism has celebrated Wilhelm Grimm's shift from indirect speech in the earliest versions of individual tales to direct speech in later and final versions. No critic has asked, "Who speaks?" or "Under what circumstances?" Even writers themselves, from whom one would expect sensitivity to nuances of language and speech patterns, have stopped at the level of plot in their scrutiny of *Grimms' Tales*.[4]

Several tales, among them the best known, purvey images of women muted narratively by the very language in which the tales are told. Alongside the frog's curt command to the princess, "Be quiet" (Sei still) in "The Frog-King" (no. 1), the reader sees the princess' numerous compliant reactions to the frog's imperious commands: to lift him to the table, to eat from her golden plate, and to take him to rest. Only when he adds that he expects to share her bed does the princess respond with spirited outrage, which turns out in fact to be Wilhelm Grimm's rather than hers.[5] In "Hansel and Gretel" (no. 15) Hansel speaks not only more often than Gretel, but also at greater length, and his first words to Gretel are "Quiet, Gretel" (Still, Gretel).

Textual silencing also exists in Rapunzel (no. 12) when Wilhelm Grimm describes her feelings rather than letting her give voice to her own reactions

---

structure. For illuminating discussions and an extensive bibliography, see Thorne, Kramarae, and Henley, eds., *Language, Gender and Society*.

4. When P. L. Travers writes that "Every woman—maiden, mother, or crone, Kore, Demeter, or Hecate—can find [in *Grimms' Tales*] her prototype, a model for her role in life," she describes only what happens in these tales, and not how these events are presented verbally ("Grimm's Women").

5. See chap. 14.

and thoughts. We learn of her "song" (Gesang) and "her sweet voice" (ihre süße Stimme), but do not hear her sing. We are told that "at first Rapunzel was terribly frightened when a man, such as her eyes had never yet beheld, came to her" (anfangs erschrak Rapunzel gewaltig, als ein Mann zu ihr hereinkam, wie ihre Augen noch nie einen erblickt hatten), but the prince cries out his surprise and his intention: "If that is the ladder by which one mounts, I too will try my fortune" (Ist das die Leiter, auf welcher man hinaufkommt, so will ich auch einmal mein Glück versuchen).

In "Cinderella" (no. 21) textual silence and powerlessness unite in the titular protagonist, despite her manifest conjuring abilities and eventual betrothal to a prince. After her piously expressed wish that her father bring her the first branch that brushes against his hat, Cinderella, aside from her formulaic incantations, says nothing. Silent at the ball, speechless among the ashes, mute when trying on the tiny slipper, Cinderella endures the barbs and jibes of her loquacious and delinquent stepsisters. It is not an overt curse that condemns her to silence; it is the pattern of discourse in *Grimms' Tales* that discriminates against "good" girls and produces functionally silent heroines.

Within the text of the collection, Grimm characterizes women's speech editorially both explicitly and implicitly. The lazy spinner's (no. 128) sloth-fulness parallels her readiness to speak: "she was always ready with her tongue" (so war sie mit ihrem Maul doch vornen), we are told, and furthermore she uses her speech to maintain her slothful ways when she tricks her husband with spooky chanting.

Implicit in most tales is the narrative, textual, and lexical silence of the biological mother. Snow-White's mother thinks to herself but never speaks (no. 53), and when her daughter is born, she dies. The same is true of Cinderella's mother, who first adjures her to be good and pious—and then dies. Hansel and Gretel's mother is entirely absent (no. 15), while the mother in "The Twelve Brothers" (no. 9) speaks once before disappearing forever from the tale, a pattern which recurs even in that ultimate tale of powerful womanhood, "The Goose-Girl" (no. 89). Opposed to these patterns established for girls and women, and especially to that of "The Lazy Spinner," is Master Pfriem's (no. 178) scolding tongue, which castigates his wife and lashes his apprentices from morning to night, both on earth and in heaven. For this shrill and strident male, punishment occurs only in a dream about heaven while his earthly life proceeds without change or chastisement.

How much speech Wilhelm Grimm accorded any single character resulted from apparently conscious choices. How that speech was introduced lexically, however, seems not to have been under any such conscious control, for the patterns that emerge, though generally regular, are not exact. Five verbs form the principal introductory group: "asked" (*fragte*), "answered" (*antwortete*), "cried" (*rief*), "said" (*sagte*), and "spoke" (*sprach*).

Asked must have represented something particularly problematic to Wilhelm, for he generally introduces questions not with *asked,* but with *said* or *spoke.*[6] *Asked* seldom introduces a woman's question; when it does make an infrequent appearance, *asked* generally introduces a question posed either by an acknowledged authority figure (St. Peter, a king, or a father) or by a character already known to be wicked or who will turn out to be wicked or disastrous in the course of the tale, such as the wife in "The Gold-Children" (no. 85).[7] Those rare occasions on which *asked* introduces a good girl's question seem to mark the fact that Wilhelm did not consciously distinguish among introductory verbs, but instead unconsciously expressed his basic feelings and beliefs about gender differences through them. Typical examples of how Wilhelm avoided using *asked* occur in "The Robber-Bridegroom" (no. 40): "Then said the bridegroom to the bride: 'Come, my darling, do you know nothing?' " (Da sprach der Bräutigam zur Braut: "Nun, mein Herz, weißt du nichts?"). Within the context of a dream, his bride then recounts having asked a question, but immediately discounts everything she has said by adding, "My darling, I only dreamt this" (Mein Schatz, das träumte mir nur). The following formulation is more typical: " 'Can you not tell me,' said the maiden, 'if my betrothed lives here?' " ("Könnt Ihr mir nicht sagen," sprach das Mädchen, "ob mein Bräutigam hier wohnt?"). Little Briar-Rose (no. 50) also uses *spoke* rather than *asked* to introduce a straightforward query: " 'What sort of thing is that, that rattles round so merrily?' said the girl" ("Was für ein Ding, das so lustig herumspringt?" sprach das Mädchen). Younger questioners use *said:*

> But the young child grew impatient and said: "Dear mother, how can I cover my father's face when I have no father in this world?"
>
> Da ward das Knäbchen ungeduldig und sagte: "Liebe Mutter, wie kann ich meinem Vater das Gesicht zudecken, ich habe keinen Vater auf der Welt?"

Answered on the other hand, is quite unproblematic on its numerous appearances. Although both men and women use it, a clear pattern emerges of the female voice as responsive to the male voice, for it appears more often in

---

6. Typical of stylistic discussions of *Grimms' Tales* is Elisabeth Freitag, *Die Kinder- und Hausmärchen der Brüder Grimm im ersten Stadium ihrer stilgeschichtlichen Entwicklung,* where she introduces her work thus: the dissertation "legt die Beobachtungen in typischen Beispielen vor, verzichtet jedoch darauf, über die Vergleichsergebnissen zu reflektieren" (p. 1, "presents observations in the form of typical examples, foregoes however reflecting on comparative results"). With reference to the question of *sagen* vs. *sprechen* she says only " . . . das bibelmäßige 'sprach' der Urform ist fast überall durch 'sagte' ersetzt . . ." (p. 55, "the Biblical *spoke* of the original version has been replaced nearly everywhere by *said*"). She avoids drawing general conclusions from her data and raises no questions concerning gender, as do most stylistic inquiries into *Grimms' Tales.*

7. Her irrepressible curiosity twice breaks the spell that has brought wealth to her and her husband, and causes it all to fade away.

good girls' mouths than in their suitors', their fathers', or their kings'. In like manner *cried (out)* introduces female speech more often than male speech, perhaps because the plots of the tales jeopardize women more often than men. Of all the introductory verbs, only *said* seems user-neutral. It introduces the speech of male and female, good and evil, high and low without distinction. *Spoke*, however, is charged with meaning.[8] Like *asked*, *spoke* is reserved primarily for acknowledged authority figures. If used too frequently to introduce female speech, it usually heralds a bad hat. The princess' first use of *spoke* in "The Three Snake-Leaves" (no. 16) presents no problem, for it introduces a question, a licit use of the verb in connection with women's speech, but its second occurrence marks the point in the narrative at which her actively evil nature becomes clear. A further and more tantalizing use of *spoke* occurs in "The Story of the Youth Who Went Forth to Learn What Fear Was" (no. 4). Here a potential social distinction emerges and suggests that working people are subject to rules different from those governing precursor (and real) princesses' and princes' speech, as the innkeeper's wife and the chambermaid each use *spoke* once, and the sexton's wife poses a question with *asked*, while the boy/king's wife remains mute.[9] She is described as annoyed but is given no direct speech to express her irritation, whereas the youth expresses a broad range of emotions in his various direct speeches.

The Grimms' *Wörterbuch der deutschen Sprache* (dictionary of the German language) distinguishes *sprechen* ("speak") from *sagen* ("say") by pointing out that *sprechen* has given way to *sagen* in general usage and has taken on a somewhat ceremonial character. Whereas *sprechen* places more emphasis on the act of speaking itself, the use of *sagen* emphasizes the content of an utterance.[10]

The five principal introductory verbs "focalize" the character who speaks, putting him or her into a certain psychological perspective.[11] Patterns in the focalizing process admit the reader to the narrator's psychological stance, while speech itself and the manner in which it is introduced form part of the textual "chain of authority." The fact that the patterns which emerge from a close reading of the fairy tales are regular but not rigorously so suggests that they represent unconscious expressions of Wilhelm Grimm's deeply held convictions. Thus, the extent of a girl or woman's association with *speak* is more important than whether the verb appears in female company at all.

---

8. As the reader has probably observed, this distinction is often erased in the process of translation.

9. This use of *spoke* for peasant, artisan, and petty bourgeois speakers recurs in jest tales (*Schwänke*). See my Appendix.

10. These definitions were not composed by the Grimms themselves, who only got as far as "E" during their lifetimes, but they correspond to the way Wilhelm Grimm uses *sagen* and *sprechen*.

11. The vocabulary of the following paragraph draws on Susan Sniader Lanser, "From Person to Persona," in *The Narrative Act*, 108–48, esp. 140–41.

Furthermore, since *asked* is regularly avoided in favor of *said* or *spoke,* the appearance of *spoke* can be further refined into those instances that represent a displacement down the scale of authority from *asked* and those that represent the act of speaking. In "The Frog-King" the frog "speaks" while the princess uses only *said* and *answered.* Both the Virgin Mary and the king use *spoke* exclusively in "Our Lady's Child" (no. 3), while the disobedient but long-suffering girl uses *spoke* twice, *answered* once, *said* twice, and *cried out* once. In "The Story of the Youth Who Went Forth to Learn What Fear Was," the first instance of the verb *spoke* marks the narrative point at which the youth assumes authority. Furthermore, the same character associates "speaking" with candid male characteristics when he calls out, "Speak, if you are an honest fellow" (Sprich, wenn du ein ehrlicher Kerl bist). The same lexical pattern emerges in "Faithful John" (no. 6), whose hero Grimm restricts to *said* and *answered* until the moment in which he acts independently and suggests a solution to the king's problems: "At length he thought of a way, and said to the king . . ." (Endlich hat er ein Mittel ausgedacht und sprach zu dem König . . .). Indeed, the adjective *candid* (*redlich*), which evokes the act of talking (*reden*) is regularly and preferentially applied to men in German from at least the Middle Ages onward. [12] This analysis of the use of *spoke* to distinguish between male and female as well as between good and evil speech holds up even in animal tales, where *spoke* introduces the bad wolf's speeches, while the frightened old nanny goat uses *said* and the endangered kids *cry out* their fear ("The Wolf and the Seven Little Kids," no. 5).

These distinctions of frequency and particularity can be used predictively with some reliability. Knowing that the plot of "Mother Holle" (no. 24) includes a beautiful diligent maiden and her ugly and lazy stepsister, one can assume that the latter will talk more often. Brief though this tale is, it, too, maintains the pattern in which bad girls talk more frequently (2:1).

To scrutinize the phenomenon of patterns of speech in *Grimms' Tales* properly, both intensive and extensive examinations are necessary. Because the collection is so popular and widely read, and because its constellation of characters conforms to general patterns in other popular tales, "Cinderella" makes an ideal choice for a close reading. [13]

12. For numerous examples see the article on *redlich* in the Grimms' *Wörterbuch der Deutschen Sprache,* 8: cols. 476–82.

13. To confirm the validity of conclusions drawn from a single tale, even though it can be taken as paradigmatic for the collection as a whole, this discussion continues with a survey of five groups of tales in the Appendix.

6

"Cinderella"

n addition to offering a plot familiar throughout the world, "Cinderella" (no. 21) exists in numerous easily accessible versions so that readers may continue the study presented here among other versions of the tale.[1] It is also a tale thought to have been collected by Wilhelm Grimm, so that a close scrutiny of the tale is not necessarily clouded by questions of a shift from Jacob's gathering to Wilhelm's editing.[2] For the European tradition as it impinges on *Grimms' Tales,* Perrault's 1697 publication serves as a convenient starting point. His heroine, like Wilhelm Grimm's, is an exemplar of kindness and virtue, whereas Basile's Zezolla in "La Gatta Cenerentola" exhibits character traits alien to later "good" fairy tale heroines in England, France, and Germany.

Of the eight tales in Perrault's original volume, seven were widely translated, adapted, and imitated. That the eighth, "Riquet à la Houppe" (Ricky of the Tuft), remained a commodity unexportable to Germany may well have to do with its subject, for it details the story of two sisters, one beautiful but *stupide,* the other ugly but articulate. In return for the beautiful princess' love, the ugly Riquet confers eloquence upon her, uniting two qualities which perfect her as a woman in Perrault's seventeenth-century French courtly vision. This romance of beautiful articulate womanhood has dropped out of the canon of children's literature and it never seems to have entered the German tradition. Of the seven other tales, however, "Cinderella" probably occupies pride of place in its many translations (Robert Samber's 1729 version introduced it to the English-speaking tradition).

The general outlines of the Grimm version of "Cinderella" belong to central and northern Europe together with the areas it influenced.[3] Consistent with

---

1. See Cox, *Cinderella: Three Hundred and Forty-Five Variants;* Rooth, *The Cinderella Cycle;* and Dundes, *Cinderella: A Folklore Casebook.*

2. Rölleke, *Kinder- und Hausmärchen* (1857), 3:451. Jacob collected approximately two-thirds of the tales in the earliest edition.

3. The Scottish tale of Rashin Coatie, for example, would seem to derive from Scandinavian sources.

Germanic beliefs in women's ability to conjure, these tales unite the powers of the godmother and the sufferings of the pariah in the figure of a cinder-girl able to lay spells. Cinderella is an effective conjurer, but as a daughter and sister, she remains conspicuously silent in the face of verbal abuse from her stepsisters and stepmother. When Wilhelm Grimm had edited "Cinderella" for the last Large Edition (1857), the text contained the following number of spontaneous direct statements, questions, or thoughts as defined not only by punctuation marks but also by pronoun use consistent with direct speech.[4]

Cinderella:	1
Stepsisters:	5
Stepmother:	7
Father:	3
Prince:	8

The prince, with eight direct statements, dominates the direct speech of this tale, while the stepmother's seven speeches mark her as a woman to beware of. The stepsisters appear as relatively undifferentiated; three of their utterances are expressed in common, while each has only a single statement of her own. Consistent with the general paternal ineffectuality one finds in *Grimms' Tales,* two of Cinderella's father's statements are unspoken but directly rendered thoughts, while the third is a kindly question. Cinderella utters five incantations in addition to responding once to her father's question concerning what she would like him to bring her from his trip.

These figures, representing the final point on a continuum of editorial reworking, are most revealing when assessed from the broader perspective of the entire editorial history of this tale, beginning with the first edition in 1812.[5] The incidence of indirect as well as direct speech follows a pattern, not, as has been asserted, a simple pattern of replacing indirect with direct speech. Rather direct speech has tended to be transferred from women to men, and from good to bad girls and women (see table 6.1). This simple tabulation counters the long-held orthodoxy that Wilhelm Grimm replaced indirect with direct speech. Instead it reveals a stark reduction in direct speech for Cinderella (from 14 to 6), her stepsisters (16–5) and the doves (10–3), with an equally notable increase in direct speech for the stepmother (4–7), the father (0–3) and the prince (4–8). Furthermore, it shows an *increase* in indirect speech for Cinderella (0–1), her stepmother (0–1) (1819), and even for her father (0–1), while the significant reduction in indirect speech for the prince in 1819 (5–2) is followed by an increase in indirect speech in 1857 (2–4).

---

4. Cinderella's formulaic incantations are considered separately.

5. The 1810 version of this tale is assumed to have been lost by Clemens Brentano. Although the Grimms subsequently refer to it in their correspondence with Brentano, it does not form a part of the Ölenberg collection.

Table 6.1: Direct Speech and Thought in "Cinderella"

		1812	1819	1857
Good Girls and Women and Their Associates				
Cinderella:	indirect	—	2	1
	direct (includes spells)	14	6	6
Doves:	indirect	—	—	—
	direct	10	3	3
Mother:	indirect	—	—	—
	direct	1	1	1
Total indirect		0	2	1
Total direct		25	10	10
Bad Girls and Women				
Stepsisters:	indirect	—	—	—
	direct	16	4	5
Stepmother:	indirect	—	1	—
	direct	4	8	7
Total indirect		0	1	0
Total direct		20	12	12
Men				
Father:	indirect	—	1	1
	direct	—	3	3
Prince:	indirect	5	2	4
	direct	4	9	8
Total indirect		5	3	5
Total direct		4	12	11

When the characters are grouped by their relationships to one another, the shifts in the number of their utterances become even more obvious. Direct speeches by good characters—Cinderella, her mother, and her agents, the doves—are reduced from 25 (1812) to 10 (1857). Utterances by the wicked female constellation—the stepsisters and their mother—are also reduced, but not as drastically, from 20 (1812) to 12 (1857), while the prince and Cinderella's father, Cinderella's two possessors, increase the number of their utterances from 4 to 11. These results indicate that the distribution of direct speech to various characters is part of a highly selective process. No clear pattern is established, however, in the incidence of indirect speech. Together, these two observations nullify a long-held belief about Wilhelm Grimm's editorial policy, for this tale shows that he did not simply animate early versions of the tales by replacing indirect with direct speech. Instead, a detailed analysis reveals that Grimm removed direct speech from women and gave it to men.

A closer inspection shows that Grimm used speech to define character. Thus, the stepmother's increased frequency of speaking defines her wicked intentions, realized when she heartlessly makes her daughters mutilate their feet to fit them into the tiny royal slipper. In one of the many internal contradictions of this and other tales, the lamed sisters subsequently walk to church and back, during which perambulation they are further savagely punished by having their eyes pecked out. By most standards of justice it should be the stepmother who suffers punishment, but, perhaps as part of its normative function, this text punishes bad girls, presumably as a warning against juvenile "wickedness and falsehood" (Bosheit und Falschheit).

The tabulated figures confirm a significant plot alteration that occurs between the 1812 and the 1819 editions and accompanies the shifts in direct speech. In the first edition (1812), as in Perrault's version, Cinderella's chief antagonists are her stepsisters. The reduction in the number of their speeches and the increase in their mother's speeches in the second edition (1819) signals the shift of antagonism from the sisters to the stepmother. The father is virtually absent as a character in 1812, but he enters as an amiable though feckless foil to his second wife in the 1819 and subsequent editions. This selective process in assigning speech produces some startling contrasts. In 1812, for example, Cinderella actively questions her situation and wonders how she can get to the ball when she says, "Oh, how can I go, I have no clothes" (Ach, ja, wie kann ich aber hingehen, ich habe keine Kleider). The same point in the text in 1857 assumes she can't go and emphasizes her obedient misery:

> Cinderella obeyed, but wept, because she too would have liked to go with them to the dance, and begged her step-mother to allow her to do so.

> Aschenputtel gehorchte, weinte aber, weil es gern zum Tanz mitgegangen wäre, und bat die Stiefmutter, sie möchte es ihm erlauben.

The stepsisters' incidence of direct speeches and thought breaks down differently in the 1812, 1819, and 1857 versions:

	1812	1819	1857
Older sister	6	1	1
Younger sister	2	1	1
Both sisters in unison	8	2	3
Total	16	4	5

As is almost always the case in fairy tales, the younger sister in the 1812 version is also the more sympathetic. Her smaller number of speeches suggests that and the text confirms it: "then the youngest, who still retained a bit of sympathy in her heart, said . . ." (da sagte die jüngste, die noch ein wenig Mitleid im Herzen hatte. . .). By 1819, however, the stepsisters have become undifferentiated antagonists, speaking less often, but more often than not voicing their taunts in unison. The overall reduction in the number of speeches Cinderella and the stepsisters have at their disposal also contracts their range of expression. This is best seen by listing all instances of their direct speech in the 1812 and the 1857 editions.

Cinderella's Direct Speech in the First Edition (1812)

"Oh," she said and sighed, "how can I go, I have no dresses."
"Ach ja, wie kann ich aber hingehen, ich habe keine Kleider."

"Oh," she said and sighed, "then I'll have to pick til midnight and I daren't shut my eyes, even if they hurt ever so much, if only my mother knew about that."
"Ach, sagte es und seufzte dabei, da muß ich dran lesen bis Mitternacht und darf die Augen nicht zufallen lassen, und wenn sie mir noch so weh thun, wenn das meine Mutter wüßte."

"Yes," answered Cinderella:
  "the bad into the crop
    the good into the pot."
"Ja, antwortete Aschenputtel:
  die schlechten ins Kröpfchen
    die guten ins Töpfchen."

"Yes," said Cinderella, "I saw the lights shimmering, that must have been really magnificent."
"Ja, sagte Aschenputtel, ich habe die Lichter flimmern sehen, das mag recht prächtig gewesen seyn."

"I stood up on the dovecote."
"Ich hab' oben auf den Taubenstall gestanden."

"Yes,—the bad into the crop,
    the good into the pot."
"Ja,—die schlechten ins Kröpfchen,
    die guten ins Töpfchen."

"Oh, my God," she said, "how can I go in my ugly clothes?
    Little tree, shiver and shake
    Throw beautiful clothes down for me."
"O du mein Gott, sagte es, wie kann ich in meinen schlechten Kleidern hingehen?"
  "Bäumlein rüttel und schüttel dich,
  wirf schöne Kleider herab für mich."

"Little tree, shiver and shake!
Take my clothes back for me."
"Bäumlein rüttel dich und schüttel dich!
nimm die Kleider wieder für dich!"

"you probably had lots of fun last night"
"ihr habt wohl gestern abend viel Freude gehabt"

"Was it perhaps the one who drove in the magnificent coach with the six black horses?"
"Ist es vielleicht die gewesen, die in den prächtigen Wagen mit den sechs Rappen gefahren ist?"

"I stood in the doorway and saw them drive past."
"Ich stand in der Hausthüre, da sah ich sie vorbeifahren."

"Yes, the bad into the crop
    the good into the pot."
"Ja, die schlechten ins Kröpfchen
    die guten ins Töpfchen."

"Little tree, shiver and shake,
throw beautiful clothes down for me."
"Bäumlein rüttel dich und schüttel dich,
wirf schöne Kleider herab für mich."

Cinderella explains, conjectures, conjures, questions, assumes, and lies in her fourteen speaking appearances in the 1812 edition. She even echoes Falada's intimation in "The Goose-Girl" (no. 89) of an unseen but powerful maternal presence: "If only my mother knew abut that" (Wenn das meine Mutter wüßte). Her extended and varied talk ends abruptly with the narrator's statement, "Cinderella well knew who the unknown princess was, but she said nary a word" (Aschenputtel wußte wohl wer die fremde Prinzessin war, aber es sagte kein Wörtchen).

Cinderella's Direct Speech in the Last Large Edition (1857)

The 1857 version presents a far different picture. Here Cinderella has nearly lost her filial voice, responding only to her father's inquiry about what he should bring her from his trip: "'Father, break off for me the first branch which knocks against your hat on your way home'" ("Vater, das erste Reis, das Euch auf Eurem Heimweg an den Hut stößt, das brecht für mich ab"). After this she twice conjures the birds:

"You tame pigeons, you turtledoves, and all you birds beneath the sky, come and help me to pick
    The good into the pot,
    The bad into the crop."

"Ihr zahmen Turteltäubchen, ihr Turteltäubchen, all ihr Vöglein unter dem Himmel, kommt und helft mir lesen,
    die guten ins Töpfchen,
    die schlechten ins Kröpfchen."

and thrice the tree:

> "Shiver and quiver, my little tree,
> Silver and gold throw down over me."

> "Bäumchen, rüttel dich und schüttel dich,
> wirf Gold und Silber über mich."

In depriving Cinderella of her voice, Grimm has further isolated her within the tale, relegating nearly all her talk with people to indirect discourse, but leaving her the unvarying incantations addressed to birds and tree.

The Stepsisters' Direct Speech in the First Edition (1812)

The stepsisters, beautiful of face but proud of heart,[6] manifest a different set of concerns in their early (1812) conversation, straying but rarely from clothing and coiffure. Snatching Cinderella's beautiful gowns away from her and giving her an old gray dress, they say:

> "that's all right for *you!*"
> "der ist gut für dich!"

> "Cinderella," they called, "come upstairs, comb our hair, brush our shoes and fasten them up, we're going to the ball to [see] the prince."
> "Aschenputtel, riefen sie, komm herauf, kämme uns die Haare, bürst uns die Schuhe und schnalle sie fest, wir gehen auf den Ball zu den Prinzen."

> [They] asked sarcastically, "Cinderella, you'd probably like to go along to the ball?"
> [Sie] fragten spöttisch: "Aschenputtel, du gingst wohl gern mit auf den Ball?"

> "No," said the eldest, "that would be a fine thing for you to be seen there, we'd certainly be embarrassed when people heard you were our sister; you belong in the kitchen. You have a dish of lentils; when we come back they have to be sorted, and watch out that not a single bad one is [left] among the good ones, otherwise you'll have nothing good to expect."
> "Nein, sagte die älteste, das wär mir recht, daß du dich dort sehen ließest, wir müßten uns schämen, wenn die Leute hörten, daß du unsere Schwester wärest; du gehörst in die Küche, da hast du eine Schüssel voll Linsen, wann wir wieder kommen muß sie gelesen seyn, und hüt dich, daß keine böse darunter ist, sonst hast du nichts Gutes zu erwarten."

On their return, the stepsisters breathlessly flaunt their pleasure in the glories of the prince's ball:

> "Cinderella, it was a joy, at the dance, the prince, the handsomest one in the world, led us out, and one of us will be his wife."

---

6. Subsequently changed to "black of heart but white of face."

"Aschenputtel, das ist ein Lust gewesen, bei dem Tanz, der Prinz, der allerschönste auf der Welt hat uns dazu geführt, und eine von uns wird seine Gemahlin werden."

When Cinderella, who has magically witnessed it all through the dovecote, knowingly comments on the chandeliers, they interrogate her: " 'Hey! how do you know that?' asked the eldest" ("Ei! wie hast du das angefangen," fragte die älteste). The next day Cinderella must help prepare them for the ball again.

Then the youngest one, who still had a bit of compassion in her heart, said, "Cinderella, when it's dark you can go out and peek in through the windows." "No," said the eldest, "that'll only make her lazy. You have a sack of vetch, Cinderella. Sort the good from the bad and work well, and if you haven't done it by tomorrow, then I'll dump them into the ashes and you'll go hungry until you've picked them all out again."

Da sagte die jüngste, die noch ein wenig Mitleid im Herzen hatte: "Aschenputtel, wenns dunkel ist, kannst du hinzugehen und von außen durch die Fenster gucken!" "Nein, sagte die älteste, das macht sie nur faul, da hast du einen Sack voll Wicken, Aschenputtel, da lese die guten und bösen auseinander und sey fleißig, und wenn du sie morgen nicht rein hast, so schütte ich dir sie in die Asche und du mußt hungern, bis du sie alle herausgesucht hast."

Their spirits dampened by the unknown princess' stunning success at the ball, the stepsisters appear morosely in the kitchen the next morning. Angered by Cinderella's disingenuous suggestion that they had again had a wonderful time, they say:

"No, there was a princess there, the prince danced with her almost the whole time, but nobody recognized her and nobody knew where she came from."

"Nein, es war eine Prinzessin da, mit der hat der Prinz fast immer getanzt, es hat sie aber niemand gekannt und niemand gewußt, woher sie gekommen ist."

Cinderella asks whether it was the princess who had arrived in the coach pulled by six black horses. " 'How do you know that?' " ("Woher weißt du das?"), they ask. She had stood in the doorway and watched them pass by.

"In the future stay at your work," said the eldest and looked at Cinderella angrily. "Why do you need to stand in the doorway?"

"In Zukunft bleib bei deiner Arbeit, sagte die älteste und sah Aschenputtel böse an, was brauchst du in der Hausthüre zu stehen."

For the third time Cinderella assists at the stepsisters' toilette, and this time she has to sort a dish of peas. " 'And don't you dare leave your work,' the eldest called out as she left" ("und daß du dich nicht unterstehst von der Arbeit wegzugehen, rief die älteste noch nach"). On their return the stepsisters querulously require Cinderella's services: " 'Cinderella, get up and light the way for us' " ("Aschenputtel, steh auf und leucht uns"). At her appearance they grumble:

"God knows who the cursed princess is, I wish she were dead and buried! The prince danced only with her, and when she was gone, he didn't want to stay any longer and the whole party was over."

"Gott weiß, wer die verwünschte Prinzessin ist, daß sie in der Erde begraben läg! der Prinz hat nur mit ihr getanzt und als sie weg war, hat er gar nicht mehr bleiben wollen und das ganze Fest hat ein Ende gehabt."

"It was as if all the lights were blown out all of a sudden," said the other.

"Es war recht, als wären alle Lichter auf einmal ausgeblasen worden," sagte die andere.

Thus ends the stepsisters' vocal participation as it is rendered in the 1812 First Edition, where the large number of speeches allows a certain complexity and differentiation of character between the younger and the more wicked older sister.

The Stepsisters' Direct Speech in the Final Edition (1857)

The textual description of the stepsisters' appearance and behavior is markedly reduced in the final (1857) form: they are described as "beautiful and fair of face, but vile and black of heart" (schön und weiß von Angesicht . . . aber garstig und schwarz von Herzen). Similarly, the incidence of and differentiation within their speeches also decreases. Spoken in unison, their first statements outline their relationship with Cinderella:

"Is the stupid goose to sit in the parlor with us?" they said.
"Soll die dumme Gans bei uns in der Stube sitzen!" sprachen sie.

"Whoever wants to eat bread must earn it; out with the kitchen-wench."
"Wer Brot essen will, muß es verdienen: hinaus mit der Küchenmagd."

"Just look at the proud princess, how decked out she is!"
"Seht einmal die stolze Prinzessin, wie sie geputzt ist!" riefen sie, lachten und führten es in die Küche.

Individually they respond greedily to their father's question about what they'd like from his trip: " 'Beautiful dresses,' said one, 'pearls and jewels,' said the second" ("Schöne Kleider," sagte die eine, "Perlen und Edelsteine" die zweite). They speak in unison once again, ordering Cinderella to serve them.

"Comb our hair for us, brush our shoes and fasten our buckles, for we are going to the wedding at the King's palace."

"Kämm uns die Haare, bürste uns die Schuhe und mache uns die Schnallen fest, wir gehen zur Hochzeit auf des Königs Schloß."

The unsisterly taunts of 1812 have disappeared from their mouths, and they seem more spoiled than evil.

The Stepmother's Direct Speech (1812)

A very different transformation is made to take place within the stepmother. In the 1812 edition the stepmother is the one who sends Cinderella off into the kitchen, who urges her daughters to maim their feet, and who denies that Cinderella might be the girl the prince seeks:

> "What's that disgusting good-for-nothing doing in the parlor . . . out with her and into the kitchen, if she wants to eat bread, she has to earn it first, she can be our maid."
> "Was macht der garstige Unnütz in den Stuben . . . fort mit ihr in die Küche, wenn sie Brod essen will, muß sies erst verdient haben, sie kann unsere Magd seyn."

> "Listen," said the mother secretly, "here's a knife, and if the slipper is still too tight for you, then cut a piece of your foot off, it'll hurt a little, but what's the harm, it'll soon pass and one of you will become the queen."
> "Hört," sagte die Mutter heimlich, da habt ihr ein Messer, und wenn euch der Pantoffel doch noch zu eng ist, so schneidet euch ein Stück vom Fuß ab, es thut ein bischen weh, was schadet das aber, es vergeht bald und eine von euch wird Königin."

> But the mother said to the second daughter, "You take the slipper, and if it's too short for you, cut the end of your toes off."
> Die Mutter aber sagte zur zweiten Tochter: "nimm du den Pantoffel, und wenn er dir zu kurz ist, so schneide lieber vorne an den Zehen ab."

> "No," said the mother, "there's only an ugly scullery maid left, she's sitting downstairs among the ashes, the slipper can't possibly fit *her*."
> "Nein, sagte die Mutter, nur ein garstiges Aschenputtel ist noch da, das sitzt unten in der Asche, dem kann der Pantoffel nicht passen".

The Stepmother's Direct Speech (1857)

In the 1857 version, malevolence concentrates and speech use expands in the stepmother as the time frame within which she speaks contracts and she fills this time by plaguing her beautiful but hapless stepdaughter.

> "You go, Cinderella!" said she; "covered in dust and dirt as you are, and would go to the festivities? You have no clothes and shoes, and yet would dance!"
> "Du, Aschenputtel," sprach sie, "bist voll Staub und Schmutz und willst zur Hochzeit? Du hast keine Kleider und Schuhe und willst tanzen!"

> "I have emptied a dish of lentils into the ashes for you, if you have picked them out again in two hours, you shall go with us."
> "Da habe ich dir eine Schüssel Linsen in die Asche geschüttet, wenn du die Linsen in zwei Stunden wieder ausgelesen hast, so sollst du mitgehen."

> "No, Cinderella, you have no clothes and you can not dance; you would only be laughed at."

"Nein, Aschenputtel, du hast keine Kleider und kannst nicht tanzen: du wirst nur ausgelacht."

"If you can pick two dishes of lentils out of the ashes for me in one hour, you shall go with us."
"Wenn du mir zwei Schüsseln voll Linsen in einer Stunde aus der Asche rein lesen kannst, so sollst du mit gehen."

"All of this will not help; you cannot go with us, for you have no clothes and can not dance; we should be ashamed of you!"
"Es hilft dir alles nichts: du kommst nicht mit, denn du hast keine Kleider und kannst nicht tanzen; wir müßten uns deiner schämen."

"Cut the toe off; when you are Queen you will have no more need to go on foot."
"Hau die Zehe ab: wann du Königin bist, so brauchst du nicht mehr zu Fuß zu gehen."

"Cut a bit off your heel; when you are Queen you will have no more need to go on foot."
"Hau ein Stück von der Ferse ab: wann du Königin bist, brauchst du nicht mehr zu Fuß zu gehen."

Herself the cause of Cinderella's destitution, the stepmother charges her with an inadequate wardrobe, and when Cinderella satisfies her senseless preconditions of picking lentils from the ashes, the wicked woman still refuses to allow her to go to the dance.

The Prince's Direct Speech (1812)

In the first edition, the prince's four utterances encompass Cinderella's experiences from the point at which she first appears at the ball to the moment when he confirms her as his betrothed. As soon as Cinderella appears at the ball, the prince reflects: " 'I'm supposed to pick out a bride for myself, I know none but this one for me' " ("Ich soll mir eine Braut aussuchen, da weiß ich mir keine als diese"). And after he finds her shoe, he comments on two of the three attempts:

"That's not the right bride, either; isn't there another daughter in the house."
"Das ist auch nicht die rechte Braut; aber ist nicht noch eine Tochter im Haus."

"Try it on! and if it fits you, you'll be my wife."
"Probier ihn an! und wenn er dir paßt, wirst du meine Gemahlin."

"That's the right bride."
"Das ist die rechte Braut."

The Prince's Direct Speech (1857)

The utterances added in subsequent editions and codified in 1857 establish not only the prince's recognition of the right bride but his proprietary interest in her, as he thrice repeats that she is *his* dancing partner.

"This is my partner."
"Das ist meine Tänzerin."

"I will go with you and bear you company."
"Ich gehe mit und begleite dich."

"This is my partner."
"Das ist meine Tänzerin."

"The unknown maiden has escaped from me, and I believe she has climbed up the pear-tree."
"Das fremde Mädchen ist mir entwischt, und ich glaube, es ist auf den Birnbaum gesprungen."

"This is my partner."
"Das ist meine Tänzerin."

"No one shall be my wife but she whose foot this golden slipper fits."
"Keine andere soll meine Gemahlin werden als die, an deren Fuß dieser goldene Schuh paßt."

"This also is not the right one," said he, "have you no other daughter?"
"Das ist auch nicht die rechte," sprach er, "habt Ihr keine andere Tochter?"

"That is the true bride!"
"Das ist die rechte Braut!"

Beyond establishing his proprietary interest in Cinderella, the prince also sets the condition for identifying his betrothed. In addition, he joins forces with the other male character, Cinderella's father, when he tells him he thinks she has leapt into the pear tree, whereupon the father chops down the tree in an effort to find and identify the mysterious princess, whom he finally suspects of being his own daughter.[7]

The Father's Direct Speech (1812)

The father's position changes more radically than any other figure's in "Cinderella," for in the 1812 version he serves only to open the tale, disappearing without a trace after the first sentence. The majority of the most popular tales share a five-person list of significant characters: good girl, mother, evil figure, father or king, and suitor. This does not mean, of course, that these tales have only five characters, but that these five usually form the base line for the plot. Part of Grimm's editorial concern in bringing the father into higher relief in this tale might have been to align "Cinderella" with this consistent pattern. The father's genteel ineffectuality links him, in any case, with other father figures in popular tales such as "Hansel and Gretel" (no. 15), "Snow-White" (no. 53), "Rapunzel" (no. 12), and "Little Briar-Rose" (no. 50).

7. Cinderella disappearing into a pear tree is a special instance of the special relationship of girls, women, and trees, which is explored in chap. 10.

The Father's Direct Speech (1857)

The 1857 version of "Cinderella" opens with a mention of the father, whose relationship with daughter and stepdaughters alike is established when he asks all three (in indirect discourse) what they would like him to bring home from his journey. Although Grimm—or Georg Reimer, his publisher—punctuates much of the girls' direct speech indirectly, he treats the father's recurring thoughts as direct speech:

> The old man thought: "Can it be Cinderella?"
> Der Alte dachte: "Sollte es Aschenputtel sein."
>
> The father thought: "Can it be Cinderella?"
> Der Vater dachte: "Sollte es Aschenputtel sein."

Neutralizing him in words as his inaction has neutralized him in the plot, his spoken words confirm his paternal ignorance of his own daughter, despite previously expressed presentiments:

> "No," said the man, "there is still a little stunted kitchen-wench which my late wife left behind her, but she cannot possibly be the bride."
>
> "Nein," sagte der Mann, "nur von meiner verstorbenen Frau ist noch ein kleines verbuttetes Aschenputtel da: das kann unmöglich die Braut sein."

This statement puts him in complete agreement with his evil wife, the stepmother, who also insists that the remaining girl could not be the one sought by the prince.

The changes discussed here represent a shift within a German-language fairy tale tradition. Fairy tales read in German by the German bourgeoisie in the early years of the nineteenth century still derived largely from French sources. The French "Cinderella" tradition, together with the English tradition based on it, has a very different narrative, textual, and lexical character and history. Cinderella's last speech is also the last direct speech in Perrault's tale, and in it she herself, highly amused because she already knows the outcome, suggests that she try on the fateful slipper: "Cinderella was looking on and recognized her slipper: 'Let me see,' she cried, laughingly, 'if it will not fit me.'"[8] An early translator into English even has the fairy godmother evaluate Cinderella's speech as praiseworthy in the following exchange: "I'll go and look into the Trapp for Rats, whether I'll find a Rat or other for a Coachman. Well said, said the Fairie. Go and see." As in the tale of "Riquet à la Houppe," beauty can also articulate its fate in the French and English tradition, while Grimm's Cinderella had to be called (mußte gerufen werden).

A close analysis of this single tale reveals a truth about the tale itself and also represents a broader phenomenon in conjunction with speech use in *Grimms'*

---

8. Taken from A. E. Johnson's translation of *Perrault's Fairy Tales.*

Tales. The incidence, distribution, and presentation of direct speech in "Cinderella" express a skewed view of the sexes and their speech use. Speech is also used to indicate inner qualities of good and evil. Together they form a pressing editorial concern that surfaces in other tales in the collection (examined in detail in the appendix).

7

Paradigms for Powerlessness

 great gulf separates the mentality producing tales in which women lay spells in order to direct natural forces from one that insistently condemns women to a silence during which they are often exposed to mortal danger. Both extremes are represented in *Grimms' Tales,* but tales in which women are narratively silenced as opposed to textually silent far outnumber those in which they conjure. [1] In the following eight text samples, the first five pertain to girls, the next three to boys.

"You must be dumb for seven years, and may not speak or laugh."
   "The Twelve Brothers" (no. 9)
. . . she could bring forth no sound.
   "Our Lady's Child" (no. 3)
"For six years you may neither speak nor laugh."
   "The Six Swans" (no. 49)
. . . but she was not to say more to her father than three words.
   "The Iron Stove" (no. 127)
"I found that speech was taken away from me by an unknown force."
   "The Glass Coffin" (no. 163)

" . . . be silent; give them no answer [until midnight]."
   "The King of the Golden Mountain" (no. 92)
. . . he must for a whole year not speak to them.
   "The Three Black Princesses" (no. 137)
"You must pass three nights in the great hall of this enchanted castle . . . without letting a sound escape you."
   "The King's Son Who Feared Nothing" (no. 121)

1. Volker Roloff addresses "Märchenmotive des Schweigens" in *Reden und Schweigen;* he discusses "The Twelve Brothers" and the variants of "The Seven Ravens," "The Six Swans," and "Our Lady's Child" in terms of origins (taboo, ritual, initiation) and asserts "den ursprüng-lichen Tabucharakter des Schweigemotivs" (p. 189, "the original taboo character of the motif of silence"). In *Beredtes Schweigen in lehrhafter und erzählender deutscher Literatur des Mittelalters,* Uwe Ruberg works out the situational distinctions in different kinds of silence and discusses the literary-historical roots of silence, first as a monastic approach to and knowledge of God (30ff.).

The subject of women and silence occupies a central position in much recent research, as an already voluminous and still growing bibliography attests.[2] It indicates that medieval writers targeted women as the recipients of their dogma of silence and silencing with wearisome regularity, because of their nearly axiomatic identity as *mulier loquax*.[3] An unbroken tradition from Ambrosius on analyzes Eve's transgression and prescribes all women's consequently necessary silencing. Heinrich Vigilis von Weissenburg pins the blame squarely on Eve in his 1497 "Von dem heilgen swygenhaltten" (Of the Holy Maintenance of silence):

> But why women should be silent and in subjection, that is from three causes. For the first: the first woman incurred guilt in Paradise, she was the first to be deceived and led astray and not the man. Eve was deceived and followed and favored him to whom by nature she has no relationship nor partnership nor heart nor love. That was the devil in the image of the serpent. But Adam was not deceived by the same [creature], but he is overcome by one who was his nature and body and life and his half part, to whom he was bound so closely with natural love that he does not grieve her.

The author continues with reasons two and three: woman is supposed to be silent because she is made from man's rib and not he from hers, and, finally, woman should be quiet because she *should* be quiet by nature![4]

Grimms' Tales demonstrates a similarly persistent pattern of silencing and silence. Chapter 5 discusses textual silences resulting from the narrator's or editor's choice in distributing direct and indirect speech as well as in conferring vocal authority lexically by the verbs which introduce direct speech. Far more conspicuous, however, are the silences within the narrative which apparent necessity—the threat of violence or a malevolent witch's influence— forces upon fairy tale heroines or heroes. How differently silencing women is viewed in *Grimms' Tales* and in Perrault's *Tales* is clear from "Le Petit Poucet" (Little Tom Thumb), where speech itself becomes a legitimate subject for the narrator:

> He threatened to beat her if she did not hold her tongue. It was not that the woodcutter was less grieved than his wife, but she browbeat him, and he was of the same opinion as many other people, who like a woman to have the knack of saying the right thing, but not the trick of being always in the right.[5]

Scholars from many disciplines have taken a peripheral interest in silence in their analyses of society and of fairy tales. Of particular importance to my

2. See "Discourse" in the Modern Language Association Bibliography or the bibliography in Freeman, "Marie de France's Poetics of Silence"; also Knüsel, "Reden und Schweigen im Märchen."

3. Ruberg, 40.

4. Ibid., 276.

5. *Perrault's Fairy Tales*, 99.

formulation of silence are linguistic studies from the 1970s and 1980s that relate language use to social power and social roles, and thus in this chapter I shall venture beyond content analysis to try to relate these patterns to the society in which they took shape. In historiographic terms, fairy tale silence can be understood as a transformation and elevation of daily experience to folk literary status. For instance, in past centuries the desperately poor have had to endure great deprivation without complaint: hunger, the possibility of sudden orphandom, and crippling disease. In this theoretical framework a historical understanding of fairy tales leads to the conclusion that insistent privation or imminent deprivation can be and have been recast into a narrative in which silence and being condemned to silence stand for the domestic, political and social experience of the poor.[6]

Both past and present folk and fairy tale scholarship has been unable or unwilling to see individual cases of silenced women as part of a broader gender-specific phenomenon. When Heinz Rölleke notes that the introductory paragraph of the 1819 edition of "The Twelve Brothers" excises mention of the queen's 1812 attempt to talk her husband out of his infanticidal intentions, he explains, "By removing the indication of the queen's rejoinder . . . the activity emanates from a single person, corresponding to the genre peculiarities of the folk tale."[7] Until recently, gender has clearly bowed to genre as an acceptable category for data and its interpretation.

Feminist literary criticism draws on sociological and anthropological thought on occasion, pursuing the relationship between art and society. "The persistent exclusion of women from significant historical events [resides] in their limited education, in their general socialization, in their internalization of restricting views of their creative potential" so that "their use of language must, no doubt, suffer."[8] A fortuitous glimpse of an image linking women's chatter to being burned to death at the stake for witchcraft emerges from a cheaply produced and much-used 1855 almanac for children:

I well know that in times of old
Many witches were burned,
But *you* are igniting yourself!
For chattering this punishment seems new indeed.[9]

6. In "Fairies and Hard Facts," Weber argues that fairy and folk tales, especially those which begin with "once upon a time" (es war einmal), tell about genuine situations in which real people were powerless to alter the course of events. "So it is not surprising that in a lot of folktales, enduring in silence is one of the most common tests a heroine (or even a hero) has to pass" (110). In assuming the similarity of male and female silences, Weber joins generations of scholars who do not or cannot perceive the distinct functional gender differentiation between male and female fairy and folk tale characters. In *Grimms' Tales* the quality, extent, and viciousness of silence and its associated images clearly breaks down along gender lines.

7. *Kinder- und Hausmärchen* (Cologne: Diederichs, 1982), 2:569.

8. Landy, "The Silent Woman," 21.

9. *Deutscher Jugend-Kalender*, ed. H. Bückner (1855), 59.

Within the folk and fairy tale tradition a comparative approach throws specific themes into high relief. When a theme, such as the extent and mode of female speech, is absent in one tradition but widely represented in another, it can be assumed to occupy an important position in the latter tradition. For instance, mute women do not appear in Perrault's collection of tales. On the contrary, eloquence is highly prized, as the little tale "Riquet à la Houppe" (Ricky of the Tuft) amply illustrates. The fact that this tale did not enter the German fairy and folk tale tradition, whereas Perrault's other tales thrived on German soil, indicates a preference for silent or silenced women in the German tradition that is realized in the name of Thomas Mann's female character in *Dr. Faustus,* Schweigestill.

Lexically, speech or its absence correlates neatly with legal personhood in German tradition. *Mündig,* one of many words linking the power of speech (*Mund*-mouth) with personal rights, refers to legal majority and underlines the potential consequences of silencing in "Our Lady's Child": "but she could bring forth no sound" (ihr war der Mund verschlossen).[10]

A verse Wilhelm Grimm inscribed for Jenny von Droste-Hülshoff (July 1813) hints that the image of beauty united with silence had particular importance for him:

In the moss grows a blossom true,
It has such eyes of blue.
It is so mute, cannot move about . . .

Im Moos wächst ein Blümlein treu,
Das hat so blaue Augen.
Es ist so stumm, ist gar nicht frei, . . .[11]

This rhyme exemplifies the same values that the Grimms' tales express and often encapsulate and that prepare us for heroines who not only do not speak but have frequently been condemned to silence, for example in "The Robber-Bridegroom" (no. 40): "The bride sat still, and said nothing" (Die Braut saß still und redete nichts).

In a purely literary sense, enforced silence can perform useful narrative services. It can retard the final resolution by postponing the moment in which all is explained, clarified, or excused. A prolonged silence can ensure plot elaboration by providing narrative time in which characters reveal themselves through situations and relationships that determine how they may act. Silence can be oral (a missed cue, no response) or epistolary (a purloined or lost letter); it can be male or female without gender bias. In *Grimms' Tales,* however, silence is almost exclusively female; enforced silence exists for both heroines

---

10. Both *Mund* and *Stimme* form compounds that relate to individual autonomy. *Mundtot* = dead in law; *Mündigsprechung* = emancipation; *stimmberechtigt* = enfranchised; *keine Stimme haben* = to have no say in the matter.

11. Quoted in Seitz, *Die Brüder Grimm: Leben, Werk, Zeit,* 72.

and heroes as a precondition for redeeming oneself or others; and it also exists as a punishment for heroines (but not heroes) and as a narrative necessity for heroines (but not heroes), as in "The Robber-Bridegroom."

In "The Twelve Brothers," the youngest sibling, a sister, must neither speak nor laugh for seven years. A single word will cause her brothers' death. She is bound to the stake about to be immolated when the last minute of the seven years passes and her brothers appear and save her. An old tale, "The Twelve Brothers" has two close relatives in the Grimms' collection: "The Seven Ravens" (no. 25) and "The Six Swans" (see chapter 3). In "The Six Swans" the sister figure accepts the condition of six years' silence—both laughter and speech are forbidden—to redeem her brothers, whom their stepmother's spell has changed into swans. Exposed to the uncertain dangers of murderous robbers in the wood, she too is powerless against the world until she marries a king. She bears children, whom her wicked mother-in-law whisks away, which leads again to the stake where she stands bound just as the last moment of the sixth year passes. Her brothers fly in to the rescue, and her mother-in-law is executed instead.

Silence is similarly enjoined in "The Iron Stove" as a precondition for redeeming an imprisoned prince whom the heroine encounters in the forest. He can be released from the iron stove in which he has been imprisoned only if she limits her conversation to three words when she visits her family before setting off with the prince. However, her joy at seeing her father is so great that she unintentionally breaks the condition.

Silence in "Our Lady's Child" appears in a problematic light.[12] In the surface message of this tale, which has been popular in Germany for generations, the Virgin Mary imposes silence to bring the disobedient girl back into the fold, thus the silence is seen as a redemptive effort. But a second and more obvious aspect of the prescribed silence is punishment. After the child, Marienkind, refuses to confess that she has opened a forbidden door, the Virgin Mary deprives her of speech and casts her out of heaven. Her muteness leaves her defenseless against the accusations of cannibalism that arise when her infants disappear one by one, taken away by the Virgin Mary. Only at the last moment, tied to the stake and about to be burned, does Marienkind submit, saving herself by confessing her misdeed.

Silence in connection with girls and women, an occasional element of other traditions, seems to have become so ingrained in the German fairy tale tradition that it grew into a narrative necessity in newly revived or composed nineteenth-century fairy tales. Thus, it appears almost compulsively in "The Glass Coffin."[13] Rather longer than other tales, it is an eighteenth-century

12. Going to the heart of the matter, the tale was entitled "The Mute Maiden" in the Ölenberg MS of 1810.

13. Dietmar Peschel discusses the textual history of this tale, first published in 1728, in "Märchenüberlieferung: Fundsachen und Einfälle zur literarischen Vorlage des Grimmschen Märchens 'Der gläserne Sarg.'"

German literary fairy tale. Motivations are accounted for, and it is full of symbolic actions, self-consciously employed magic, the sophistication of a frame tale, and the particularity absent from most fairy tales. As in "Our Lady's Child," the heroine is struck dumb in conjunction with her willful refusal to comply with a demand. In "Our Lady's Child" the text justifies the punishment by reference to the nature of the transgression—Marienkind has opened a door forbidden her by no less a personage than the Virgin Mary herself—while in "The Glass Coffin" the female protagonist loses her voice at the appearance of the man who wishes to claim her hand in marriage. This tale's use of the theme of silence in conjunction with marriage links it with a persistent European tradition of folk tales, beginning in the Middle Ages, in which the heroine loses her voice at betrothal, marriage, or childbirth.

Male silence exists, too, but it is far briefer and much less restrictive. For instance, in "The King of the Golden Mountain," a merchant's son can break the magic spell binding a princess only if he silently endures the torments inflicted by twelve black men for three nights in a row. Similarly, the poor fisher's son in "The Three Black Princesses" may not speak for the space of a year to the three princesses he has undertaken to redeem, but during that time he is bound by no other proscription against speech. A similar plot drives "The King's Son Who Feared Nothing." He too must silently endure whatever terrifying sights and sounds confront him in an enchanted castle in order to redeem a princess who is beautiful by day but black by night. And, finally, in one of the legends appended to *Grimms' Tales*, "Poverty and Humility Lead to Heaven" (leg. 4), we become acquainted with a prince who renounces not only his position at court but also everyday speech, spending seven years praying to God.

Female and male silence differ markedly from one another in the foregoing tales. The redemptive female silences of "The Twelve Brothers" and "The Six Swans" last for years, but redemptive male silence is both brief and attenuated. The putatively self-redemptive silence of "Our Lady's Child" is prescribed as a punishment that generates the threat of a graver punishment in secular society—being burned at the stake. On the other hand, a genuinely self-redemptive male silence is taken on voluntarily. In social terms, women and girls at every level from peasant to princess may be deprived of speech, whereas the two men on whom silence is imposed as a redemptive precondition both emerge from lower social orders (artisan and merchant families).

It becomes clear through a detailed examination of the editorial history of one tale, "Our Lady's Child," that depriving a girl of speech is particularly effective in breaking her will. This completes the equation of speech with individual power and autonomy. It is precisely the deprivation and transformation of power that seems to motivate the shifts evident in the transformation of individual folk and fairy tale heroines during the Early Modern period in European history. Positively presented, powerful female figures either were deprived of their inherent power or else had their power transformed in the tales into the godless potency of witchcraft, punishable by unimaginably vicious executions; on the other hand, a large proportion of "happy" endings were preceded by the loss or deprivation of female speech. [14]

The images associated with muted girls and women clearly establish the relationship between language and autonomy. The pawn of external forces, Marienkind is banished from heaven, imprisoned by an impenetrable thorn hedge, nourished on roots and berries, exposed naked to ice and snow, condemned as a cannibal, and tied to a stake with flames beginning to burn. The sister in "The Twelve Brothers" also ends up bound to the stake:

> And when she was bound fast to the stake, and the fire was licking at her clothes with its red tongue . . .

> Und als sie schon an den Pfahl festgebunden war und das Feuer an ihren Kleidern mit roten Zungen leckte . . .

The youngest sibling, the sister in "The Six Swans," experiences the same fate, though in her case the fire has not yet been lit as she stands on the faggots. The nine days' hunger endured by the princess in "The Iron Stove" as a punishment for speaking more than the allotted three words to her father seems mild in comparison to those ghastly conclusions.

Sexual vulnerability also permeates tales of muteness. Marienkind's clothes rot and fall off her body in the several years she spends in the forest, before a king out hunting discovers her. Wielding a sword, he hacks his way through the thicket and carries her off naked to his castle. The central fact of the girl's sexual vulnerability, her nakedness, is raised in high relief when it is retained in "The Six Swans," where against all contemporary logic the treed girl tries to drive off the king's hunters by throwing her clothes down at them, piece by piece, until only her shift is left.

> The huntsmen, however, did not let themselves be turned aside by that, but climbed the tree and fetched the maiden down and led her before the king.

> Die Jäger ließen sich aber damit nicht abweisen, stiegen auf den Baum, hoben das Mädchen herab und führten es vor den König.

The evident fact that no amount of security is protection enough for a woman emerges from my reading of "The Glass Coffin," where the onset of speechlessness coincides with the revelation of the young woman's vulnerability, that is, her powerlessness against an intrusion that can be read sexually as well as spatially:

> Hardly had I fallen off to sleep, when the sound of faint and delightful music awoke me. As I could not conceive from whence it came, I wanted to summon my waiting-

---

14. See Bottigheimer, "The Transformed Queen."

maid who slept in the next room, but to my astonishment I found that speech was taken away from me by an unknown force. I felt as if a nightmare were weighing down my breast, and was unable to make the very slightest sound. In the meantime, by the light of my nightlamp, I saw the stranger enter my room through two doors which were fast bolted.

Kaum war ich ein wenig eingeschlummert, so weckten mich die Töne einer zarten und lieblichen Musik. Da ich nicht begreifen konnte, woher sie kamen, so wollte ich mein im Nebenzimmer schlafendes Kammermädchen rufen, allein zu meinem Erstaunen fand ich, daß mir, als lastete ein Alp auf meiner Brust, von einer unbekannten Gewalt die Sprache benommen und ich unvermögend war, den geringsten Laut von mir zu geben. Indem sah ich bei dem Schein der Nachtlampe den Fremden in mein durch zwei Türen fest verschlossenes Zimmer eintreten.

Many silenced heroines, fleeing from wild animals or pursued by men or by witches, take refuge in trees, and fill their quiet hours with spinning and sewing, traditional female occupations. Some of the most stringent silencings occur in a Christian framework or with a Christian coloration, easily anticipated given the specific prohibitions against female speech in the New Testament epistles. For example, Paul's letter to the Corinthians urges:

As in all congregations of God's people, women should not address the meeting. They have no license to speak, but should keep their place as the law directs. If there is something they want to know, they can ask their own husbands at home. It is a shocking thing that a woman should address the congregation. (I Cor. 14:34–35)

One tale in Grimms' collection contradicts the foregoing conclusions. Danish in origin, "Maid Maleen" (no. 198) incorporates an autonomous heroine within a traditional set of themes and motifs. For defying her father's wishes, she is walled into a tower for seven years to break her stubborn spirit. Windowless and sunless, her chamber is completely cut off from the world. But unlike the imprisoned queen in "The Pink" (no. 76) this princess is given seven years' provision; and unlike the total isolation of every other fairy tale heroine being punished, this princess has the company of her maid-in-waiting. When the seven years approach their end, as they knew

by the decline of food and drink . . . and [they] saw a miserable death awaiting them, Maid Maleen said: "We must try our last chance, and see if we can break through the wall."

an der Abnahme von Speise und Trank . . . und [sie sahen] einen jämmerlichen Tod voraus, da sprach die Jungfrau Maleen: Wir müssen das letzte versuchen und sehen, ob wir die Mauer durchbrechen.

Here, at last, is a fairy tale heroine among Grimms' girls who has retained both voice and initiative, who acts on her own behalf, who senses danger and takes measures to avert disaster, and who does not wait passively. Maid Maleen took up the bread-knife, and picked and bored at the mortar of a stone, and when she was tired the waiting maid took her turn . . . and when three days were over the first ray of light fell on their darkness.

das Brotmesser, grub und bohrte an dem Mörtel eines Steins, und wenn sie müd war, so löste sie die Kammerjungfer ab . . . und nach drei Tagen fiel der erste Lichtstrahl in ihre Dunkelheit.

The two emerge into a desolate wasteland. Her father and family gone, the princess wanders to a foreign kingdom, where she finds work in the royal scullery, but she falls prey to the machinations of an evil false bride who "told the servants that the scullery-maid was an impostor, and that they must take her out into the court-yard and strike off her head" (sagte den Dienern, das Aschenputtel sei eine Betrügerin, sie sollten es in den Hof abführen und ihm den Kopf abschlagen). A new voice emerges: Maid Maleen shouts for help.

The servants laid hold of Maid Maleen and wanted to drag her out, but she screamed so loudly for help, that the King's son heard her voice.

Die Diener packten es und wollten es fortschleppen, aber es schrie so laut um Hilfe, daß der Königssohn seine Stimme vernahm.

Female silence has been shattered in the 198th tale. In no other tale in the Grimms' collection does the innocent victim raise her voice to protest or to seek help. What is the significance of this lone exception?

Maid Maleen is part of a Danish tradition of feisty and independent active heroines that includes Proud Elin, Proud Senild, Proud Lyborg, and Proud Signild, as well as Little Christel. Wilhelm Grimm had certainly been acquainted with these active and articulate heroines at least since 1811, when he published *Altdänische Heldenlieder, Balladen und Märchen* (Ancient Danish Hero Lays, Ballads, and Tales). [15] Although some of these heroines (e.g., no. 64) fall victim to their mothers-in-law, like their German counterparts, others hold their ground against malevolent older female relatives (no. 84). Yet others find help and succor with their mothers (no. 64) or mothers-in-law (no. 55). Homicidal antagonism more often arises between husband and wife (nos. 50, 44), and this relationship can end with the wife returning to her own realm (nos. 64, 50).

Wilhelm Grimm was under pressure from two directions to expand his collection. The Hessian core of the first volume of the first edition was probably too restricted geographically for his expanding sense of the German nation. In 1850, when he added "Maid Maleen" to the *Tales,* he and his brother Jacob had already lived in Berlin in the service of the King of Prussia for ten years. Frederick William IV was laying covetous eyes on the Duchy of

---

15. There is no stylistic distinction in the texts between the "ballads" and "tales" of the title. They are both in rhymed meters characteristic of ballads, but are designated "ballads and tales" because of their more recent genesis, according to Wilhelm.

Schleswig-Holstein, the focus of a controversial inheritance. Jacob himself had concluded that his monarch was eminently justified in claiming Schleswig-Holstein, though he legitimated the grab not dynastically but philologically. He held that language defined race: since the people of Schleswig-Holstein spoke German, they were ipso facto German and should be governed not by King Christian of Denmark but by King Frederick William of Prussia. At about this time, "Maid Maleen" came to Wilhelm Grimm's attention—it was published in Karl Müllenhoff's volume, *Sagen, Märchen und Lieder der Herzog-thümer Schleswig, Holstein und Lauenburg* (Kiel, 1845). The tale itself was rendered in German but was socioculturally Danish, having been collected in the village of Meldorf in Holstein, which had been under Danish rule for three generations.[16] Thus, Wilhelm's including "Maid Maleen" in his volume in 1850 was a political act. In his foreword to the sixth edition (1850), Wilhelm Grimm states that he has added six new tales and that he has been at pains to incorporate sayings and indigenous idioms of the people. Whereas he dated each of the other editions from his legal residence (Cassel, Göttingen, or Berlin) this foreword is dated "Erdmannsdorf in Schlesien." Silesia (Schlesien), an annexation of the previous century by Frederick the Great, may covertly refer to Wilhelm's support for the future military annexation of Schleswig-Holstein, thus adding his own to Jacob's vociferous support of this expansionist political venture.

Whatever the political import of the inclusion of "Maid Maleen," literarily it clearly reveals its foreign provenance in preserving an active and autonomous heroine familiar from so many Scandinavian tales.[17] The Danish and Norwegian tales contain familiar folkloric material in terms of motif and theme but not the insistent and pervasive requirements for female silence found in *Grimms' Tales*. The heroine of "The Twelve Wild Ducks" (no. 33 in the collection *Norske Folkeeventyr*), an analogue of the Grimms' "The Twelve Brothers," saves her own life by begging "so prettily," whereas in the Grimms' version, the girl's brother Benjamin speaks on her behalf.[18] Both the Danish and the Norwegian heroines freely question, comment, and respond, suffering occasionally from traditional narrative silences but not from textual silencing. Like Maid Maleen, they shout for help and devise their own solutions for escape. The Danish voice we hear in "Maid Maleen" thus contrasts with and confirms the German silence of so many heroines in the rest of the collection. In *Grimms' Tales* silence prevails where in other tale traditions speech had carried the day.

16. Walter Liungmann also asserts that "Maid Maleen" is a Danish tale. See his comments appended to Ranke, "Der Einfluß der Grimmschen 'Kinder- und Hausmärchen' auf das volkstümliche deutsche Erzählgut," 134.

17. *East o' the Sun and West o' the Moon*, a translation from Asbjørnsen and Jørgen Moe, *Norske Folkeeventyr* (1852).

18. *East o' the Sun*, 54.

8

Prohibitions, Transgressions, and Punishments

general pattern of exculpating men and incriminating women permeates *Grimms' Tales*. This pattern is clearly evident in the post-1819 versions of "Hansel and Gretel" (no. 15), "Snow-White" (no. 53) and "Cinderella" (no. 21), each of which provides a stepmother who assumes the burden of blame while the father, virtually absent, shoulders no share of the responsibility for his children's fates.[1] The theme of prohibition, transgression, and punishment offers an incisive example of this more generalized pattern. "Our Lady's Child" (no. 3) and "Brother Lustig" (no. 81) are two of several tales that embody and exemplify the gender-specific consequences of transgressing prohibitions.[2] "Our Lady's Child" and "Brother

---

1. "Snow-White" and "Hansel and Gretel" both add a stepmother figure to exculpate the natural mother. The good biological mothers' early deaths do not alter the fact that succeeding versions of these two tales exculpate the father-figures who remain alive but do nothing to protect their children against the evil machinations of their second wives. This contrasts sharply with Ludwig Bechstein's contemporary and very popular collection, *Deutsches Märchenbuch,* in which mothers and fathers routinely share both guilt and responsibility. See for example a "Hansel and Gretel" analogue, "Der kleine Däumling": "Da beratschlagten eines Abends, als die Kinder zu Bette waren, die beiden Eltern miteinander was sie anfangen wollten, und wurden Rates, die Kinder mit in den Wald zu nehmen wo die Weiden wachsen, aus denen man Körbe flicht, und sie heimlich zu verlassen" (1857: "When the children were in bed one evening, both parents discussed what they should do, and they decided to take the children along into the wood where the willows grow from which one weaves baskets and to leave them there on the sly").

For a further contrast, see Perrault's "Hansel and Gretel" analogue, "Little Tom Thumb" (Le Petit Poucet), where the mother openly accuses the father of being a monster for suggesting—even if sorrowfully—that they abandon their children in the woods.

2. These gender distinctions echo those in tales where the wicked mother-in-law is discovered to be a witch/cannibal. She is generally executed summarily amid astonishingly gory detail—a pit of vipers, boiling oil, a nail-studded barrel in which she is rolled downhill, a blazing pyre—whereas in the one tale in which a male cannibal is caught, he is turned over to the authorities and executed, but no details are given. Even the detested Jew in "The Jew

Lustig" alone contain a specific prohibition, clearly presented to a character, that functions solely to determine his or her obedience. Both the heroine and the hero knowingly violate this prohibition, but only the heroine is punished; the hero is rewarded.[3]

A comparison of the consequences of transgressing prohibitions in *Grimms' Tales* with those in other popular children's books of the nineteenth century— *Max und Moritz* or *Struwwelpeter,* for example—indicates that only the Grimms' are gender-specific. In other German children's literature of the nineteenth century, bad boys and bad girls alike suffer the grisly consequences of their disobedience: Paulinchen plays with matches and burns to a crisp, Kaspar refuses his soup and promptly dies of starvation, while Max and Moritz end their Spitzbuben careers ground up as feed for their neighbors' geese.

Male transgressors who go scot-free recall the trickster figure, whose real ability is "the power of avoiding consequences."[4] On the surface, the literary history of the traditional male trickster figure would appear to account for the gender specificity of punishment in *Grimms' Tales,* but in the following discussion I conclude that all male figures in *Grimms' Tales,* whether tricksters or not, enjoy the boon of exoneration as well as the trickster's capacity to escape.

The two tales, "Our Lady's Child" and "Brother Lustig," differ in form: the first is a spare sequence of events that precipitates its female protagonist into mortal danger; while the second, a humorous tale, recounts the outrageously artful stratagems of a vagabond soldier who tricks his way into heaven. "Our Lady's Child" appeared both in the Large Edition intended for a scholarly audience and in the Small Edition, fifty tales selected by Wilhelm Grimm for a young readership, but "Brother Lustig" appeared only in the Large Edition, which suggests that Wilhelm Grimm had reservations about the morality expressed by the latter and chose to keep it from young children's eyes.

In 1807, twenty-one-year-old Wilhelm Grimm sat with Gretchen Wild, then twenty, transcribing the simple tale she told about a poor woodcutter's child whom the Virgin Mary saves from starvation and carries off to heaven. Until her fourteenth year the child plays with angels and wears golden clothes, but one day she opens a forbidden door behind which the Trinity sits in indescribable glory. For denying her deed, the girl is banished from heaven,

---

Among Thorns" (no. 110) is spared the indignity of summary execution; a judge must first pronounce the sentence and justify it, even if he does so in violently anti-Semitic terms. Gender prevails over justice. Males inhabit the public sphere and women are subject to private justice. See chaps. 9 and 12 for a detailed discussion.

3. Walter Scherf points out that "eine gründliche Untersuchung des Märchentyps vom Marienkind steht noch aus" (275). See "Marienkind" in *Lexikon der Zaubermärchen,* 273–76.

4. Welsford, *The Fool,* 50–51.

and cast—mute—into a great forest, where she remains for years until a king hunting in the forest discovers her, takes her to his castle, and marries her. At the end of her first year of marriage, the mute queen bears a son, but in the following night the Virgin Mary appears, warning her that unless she acknowledges her former transgression, her son will disappear. The queen refuses, the Virgin Mary takes her son away, and on the following day the king's ministers advise burning her at the stake for having—they are convinced—devoured the missing child.

In the following two years the same sequence of events is repeated, and the king can protect her no longer. She is condemned to be burned at the stake. As she stands on the faggots, the desire to confess overcomes her. At that moment the Virgin Mary appears with her children, asking once again if she will confess. "Yes," answers the queen. Mary returns her children, the queen regains her speech and lives happily ever after.

Eight years later, one of Jacob Grimm's Viennese Wollzeilergesellschaft friends, Georg Passy, a bookseller, brought in a humorous narrative he had heard from an aged Viennese woman. Called "Brother Lustig," it tells of an old soldier discharged from the army with a paltry severance pay of one loaf of bread and four kreuzers. Nonetheless, he generously shares money and bread with a beggar, who is actually St. Peter in disguise. Rewarding him for his generosity, St. Peter offers to share his earnings from the practice of medicine with the soldier, though he stipulates that they limit their earnings to what they need for their subsistence. Their first case is paid for with a lamb, which St. Peter gives to Brother Lustig to cook; St. Peter enjoins him not to eat any of it, then leaves him in charge of the pot while he steps out for a walk. Thinking that St. Peter will never miss the heart, Brother Lustig sneaks it from the pot, but on his return St. Peter asks for the lamb's heart. Brother Lustig not only denies that he has eaten it, but he also lies, asserting that lambs have no hearts! No amount of pressure can make Brother Lustig confess. Next St. Peter restores a princess to life. He refuses a reward, but the soldier cunningly gets the king to fill his own pack with gold. St. Peter takes the gold and cleverly divides it into three piles, one for himself, one for the soldier, and one for the person who has eaten the lamb's heart. "Oh, that was me," replies the soldier coolly, scooping up the gold and revealing, but not confessing, his guilt.

Some time later Brother Lustig, having run out of money, hopes to obtain a substantial reward by restoring a princess to life on his own; however, he fails. Suddenly, St. Peter appears, resurrects the princess himself, and saves the soldier from ignominy, but forbids him to solicit or to accept the smallest reward from the king. "By hints and cunning" (durch Anspielung und Listigkeit), however, Brother Lustig gets his pack filled with gold. Thereafter, to protect the soldier from treading "in forbidden paths" (auf unerlaubten Wegen), St. Peter gives him the power to fill his pack with whatever he wants simply by wishing for it. Years later, the soldier begins thinking about his impending death, tries to get into hell but is rejected, and as his final trick, gets past St. Peter by tossing his pack into heaven and wishing himself into it.

One might question whether a socially sanctioned moral has been expressed in "Brother Lustig." The tale might be thought to detail the idea that grace, once bestowed, cannot be rescinded. Yet this Calvinist thought would ill accord with the tale's provenance in Catholic Vienna. Reasoning that the nature of the German humorous genre (*Schwank*) carries within itself the requirements for caricaturing society's norms, one is led to question why two homologous tales dealing with the themes of prohibition, transgression, and punishment divide neatly along gender lines with the Schwank populated by men and the polished morality tale acted out by women. This formal genre distinction corroborates structurally the gender-related differentiation between "Our Lady's Child" and "Brother Lustig": the Schwank, an infinitely extensible catalog of picaresque encounters, is made to parallel male experience, whereas the morality tale, with its tightly constructed closed form, expresses female experience. Although the genres differ sharply, the two tales' plots were homologous at their first appearance and remained so from edition to edition, as table 8.1 indicates.

Lexical similarities underscore plot similarities. Gold itself signals each character's transgression: in "Our Lady's Child" Marienkind's finger is gilded by the Trinity's fire and splendor and in "Brother Lustig" the soldier's pack is filled with gold. The Trinity accelerates the plot in both tales. It reveals the girl's transgression in "Our Lady's Child" and brings about the princess' resurrection when St. Peter invokes it in "Brother Lustig." In addition, keys, a castle, and apostle(s) appear in each tale, though in dissimilar functions. In both tales, a triple denial occurs twice. Both tales contain allegorical elements in conjunction with a symbolic prohibition (the thirteenth door and the heart of the lamb) as well as familiar images from seventeenth-century European religious literature, such as the binary opposition of the divinely appointed castle versus the worldly inn and the broad way versus the narrow way.

The elemental images of fire and water, sometimes implied, sometimes explicit, course through both tales. The girl's father, a woodcutter, provides fuel for burning; the Trinity appears in fire and splendor (Feuer und Glanz); the girl's sin involves touching heavenly fire (Berührung des himmlischen Feuers); and at the conclusion, Marienkind, now a queen, stands bound to the stake surrounded by flames. In "Brother Lustig" fire appears realistically as well as symbolically. He lights a fire (machte Feuer) to cook the lamb. Fire and water are likewise united in scenes that depict boiling the princesses' flesh from their bones to restore them to life, which like the fire and water of the rain extinguishing the flames in "Our Lady's Child" can be understood to mediate a rebirth, a return to life.

Table 8.1

Element or theme	Our Lady's Child	Brother Lustig
impoverished isolated protagonist	only child	single soldier
intervention	by the Virgin Mary	by St. Peter
immediate reward	sweet bread, fresh milk, golden dresses, angelic playmates	lamb
prohibition + temptation	13th door not to be opened (key given into Marienkind's sole care)	lamb not to be eaten (given into B.L.'s sole care)
transgression	yes	yes
triple denial of guilt	yes	yes
punishment	banishment from heaven, deprivation of speech, comfort	none
second prohibition	none	may not accept or request gold for restoring princess to life
second transgression	none	gets pack filled with gold by guile
second punishment	none	none
third prohibition	none	must not accept or request gold for restoring princess to life
third transgression	none	gets pack filled with gold
third punishment	none	none
first encounter with divine justice	leads to punishment: opportunity to confess, refusal, removal of 1st child	results in gifts: given power to wish into pack whatever he wishes, and goose
second encounter with divine justice	further punishment: 2nd opportunity to confess, refusal, removal of 2nd child	leads to successful picaresque adventure: victory over demons in accursed castle
third encounter with divine justice	further punishment: 3rd opportunity to confess, refusal, removal of 3rd child	comic victory: denied admission to hell by terrified demons
resolution	confession at the stake followed by return of children and restoration of speech.	entry into heaven by trickery

And finally, the word "heart" (Herz) permeates both tales. In "Our Lady's Child" the girl/queen's heart is filled with longing; her heart beats hard and the Virgin lays her hand on it; the girl abandoned in the forest wins the king's heart; and in the final scene a heart is moved to repentance. Repeated reference to the heart of the lamb in "Brother Lustig" conjures up images of the heart of the symbolic lamb, Jesus. In this sense, it appears twenty times, while the soldier addresses Peter three times as "heart's brother" (Bruderherz).

Lexical similarities buttress the hypothesis that up to a point the two tales tell the same story. They differ in only a few essential respects, namely, in different gender-specific patterns of behavior as well as in the equally different and gender-specific consequences of transgressing prohibitions. For a single transgression Marienkind is repeatedly punished over many years, from her expulsion from heaven until the moment when the faggots are ignited; but for first contravening St. Peter's wishes and then transgressing his express prohibition, Brother Lustig is *not* punished but is rewarded in ways that lead to his eventual salvation.

A vocabulary laden with ethical and religious values, ecclesiastical imagery, and a divine cast of characters—the Virgin Mary, angels, all twelve apostles, and the Trinity—reinforce Mary's pious judgment on the offending Marienkind: "You have not obeyed me, and besides that you have lied; you are no longer worthy to be in heaven" (Du hast mir nicht gehorcht und hast noch dazu gelogen; du bist nicht mehr würdig, im Himmel zu sein). The child has previously promised to be obedient (gehorsam zu sein), which within the context of the tale justifies Mary's subsequent actions when she thrice appears, saying:

> If you will tell the truth and confess that you did unlock the forbidden door, I will open your mouth and give you back your speech, but if you persevere in your sin, and deny it obstinately, I will take your newborn child away with me.
>
> Willst du die Wahrheit sagen und gestehen, daß du die verbotene Tür aufgeschlossen hast, so will ich deinen Mund öffnen und dir die Sprache wiedergeben; verharrst du aber in der Sünde und leugnest hartnäckig, so nehme ich dein neugeborenes Kind mit mir.

When faced with imminent death, the queen wants to repent, Mary responds, "He who repents his sin and acknowledges it, is forgiven" (Wer seine Sünde bereut und eingesteht, dem ist sie vergeben). The Biblical ring of this statement is prefigured by several Gospel-invoking lines. The poor woodcutter and his wife no longer have "their daily bread" (das tägliche Brot, see Matt. 6:11), and Marienkind, in heaven, "examined the dwellings of the kingdom of heaven" (besah die Wohnungen des Himmelreiches): directly borrowed from John 14:2. In stark contrast to this highly elaborated ethical and religious framework, Brother Lustig operates beyond ethics and on the fringes of morality, despite allegorical allusions both to Jesus and the path to heaven as well as the presence of St. Peter. Other differences in the two tales also support gender distinctions. From the beginning the girl/queen recognizes that her patroness, the Virgin Mary, is clothed in the glory of heaven and wields formidable power, whereas Brother Lustig either doesn't know or doesn't wish to acknowledge the identity of the comrade who can see into his heart, raise the dead, and grant wishes.

The depiction of food in the two tales likewise differs, for in "Our Lady's Child" it remains delightfully but unnutritiously symbolic—sugar cakes and sweet milk (Zuckerbrot und süße Milch)—whereas Brother Lustig's bread, beer, lamb, and goose nourish a great appetite. Prominent in "Our Lady's Child" but absent in "Brother Lustig" is the desirability of calm, repose, punishment, and muteness. This narrative contrast clearly delineates both the girl/queen's passivity and the abject suffering necessary for her to regain life, whereas Brother Lustig always appears as an active protagonist flouting authority and disregarding prohibitions.

The foregoing narrative and lexical analyses also indicate the gender-differentiated consequences of transgression. The message is clear and unambiguous. Norms buttressed by society and religion bind women of all degrees from poverty to majesty, and a woman's transgression of these norms results in profound deprivation of selfhood, that is, muteness or the possibility of death itself.[5] A man, however, may ignore prohibitions without consequence. Editorial alterations in edition after edition loaded the text of "Our Lady's Child" with an ethicoreligious vocabulary. Between 1807 and 1812, the tale underwent considerable change. The plot remained constant, but shifts in vocabulary and motivation depersonalized the heroine and intensified her suffering and isolation. The consistent direction of editorial change, the decision to include it, but not "Brother Lustig," in the Small Edition, as well as Wilhelm Grimm's characterization of the collection as a childrearing manual (Foreword to the 1819 edition) all indicate a well-honed gender-differentiated design for substituting compliant for obstinate behavior in his young female readership.

Prohibitions of three kinds occur in *Grimms' Tales*. The first is an explicit prohibition set by a figure generally acknowledged to be morally and/or religiously good or naturally inclined to benevolence, such as the Virgin Mary, St. Peter, God, natural mothers, or supernatural helpers. The second is an explicit prohibition set by a sinful malevolent character, such as the murderous bridegroom in "Fitcher's Bird" (no. 46) or the devil. The third type of prohibition is implicit, inhering in broadly recognized rules of conduct, for example, the Ten Commandments' prohibitions against theft.

Each of the three types of prohibition is accompanied by regular patterns of gender-specific behavior. In *Grimms' Tales* girls and women are always sup-

5. See chap. 9.

posed to obey prohibitions set by good figures, but male characters move with considerably more freedom among these prohibitors. Prohibitions set by a malevolent figure may be ignored by girls and boys, women and men alike. Implicit prohibitions, on the other hand, are regularly honored by women and contravened with impunity by men. For example, in "The Thief and His Master" (no. 68), the son sets about learning "witchcraft and thieving thoroughly" (hexen und gaudeifen gut), to which he adds murder when necessary. Like "Brother Lustig" this is clearly a Schwank, and it has a male cast of characters. In a second tale, "Thumbling's Travels" (no. 45), from the first edition onward Thumbling steals without conscience, compunction, or consequence. He limits himself to stealing one kreuzer from the king's treasury, only "because he could not carry more" (weil es nicht mehr tragen konnte). And in "The Master-Thief" (no. 192) the trickster proves his skill in three imaginatively intricate thefts and gains a reward for outwitting the count and his entire retinue.

Transgressions can be carried out knowingly or unwittingly. Conscious transgressions by girls occur in at least four tales; in two the girls are punished and in two they escape. These two possible outcomes correspond with the good or evil nature of the prohibitor. In "Frau Trude" (no. 43), the bad end of a girl who knowingly disobeys her parents is foretold in the first sentence:

> There was once a little girl who was obstinate and inquisitive, and when her parents told her to do anything, she did not obey them; so how could she fare well?

> Es war einmal ein kleines Mädchen, das war eigensinnig und vorwitzig, und wenn ihm seine Eltern etwas sagten, so gehorchte es nicht; wie konnte es dem gut gehen?

She ends up as a block of wood thrown onto Frau Trude's fire.

In "The Willful Child" (no. 117) a child willfully disobeys the dictates of death itself, and its parents must beat it back into the grave with a rod.[6] On the other hand, conscious disobedience of a malevolent captor in "Fitcher's Bird" (no. 46) and in "The Robber-Bridegroom" (no. 40), although it produces grave interim consequences for the protagonist's older sisters, ultimately leads to a successful escape for all three sisters in both tales.

Boys get off much more lightly. Their conscious violations of prohibitions set either by good supernatural helpers or by evil figures bring no punishment in their train. In "The Golden Bird" (no. 57) the youngest prince repeatedly disregards a fox's prohibitions and injunctions yet each time is given another chance. In "The Gold-Children" (no. 85) a fish enjoins a man to strict secrecy about the source of his sudden good fortune, warning, "if you speak but a

---

6. "The Willful Child" is a problematic example because gender is not specified in the German tale. No pronoun identifies the child as a boy or as a girl, but the Hunt/Stern translation unwittingly absorbs the generally expressed gender bias in *Grimms' Tales* and translates *es* as "she."

single word, all [good luck] will be over" (sprichst du ein einziges Wort, so ist alles vorbei). Twice the man blurts out the secret of his newfound wealth, because his wife goads him to uncontrollable anger (itself an implicit exculpation of his failure to meet the conditions), and twice the fish grants a reprieve. On their third encounter, the fish ensures that the man will not subvert his own good fortune. He literally incorporates his golden wealth into their family by causing the birth of two golden children, two golden foals, and the growth of two golden lilies in the dooryard, at which point the tale begins an entirely new narrative cycle.

Like girls and women, boys and men do not suffer from disobeying the prohibitions of evil characters. But while girls and women merely escape, boys and men gain rich rewards. A good example of this pattern emerges from "The Devil's Sooty Brother" (no. 100). Here the devil forbids a discharged soldier to look into some kettles and then departs.

> The soldier now took a good look on every side. . . . He would have given anything to look inside [the kettles], if the Devil had not so particularly forbidden him: at last he could no longer restrain himself, slightly raised the lid of the first kettle, and peeped in, and there he saw his former corporal sitting.

> Der Soldat schaute sich nun einmal recht um. . . . Er hätte für sein Leben gerne hineingeschaut, wenn es ihm der Teufel nicht so streng verboten hätte; endlich konnte er sich nicht mehr anhalten, hob vom ersten Kessel ein klein bißchen den Deckel auf und guckte hinein. Da sah er seinen ehemaligen Unteroffizier darinsitzen.

Moreover, the devil well knows the soldier has violated the prohibition, for he says on his return, "But you have peeped into the kettles as well" (Aber du hast auch in die Kessel geguckt). But he exculpates the soldier, since he has shown no mercy to his former officers:

> it is lucky for you that you added fresh logs to them, or else your life would have been forfeited.

> dein Glück ist, daß du noch Holz zugelegt hast, sonst war dein Leben verloren.

The sweepings with which the soldier fills his knapsack turn to gold, and by singing the sweet song he learned in hell, he wins the king's heart, marries his youngest daughter, and inherits the realm.

Unwitting or involuntary transgressions also produce differential results dependent on gender. The pathetic little tale "The Ear of Grain" [RBB] (no. 194) details how a little girl fell into a puddle one day as she and her mother were passing a grain field:

> the mother tore up a handful of the beautiful ears of grain [RBB], and cleaned the frock with them. When the Lord, who just then came by, saw that, he was angry and said: "Henceforth shall the stalks of grain [RBB] bear no more ears; people [RBB] are no longer worthy of heavenly gifts." The by-standers who heard this were

terrified, and fell on their knees and prayed that he would still leave something on the stalks, even if the people were undeserving of it, for the sake of the innocent chickens which would otherwise have to starve.

Da riß die Mutter eine Handvoll der schönen Ähren ab und reinigte ihm damit das Kleid. Als der Herr, der eben vorbeikam, das sah, zürnte er und sprach: "Fortan soll der Kornhalm keine Ähre mehr tragen: die Menschen sind der himmlischen Gabe nicht länger wert." Die Umstehenden, die das hörten, erschraken, fielen auf die Knie und flehten, daß er noch etwas möchte an dem Halm stehen lassen: wenn sie selbst es auch nicht verdienten, doch der unschuldigen Hühner wegen, die sonst verhungern müßten.

The mother's imputed guilt and implicitly conveyed responsibility for reducing earthly grain yields from four- or five-hundred-fold to fifty or sixty (vier- bis fünfhundertfältig [auf] fünfzig-oder sechzigfältig) shows how far the limits of credibility could be strained in the effort to incriminate women. No prohibition had been set in this tale; the woman's deed welled out of maternal care; and God's response is at best capricious and at worst irascible.

An equally unintentional transgression by a boy in a different narrative framework appears in "Iron Hans" (no. 136) but with diametrically opposed results. What happens to him offers an instructive and revealing contrast to Marienkind's fate in "Our Lady's Child." Iron Hans clearly specifies the prohibition:

"Behold, the gold well is as bright and clear as crystal, you shall sit beside it, and take care that nothing falls into it, or it will be polluted. I will come every evening to see if you have obeyed my order." The boy placed himself by the brink of the well . . . and took care that nothing fell in. As he was thus sitting, his finger hurt him so violently that he involuntarily put it in the water. He drew it quickly out again, but saw that it was quite gilded, and whatsoever pains he took to wash the gold off again, all was to no purpose. In the evening Iron Hans came back, looked at the boy, and said: "What has happened to the well?" "Nothing, nothing," he answered, and held his finger behind his back, that the man might not see it. But he said: "You have dipped your finger into the water, this time it may pass, but take care you do not again let anything go in."

"Siehst du, der Goldbrunnen ist hell und klar wie Kristall: du sollst dabeisitzen und achthaben, daß nichts hineinfällt, sonst ist er verunehrt. Jeden Abend komme ich und sehe, ob du mein Gebot befolgt hast." Der Knabe setzte sich an den Rand des Brunnens . . . und hatte acht, daß nichts hineinfiel. Als er so saß, schmerzte ihn einmal der Finger so heftig, daß er ihn unwillkürlich in das Wasser steckte. Er zog ihn schnell wieder heraus, sah aber, daß er ganz vergoldet war, und wie große Mühe er sich gab, das Gold wieder abzuwischen, es war alles vergeblich. Abends kam der Eisenhans zurück, sah den Knaben an und sprach: "Was ist mit dem Brunnen geschehen?" "Nichts, nichts," antwortete er und hielt den Finger auf den Rücken, daß er ihn nicht sehen sollte. Aber der Mann sagte: "Du hast den Finger in das Wasser getaucht: diesmal mag's hingehen, aber hüte dich, daß du dich nicht wieder etwas hineinfallen läßt."

If one disregards motivation (Marienkind's curiosity versus the prince's overpowering pain), as Wilhelm Grimm apparently did, then this tale seems similar indeed to "Our Lady's Child." The transgressor hides his/her gilded finger, but the inquisitor knows all. After two subsequent violations of the prohibition, treated as equally unavoidable (remember that Marienkind only violated the prohibition once), the boy is ejected from this protected realm, as Marienkind was ejected from Heaven:

> let the boy excuse himself as he might, it was of no use. "You have not stood the trial, and can stay here no longer. Go forth into the world, there you will learn what poverty is. But as you have not a bad heart, and as I mean well by you, there is one thing I will grant you; if you fall into any difficulty, come to the forest and cry: 'Iron Hans,' and then I will come and help you."

> "Du hast die Probe nicht bestanden und kannst nicht länger hierbleiben. Geh hinaus in die Welt, da wirst du erfahren, wie die Armut tut. Aber weil du kein böses Herz hast und ich's gut mit dir meine, so will ich dir eins erlauben: wenn du in Not gerätst, so geh zu dem Wald und rufe 'Eisenhans,' dann will ich kommen und dir helfen."

Both Marienkind and the prince must experience poverty, but whereas the isolated girl is walled in by a thorn hedge, the boy wanders the world. For her the forest is a prison, for him it offers release in time of danger. Expulsion clearly leads to different experiences for girls than it does for boys.

The degree and extent of punishment also shifts radically depending on the sex of the offender. Sitting forlorn, eating roots and berries, wearing clothes that rot and fall off, and being exposed to freezing rain, Marienkind's punishments contrast with those meted out to male offenders. When Gambling Hansel (no. 82) lies to the Lord and St. Peter, they grant him three favors! His gambling habits are so entrenched that he is eventually expelled from heaven, but he is nonetheless granted a form of immortality: "his soul broke into fragments, and went into the gambling vagabonds who are living this very day" (is in d'onnen Spiellumpen g'fohrn, döi non bis date lebend).

Punishment is so much a part of female experience that it can be meted out whimsically, for no transgression at all.[7] "The Beam" (no. 149) recounts a tale of a sorcerer amazing a crowd of gaping onlookers by lifting a heavy beam and carrying it around as if it were only a feather.

> But a girl was present who had just found a four-leaved clover, and had thus become so wise that no deception could stand out against her, and she saw that the beam was nothing but a straw.

7. The special need for chastising females may, in part, be related to the absolute need for female chastity, because of the risk pregnancy posed as publicly perceivable sin. The sixteenth-century text, Der bösen weiber / Zuchtschul . . . specifically addresses the need to chastise children, "und sonderlich dein mägdlein dz sie nit etwan in ein bühlerey geraten und zu schentlichem fal kommen" ("and especially your girls [includes both daughters and maids] that they don't get into [sexual] mischief and come to a shameful pass").

> Nun war aber ein Mädchen, das hatte eben ein vierblättriges Kleeblatt gefunden und war dadurch klug geworden, so daß kein Blendwerk vor ihm bestehen konnte, und sah, daß der Balken nichts war als ein Strohhalm.

Full of anger at being exposed, the sorcerer determines to revenge himself on the girl. On her marriage day, he causes her to see a mirage: she mistakes a field of blue flax flowers for a swollen stream, through which she "wades," hiking her wedding gown up high. Suddenly

> her eyes were opened, and she saw that she was standing with her clothes lifted up in the middle of a field. . . . Then all the people saw it likewise, and chased her away with ridicule and laughter.

> gingen ihr die Augen auf, und sie sah, daß sie mit ihren aufgehobenen Kleidern mitten in einem . . . Feld stand. Da sahen es die Leute auch allesamt und jagten sie mit Schimpf und Gelächter fort.

There is not a single tale in the collection in which a boy suffers an equally unmerited fate under similarly humiliating circumstances.

The question of Wilhelm Grimm's goal in defining motivation and outcome naturally arises given the abundant evidence of gender differentiation involving prohibitions, transgressions, and punishments. The potential for reformulation always lies at hand for an editor, and there is some evidence in the vocabulary of the final versions of the texts that the process at work was systematic. For instance, prohibitions in tales about men tend to be morally or ethically diluted or altogether absent; when the Lord and St. Peter tell Gambling Hansel to go out and buy bread with three groschen that he instead loses at the gambling table, St. Peter turns to the Lord and says on three separate occasions, "Lord, this thing must not go on" (Herr, dos Ding tuet koan guet), but they avoid laying a prohibition directly on him. In "The Golden Bird," the fox refers to his clearly articulated prohibition as "advice" (Rat), while the fish in "The Gold-Children" calls his prohibition a "condition" (Bedingung).

Transgressions appear to be similarly shaped according to gender. Beyond the fact that a girl is always punished after only one misdeed while a boy often bears off a reward after three to five offenses, Grimm colors the misdeeds darkly or lightly according to gender. Marienkind's curiosity "gnawed [at her heart] and tormented her, and let her have no rest" (nagte [in seinem Herzen] und pickte ordentlich daran und ließ ihm keine Ruhe), while the young prince in "Iron Hans" transgresses "involuntarily" or "unhappily" and "was terrified" (unwillkürlich, unglücklicherweise, erschrak). Within Grimm's comprehension of tales as sets of motifs, such adverbial alteration probably did not represent tampering. Such changes and exculpating devices would have seemed entirely licit to him, the assembler of authentic expressions of the people's voice. Since Wilhelm cleared his desk and disposed of notes and notations after each edition had appeared, subsequent readers of his published tales can only infer the precise form of the material he had at his disposal in preparing each new edition. His own notes (1812, 1815, 1822, and 1856) generally offer the plot in outline, with special attention paid to variations in motifs in conjunction with their geographical distribution. For example, his notes to "Iron Hans" mention variants of this tale all over Central Europe, but we no longer have access to the precise wording of the variants he used to add to the original brief dialect version appearing in volume 2 of the First Edition in 1815. Nor would versions of the tale published after *Grimms' Tales* made their appearance necessarily reveal this to us, for once his collections were published, they themselves sometimes reshaped folk narratives in other countries. However, one published form that preceded his own offers us a glimpse of "The Iron-Man" in a pre-Grimm form, which he knew.[8] In a line reminiscent of the spirit of *The Magic Flute,* the iron man reminds Salkar, the prince, "Only blind obedience in everything that I will order you to do will bring this about." Thus the theme of obedience remains, though Vulpius treats it in 1791 in a manner markedly different from Wilhelm Grimm's in 1815 and after. In one other instance, however, archival evidence remains to highlight Grimm's own shifts away from his sources. A North German version of "Gambling Hansel" records an actual prohibition directed at Hans by God and St. Peter, which has been deleted in Grimm's own final version.[9] Thus, Grimm regularly makes male transgression into an unwitting act which is rewarded.

Subsequent generations and later analysts have understood the Grimms' individual tales as revelations of inherent and transcendent truth. This mindset emerges clearly from the title of Pierre Bange's article, "Comment on devient homme: Analyse semiotique d'un conte de Grimm: 'Les Douze Frères,'" in which he argues that the changes introduced by Grimm into the 1819 and subsequent texts formulate a moral code as opposed to the immoral code that preceded it, and that furthermore it appears to be necessary for boys to break interdictions in order to mature.[10] Bange's argument founders on the existence of numerous amoral tales within the canon of *Grimms' Tales.* Reclassifying all amoral or immoral tales in which the protagonist escapes punishment as humorous tales (*Schwänke*) allows one to establish a "code moral"[11] but ignores the unavoidable question about gender distinctions that characterize the two groups.

8. See his notes to the tale. It was Christian August Vulpius' volume of *Ammenmärchen* (1791), which includes "Der eiserne Mann, oder:—der Lohn des Gehorsams" (The Iron Man, or the Reward of Obedience).

9. Nachlaß Grimm, 1757.

10. In G. Brunet, ed., *Études allemandes,* 93–138.

11. Bange, 118.

If there is a moral code in these tales, how can it be understood?[12] Within the 210 tales of the Grimms' collection, a witch-burning notion of eradicating (generally female) evil coexists with an indulgent tolerance of (generally male) malefaction. Plots routinely circumscribe girls' and women's sphere of activity by laying prohibitions on them, and the language of the text exhibits an effort to avoid laying prohibitions on boys and men. Obedience is necessary for females but not for males. Girls and women are regularly punished in *Grimms' Tales,* and the punishment itself often seems to take precedence over the transgression that is supposed to have occasioned it, as does an apparent inner drive to incriminate females. At the same time, the text systematically exonerates males from guilt and repeatedly returns them to customary and acceptable paths.

One essential image might account for the skewed values which inhere in the gender-specific consequences of the prohibition/transgression/punishment paradigm: Eve herself. An interpretation of the original woman as the introducer of sin to the world and as the instrument of Adam's fall from grace would account for many of the peculiar characteristics of the gender-specific aspects of the paradigm, particularly if all women were identified with Eve's wrongdoing and all men with Adam's essential and inborn innocence. From this pivotal moment, girls and women in *Grimms' Tales* seem to derive their identity as delinquent and their destiny as punishable, while boys and men seem to acquire a blanket excuse together with forgiveness for their transgressions. This premise is nowhere stated in *Grimms' Tales,* but it is consistent with the patterns that emerge from the collection and also with exegetic material in many children's Bibles, catechisms, and chapbooks in Germany. Thus *Grimms' Tales,* which incorporates so many of the values of its contemporary society, would appear to be a volume well suited to understanding implicit nineteenth-century German social and moral values.[13] Its use as a sourcebook for the psychology of children and adults beyond those borders, however, is at best open to question and at worst fundamentally misleading.

12. Walter Scherf poses a similar question in the *Lexikon der Zaubermärchen:* "Warum wird das stumm gewordene Mädchen so grausam von der Gottesmutter bestraft?" (274), calling it a "moralisch-unmoralisches Beispiel" (275), i.e., finding no underlying explanation.

13. A fundamental problem in Bruno Bettelheim's reasoning in *The Uses of Enchantment* is his assumption that the values expressed in fairy tales, in particular in those of *Grimms' Tales* that he cites, represent transcendent developmental paradigms and norms. Children reared in a society that expresses the values outlined in this and other chapters of this study will undoubtedly incorporate them into their developing sense of themselves as individuals. *Grimms' Tales* may indeed offer insights into the psyches of children reared unquestioningly along the gender-specific lines that the volume formulates, but certainly not into the psyches of children in cultures with differing views of what characterizes appropriate male and female behavior.

9
Deaths and Executions

ntimely deaths initiate some of the best known of the Grimms' tales, murder moves the plot along in several others, and executions figure importantly in the final resolution of a score or more.[1] Atrocities abound—they are narratively gruesome, textually bloodless, and gender-linked.[2]

In tales where she figures at all, the heroine's true mother rarely survives the first page, always with disastrous results for her beautiful daughter. Her pious mother's illness and early death exposes Cinderella (no. 21) to the mocking degradation of stepsisters and stepmother; we barely meet Snow-White's (no. 53) mother before she sickens and dies; Allerleirauh's (no. 65) mother becomes ill and sets the condition that precipitates the tale's initial conflict.[3]

1. Jessen, "Das Recht in den 'Kinder- und Hausmärchen,' " discusses penalties (152–77) and trial forms (177–205), though without noting the gender specificity worked out in this chapter.

2. A discussion of horror and atrocity (*Grausamkeit*) by Walter Scherf can be found in "Was bedeutet dem Kind die Grausamkeit der Volksmärchen?," in Rötzer, ed., *Märchen*, 98–109; orig. in *Jugendliteratur: Monatshefte für Jugendschrifttum* 6 (1960): 496–514. Scherf claims that in fairy and folk tales, atrocities take on the narrative functions of menaces, jeopardy, and the opportunity to prove oneself. Stylistically they are an integral component of the genre (99). Scherf draws up separate lists for heroes and heroines as part of a discussion of "isolating elements"; he treats tests under the grammatically masculine heading "heroes" although those tested are of both sexes; and he discusses atrocity as a restoring element (which encompasses executions) in generally non-gender-specific terms (102–04). Scherf uses categories different from those I establish in this chapter. See also Lüthi, "Belohnung, Lohn" (*EM*, which discusses punishment as negative reward), "Extreme," and *So leben sie heute noch*, 33; Ranke: "Betrachtungen zum Wesen und zur Funktion des Märchens"; Lutz Röhrich: "Die Grausamkeit im deutschen Märchen," 219; and Birgit Stolt's commentary on the preceding in "Textsortenstilistische Beobachtungen zur 'Gattung Grimm' " in *Die Brüder Grimm—Erbe und Rezeption*, ed. Astrid Stedje.

3. The biological mother's death also initiates "The Juniper Tree" (no. 47). Only rarely does a father's death begin any of the Grimms' tales, although Ludwig Bechstein occasionally includes paternal death in his four volumes of fairy tales: *Thüringische Volksmärchen*, 1823; *Deutsches Märchenbuch*, 1845; *Neues Deutsches Märchenbuch*, 1856; and *Deutsches Märchenbuch*, 1857.

Attempted and actual murders occur in tales too numerous to list, but a few examples will illustrate my point. To induce a soldier to climb down a deep well and fetch a magical lamp, a witch pretends compassion, but she immediately abandons him to what she believes will be certain death. In "The King's Son Who Feared Nothing" (no. 121), a companionable lion saves his master by pushing a threatening giant over a precipice "so that he was thrown down and fell, dashed to pieces, on the ground" (daß er hinabstürzte und zerschmettert auf den Boden fiel). Another "animal," an enchanted prince in the shape of a bear, gives an ungodly dwarf "a single blow with his paw" (einen einzigen Schlag mit der Tatze) so that "he did not move again" (er regte sich nicht mehr). Some murders occur not in the middle but at the end of a tale as an unarticulated but effective punishment for calculated crimes or character faults. Greed and sudden death keep close company in "Simeli Mountain" (no. 142) and "The Griffin" (no. 165), while an evil nature leads directly to drowning in "Fundevogel" (no. 51) and "Strong Hans" (no. 166).

Death functions as a release in "The Pink" (no. 76), where the much abused queen prefers God's company to that of the husband who had unjustly imprisoned and starved her through seven long years. In six of the ten religious legends appended to Grimms' two hundred tales, death rewards piety, and in a seventh, "St. Joseph in the Forest" (leg. 1), it overtakes a greedy child in the shape of lizards and snakes who sting her to death.[4]

Of all these fatal conclusions, however, execution is the most frequent, the most colorful, and certainly the most memorable. A clear intention to kill links execution to murder, but whereas murder is an individual act, execution is carried out through recognized and established channels. In textual terms it occurs in the final paragraph, often in the concluding sentences; it frequently accompanies a statement of a young couple's blossoming future; and in one category, judicial versus summary executions, it incorporates a gender-linked component.

In a monarchy the principal agent of execution is the ruler, in whose person ultimate judicial authority resides. Any killing he authorizes becomes ipso facto an execution when he "has" (lassen) the sentence carried out by others. Although the king (but never the queen) most frequently decrees the dispatch of criminal characters, other agents of execution include councilors, judges, a mayor, magistrates, the court, and the community.

Methods of execution appear in imaginative, brutal, and sometimes irrational variety. Shooting, or drowning in a sack, in a perforated barrel rolled into a river, or in a perforated ship, provide quick conclusions.[5] Letting animals carry out the sentence protracts and increases suffering and provides a

---

4. The six are "The Rose" (leg. 3), "Poverty and Humility Lead to Heaven" (leg. 4), "God's Food" (leg. 5), "The Three Green Twigs" (leg. 6), "The Aged Mother" (leg. 8), and "The Heavenly Wedding" (leg. 9).

5. "The Water of Life" (no. 97); "The Singing Bone" (no. 28); "The Little Peasant" (no. 61); and "The Three Snake-Leaves" (no. 16), respectively.

vivid spectacle, as does evoking the original serpent in those sentences which use snakes to end malefactors' lives.[6] Burning seems conventional in comparison, although dancing to death in red hot shoes varies that motif vividly.[7] Decapitation occurs once, immurement with or without food for seven years takes place twice, and hanging three times; unspecified manners of execution follow condemnation in six cases.[8] The most terrifying executions by far, however, are devised by the evildoers themselves. To turn viciousness upon itself, kings cunningly ask malefactors how certain crimes should be punished. The punishments are horrifying.

> . . . the aged king asked the waiting-maid as a riddle, what punishment a person deserved who had behaved in such and such a way to her master, and at the same time related the whole story, and asked what sentence such a person merited. Then the false bride said: "She deserves no better fate than to be stripped entirely naked, and put into a barrel which is studded inside with pointed nails, and two white horses should be harnessed to it, which will drag her along through one street after another, till she is dead." "It is you," said the aged King, "and you have pronounced your own sentence, and thus shall it be done unto you." (The Goose-Girl," no. 89)

> . . . der alte König [gab] der Kammerfrau ein Rätsel auf, was eine solche wert wäre, die den Herrn so und so betrogen hätte, erzählte damit den ganzen Verlauf und fragte: "Welches Urteils ist diese würdig?" Da sprach die falsche Braut: "Die ist nichts Besseres wert, als daß sie splitternackt ausgezogen und in ein Faß gesteckt wird, das inwendig mit spitzen Nägeln beschlagen ist; und zwei weiße Pferde müssen vorgespannt werden, die sie Gasse auf Gasse ab zu Tode schleifen." "Das bist du", sprach der alte König, "und hast dein eigen Urteil gefunden, und danach soll dir widerfahren."

The wicked witch in "The White Bride and the Black Bride" names a similar fate for herself, though in her case the punishment is never-ending torture,

6. Tearing the condemned into four pieces occurs in "The Pink" and "The Skillful Huntsman" (no. 111). Tearing to pieces ends the life of the wicked witch's daughter in "Brother and Sister" (no. 11); four bulls pull the body of the faithless marshall apart in "The Two Brothers" (no. 60). Adders and snakes' nests do the job in "The White Bride and the Black Bride" (no. 135); lizards and snakes kill the little girl in "St. Joseph in the Forest"; while the self-defeating barrel of boiling oil with vipers dispatches the wicked stepmother in "The Twelve Brothers" (no. 9).

7. The two false sisters are burnt in "The Three Little Birds" (no. 96), the wicked mother-in-law is burnt to ashes at the stake in "The Six Swans" (no. 49), while arson ends the life of the wizard in "Fitcher's Bird" (no. 46). In "Snow-White" the evil stepmother dances to death.

8. The murderous innkeeper is beheaded in "The Three Apprentices" (no. 120). Maid Maleen's father walls her up together with her maid and seven years' provision (no. 198), but the king in "The Pink" intends to starve his wife to death when he has her put into a high windowless tower. Two false brothers are hanged in "The Gnome" (no. 91), and the titular Jew must mount the scaffold in "The Jew Among Thorns" (no. 110). Executions also occur in "The Robber-Bridegroom" (no. 40), "The Golden Bird" (no. 57), "The Bright Sun Brings It to Light" (no. 115), "The Blue Light" (no. 116), "Sharing Joy and Sorrow" (no. 170), and "Old Rinkrank" (no. 196).

since she does not die. The stepmother in "The Three Little Men in the Wood" (no. 13) adds being rolled into the water, while the wicked one-eyed captain in "The Skillful Huntsman" pronounces his own sentence when he says: "He should be torn in pieces" ("Der gehört in Stücken zerrissen zu werden").

Execution can be divided neatly into two procedural categories: summary and judicial. In summary execution the king himself generally functions as executioner, though "brothers and kinsmen" (Brüder und Verwandte) in "Fitcher's Bird" can also dispatch evildoers. On rare occasions, the agent is implied rather than explicitly identified, as in "Snow-White" where the prince himself must have ordered the stepmother's horrible dance of death in red-hot iron slippers, since no king inhabits his castle, and no instances of a queen ordering an execution exist in the collection.

The victims of summary execution are more or less evenly divided between women and men. Those who fall to instant punishment are a stepmother and her daughter (no. 13), a princess (16), a stepmother alone (49), a queen (53, 76), a false maid married to a king (89), two false sisters (96), and a witch and her daughter (135). Executed males include wicked or false brother(s) (28, 57, 91), a wizard (46), a cook (76), a wicked captain (111), and a dwarf (196). Although the blood of princesses and queens may flow when angry sentences are pronounced, princes and kings are notably absent from this listing of summarily executed victims.

Judicial execution, on the other hand, implies an orderly process, which "The Three Apprentices" outlines. Accused of murder, the three apprentices are first taken to prison to await trial, then they are led to the bar, where the judge questions them. They apparently confess and are led to execution. At the place of execution, the executioner's men lay hold of them to lead them to the scaffold, where the executioner stands waiting with his naked sword. In such a judicial process, the authorized persons can be a judge (Richter) (nos. 9, 11, 110, 116, 120); a court (Gericht) (40, 57, 115); councilors (Räte) (60); a mayor (Schultheiß) (61); the king's court (Hof) (97); or magistrates (Obrigkeit, Richter) (170).

Whereas the victims of summary execution divide more or less evenly between men and women, males predominate among the subjects of judicial executions. Those who are to swing, boil, burn, or drown are a robber and his troop (no. 40), a youth (57), a wicked marshall (60), a peasant (61), a prince (97), a Jew (110), a tailor (115, 170), a soldier (116), and an innkeeper (120).[9] Judicially dispatched women are clearly in the minority and comprise only a wicked stepmother (9), a witch and her daughter (11) and a witch alone (116).

The vocabulary of executions provides a regular litany of Schadenfreude as far as women are concerned. The mother-in-law in "The Twelve Brothers" (no.

---

9. Of these, the soldier and the prince are wrongly condemned and eventually escape execution.

9) "died an evil death" (starb eines bösen Todes) like her sister under the skin in "Brother and Sister" (no. 11), who was "miserably burnt" (mußte jammervoll verbrennen). On the male side dry reportage is more common: "The marshall was therefore executed" (Also ward der Marschall gerichtet; no. 60) or "the tailor was brought to trial and condemned" (der Schneider kam vors Gericht und ward gerichtet; no. 115). The most brutal of criminals, the Robber-Bridegroom, who first intoxicates his young and beautiful victims, then butchers, salts, and eats them raw, is delivered "over to justice. Then he and his whole troop were executed for their infamous deeds" (den Gerichten. Da ward er und seine ganze Bande für ihre Schandtaten gerichtet). An inchoate value judgment inheres in "infamous deeds," a change from the earliest versions in which they are executed "as a reward for their tricks" (zu Lohn für ihre Bubenstücke). "Infamous deeds" characterizes the act, whereas "punishment" (Strafe) drily delineates the nature and intent of the response. The word makes a rare appearance in association with a man in "The Robber-Bridegroom"; but "punishment" habitually accompanies the execution of women, an extreme example of the selective punishment of girls and women outlined in the last chapter. In "The Six Swans," "as a punishment, the wicked mother-in-law was bound to the stake, and burnt to ashes" (die böse Schwiegermutter wurde zur Strafe auf den Scheiterhaufen gebunden und zu Asche verbrannt), but male execution is never referred to in such harsh and gloating terms.

The executions in *Grimms' Tales* differ markedly not only from those in other European narrative traditions but also from other tale collections within Germany. Chief among contemporary traditions are Ludwig Bechstein's collections of fairy tales, which far outsold the Grimms' *Kinder- und Hausmärchen* on their first appearance. In part their popularity may have derived from Ludwig Richter's charming illustrations, but tender parents may well have preferred Bechstein's ambiguous or veiled endings for evil characters. Typically, a roebuck knocks off a witch's magic ring, causing her to disappear, or the wicked mother-in-law must suffer seven years in a cave, the same fate she had forced upon her innocent daughter-in-law. [10] To be sure, Aschenbrödel's sisters still have their eyes pecked out, Gretel still pushes the witch into the oven, and the stepmother in Bechstein's version of "The Juniper Tree" is still crushed by a falling mill stone, but the unpalatable detail of endless executions simply does not appear. [11]

10. "Die Hexe und die Königskinder" and "Die sieben Schwanen," *Deutsches Märchenbuch*, 1857.

11. This is not to say, however, that Bechstein's *Deutsches Märchenbuch* contains no fearsome material. In "Vom Zornbraten" a knight endures his wife's scolding tongue for several years, then revenges himself on her by slicing off a portion of her buttocks, claiming that that is where her anger resides, and that should she express herself in an untoward manner in the future, he can simply excise again. This tames her effectively. Compare to Shakespeare's *Taming of the Shrew*, which stops far short of surgical intervention for mood control.

Grimms' Tales documents the gorier of at least two competing narrative traditions. Eventually the gentler tales, exemplified by Bechstein's collections, receded in prominence, leaving the Grimms' collection a ready-made handbook confirming an ethic of public man and private woman, symbolized by gender-skewed access to judicial procedures. If previous scholars have noticed such profound gender-based divisions in this collection, they have neither written nor spoken of them. Contemporary scholars discuss the blood and gore but avoid the gender; for instance, Heinz Rölleke writes that "normally a child doesn't note in detail the drastic [ends], particularly since grotesque performances such as the "symmetrically" bloodless end of the demon Rumpelstiltskin (no. 55), the stupid witch who creeps into her own oven (no. 15), or the barrel hurtling downhill (no. 13) makes any trace of sadism impossible." [12] Common sense, however, suggests that it is not sadism which is in question here, but an entire text of socially sanctioned gender-skewed violent conclusions.

12. Heinz Rölleke, "Nachwort" (1857), *Kinder- und Hausmärchen* (1980), 3:615.

10

Towers, Forests, and Trees

he single most pervasive image evoked in the popular mind by the word *fairy tale* is probably that of a maiden in distress leaning from a tower window and searching the horizon for a rescuer. *Grimms' Tales* provides several immured, incarcerated, or sequestered heroines who fit this description.[1] Maid Maleen's father (no. 198) walls her in; the king imprisons his wife in "The Pink" (no. 76); Dame Gothel hides twelve year-old Rapunzel (no. 12) from the world and so does the old woman the fifteen year-old sleeping beauty in "Little Briar-Rose" (no. 50).

The enclosure that girls and women endure is not inferred but presented to the reader with painful clarity. When Rapunzel is twelve years old, "the enchantress shut her into a tower, which lay in a forest, and had neither stairs nor door, but quite at the top was a little window" (schloß es die Zauberin in einen Turm, der in einem Walde lag und weder Treppe noch Türe hatte, nur ganz oben war ein kleines Fensterchen).

In those tales in which women are enclosed in a socially created architectural structure like a tower rather than in a natural setting, they go on to suffer further deprivations, but none of them leads to the possibility of death by fire, a mortal threat sometimes carried out against women in forests or trees.[2]

1. For essays representative of enclosing and isolating practices from an anthropological perspective, see Ardener, ed., *Women and Space*. Some critics see fairy tale enclosure or isolation as a remnant of archaic or exotic sequestrations experienced by pubescent girls and adolescent boys before marriage. See Peuckert, *Deutsches Volkstum in Märchen und Sage, Schwank und Rätsel*, 19–20. However, in *Grimms' Tales* females of all ages are sequestered, whereas such isolation is vanishingly evident in association with males.

2. Both legal scholars (see bibliography in Gerhard O. W. Mueller, "The Criminological Significance of the Grimms' Fairy Tales," in Bottigheimer, ed., *Fairy Tales and Society*) and fairy tale scholars (e.g., Walter Scherf, "Was ist Grausamkeit, und ist sie für das Kind vielleicht etwas anderes als für den Erwachsenen?," in Rötzer, ed., *Märchen*) have attributed the association of witches with death at the stake with a collective folk memory of witch trials and executions from the late Middle Ages and the early modern era. My work in this area indicates that it is women in general, only a few of whom are witches, who are associated with death at the stake. Furthermore, several women condemned to the stake as witches in the 1857 edition are

Rapunzel, Maid Maleen, the queen in "The Pink," and the queen in "The Three Little Birds" (no. 96) each provide a confirmatory example of this distinction.

Essential textual images in *Grimms' Tales* are the great German woods and forests, which provide the setting for many more heroines. The bosky isolation of "Brother and Sister" (no. 11) offered so central an image for Wilhelm Grimm that he chose it as the frontispiece for volume 1 in every Large Edition from 1819 onward. The hut in which Little Sister waits alone all day for her brother's return is the generic cottage in the woods found in several well known and lesser known fairy tales, for example, "The Girl without Hands" (no. 31), "Little Red Riding Hood" (no. 26) and "Snow-White" (no. 53). In each of these tales, a girl passes her days alone, a state that the seven dwarves emphasize in their repeated injunctions to "be sure to let no one come in" (laß ja niemand herein); to "let no one come in when we are not with you" (laß keinen Menschen herein, wenn wir nicht bei dir sind); or "to be on her guard and open the door to no one" (auf seiner Hut zu sein und niemand die Türe zu öffnen). In each of these tales, visits that might relieve the daily tedium of solitude are more often perceived as sources of danger than as forms of amusement. Wolves and witches alike threaten these cloistered girls and women.

Little Sister fares no better. "She walked deeper and deeper into the forest" (ging immer tiefer in den Wald hinein) and finds a tiny empty house, where each day she fearfully awaits her brother's return from his hazardous forays into the forest. Her lonely isolation, as such, is quite acceptable to the tale's narrator, for "if only the brother had had his human form it would have been a delightful life" (Und hätte das Brüderchen nur seine menschliche Gestalt gehabt, es wäre ein herrliches Leben gewesen).

The forest embodies and expresses noncommunity and thus harbors egregious creatures like witches, as in "Hansel and Gretel" (no. 15); murderers and robbers, as in "The Robber-Bridegroom" (no. 40) and "Fitcher's Bird" (no. 46); as well as dwarves and wolves, like those in "Snow-White" and "Snow-White and Rose-Red" (no. 161). If individual tales are analyzed without reference to the collection as a whole, the dangerous and threatening forest can take on the identity of an intercommunity, through whose uncertainties and perils the hero(ine) must pass before establishing a new kingdom. Taken as a

not witches in earlier versions (see chap. 9). Mueller's and Scherf's conclusions suggest that they investigated only the 1857 edition of *Grimms' Tales*. It is not women's identity as witches that exposes them to death at the stake, but their gender—this has been obscured in the final edition of 1857, however, by declaring the executed women to be witches. Thus a whole set of conclusions is turned on its head. Rather than a folk memory of witches' just desserts, the fairy tales memorialize the idea that women are subject to a summary dispatch that can be justified by declaring them to be witches.

group, however, the tales in the collection outline very different relationships to forest isolation for male and for female protagonists.

Max Lüthi defined isolation as a central stylistic principle in fairy tales, yet to date no attempt has been made to analyze and characterize social isolation as it occurs narratively in the corpus of *Grimms' Tales*.[3] The isolating trees and forests among which young girls are squirreled away differ radically from the home-grown trees that willingly bend to serve their mistress in "One-Eye, Two-Eyes, and Three-Eyes" (no. 130) or that magically provide ball gowns for Cinderella (no. 21). Instead of linking a girl to natural powers whose visible sign is gleaming gold, these trees form part of a forest, a dark *locus separatus*. "The Two Brothers" (no. 60) clearly expresses these polarities.

> Then they seized the witch, bound her and laid her on the fire, and when she was burnt the forest opened of its own accord, and was light and clear, and the King's palace could be seen at about the distance of a three hours' walk.

> Dann griffen sie die Hexe, banden sie und legten sie ins Feuer, und als sie verbrannt war, da tat sich der Wald von selbst auf und war licht und hell, und man konnte das königliche Schloß auf drei Stunden Wegs sehen.

The threatening witch's domain counterbalances the king's palace, darkness gives way to a clearing, the trackless forest suddenly yields a path. Above all, a gender opposition of female witch versus male monarch dominates this scene.

Fairy tale heroines enter or remain in forests with remarkable frequency and great unwillingness. Snow-White is taken there to be murdered, but even after tearful pleas move the huntsman to sheath his knife,

> the poor child was all alone in the great forest, and so terrified that she looked at all the leaves on the trees, and did not know what to do. Then she began to run, and ran over sharp stones and through thorns and the wild beasts ran past her, but did her no harm.

> Nun war das arme Kind in dem großen Wald mutterselig allein, und ward ihm so angst, daß es alle Blätter an den Bäumen ansah und nicht wußte, wie es sich helfen sollte. Da fing es an zu laufen und lief über die spitzen Steine und durch die Dornen, und die wilden Tiere sprangen an ihm vorbei aber sie taten ihm nichts.

In "Strong Hans" (no. 166), robbers "seized the mother and child, and carried them far away into the black forest, where no one ever came from one year's end to another" (packten die Mutter und das Kind und führten sie tief in den schwarzen Wald, wo jahraus, jahrein kein Mensch hinkam). Likewise, a princess accidentally bewitched by her mother's hasty wish "flew into a dark forest, and stayed in it a long time" (flog aber in einen dunkeln Wald und blieb

---

3. See *Volksmärchen und Volkssage:* "Mit dem Begriff der Isolierung sind wir ins Zentrum des Märchenstils vorgestossen" (36), as well as the discussion of isolation as a stylistic device that permeates *The European Folktale*.

lange Zeit darin), and the first effort to help her comes from a man who tells her to go still farther into the forest ("The Raven," no. 93).

As in "Brother and Sister," editorial commentary within the narrative presents female isolation in the depths of the forest as a rare idyll, much to be desired. After witnessing the murder of every member of the family whom she serves as maid, a poor servant girl fears starvation in the trackless forest, but a dove brings her three golden keys. Each opens a tree, which produces the necessities of life. "She lived there for some time . . . and it was a quiet good life" (Also lebte es da eine Zeitlang . . . und war das ein stilles, gutes Leben).[4]

Of all the Grimms' sylvan and arboreal images, however, the oddest is that of a girl or woman in the branches of a tree. In two tales the heroine spends long years perched birdlike in a tree. To comply with an old woman's formula for saving her twelve brothers (no. 9), the sister "went and sought a high tree and seated herself in it and spun, and neither spoke nor laughed" (ging und suchte einen hohen Baum, setzte sich darauf und spann, und sprach nicht und lachte nicht), remaining there seven years. The same motif recurs in "The Six Swans" (no. 49). The maiden "left the hut, went into the midst of the forest, seated herself on a tree, and there passed the night" (Es verließ die Waldhütte, ging mitten in den Wald und setzte sich auf einen Baum und brachte da die Nacht zu). The girl spends "a long time" (lange Zeit) there, probably several years, working at her magic task.

Closely related to these odd forms of isolation is Allerleirauh's (no. 65) hiding place inside a hollow tree. Wearing a mantle made from a thousand different animal skins, her face blackened with soot, she is found by the king's hunting dogs. They sniff and run barking around their terrified quarry, the noise of which brings the king's huntsmen who lay hold of the girl. Similarly, the girl in "Our Lady's Child" (no. 3) sits mute and naked year after year in the forest fastness until a king out hunting forces his way into her thorny enclosure.

Each of these isolated fairy tale heroines suffers from a variety of other deprivations, but the greatest discomfort or danger comes from the threat of imminent execution.[5] Though grievous, the danger is temporary, and in each case, rightful identities are reestablished, lawful wedlock triumphs, and evil is vanquished. Nonetheless, each of these heroines has had to endure physical as well as social isolation, and each has perilously approached loss of life or social position.

4. This tale, "The Old Woman in the Wood" (no. 123) maintains several characteristic themes of tales about girls or women isolated in woods. The girl must maintain silence at one brief juncture and the tree becomes the locus of recognition when, inverting young Daphne in every respect, it turns into a young man, and its branches become arms that embrace her.

5. In two further tales a princess must serve in the scullery, and in the latter, the princess, thought to be dead, is forgotten and must await the chance to make herself known as the true bride of her forgetful fiancé.

On occasion an old hag rather than a young woman appears in a tree, as in the long and convoluted tale, "The Two Brothers."[6] When a young king loses his way in the woods, he makes a fire under a tree and seems to hear a human voice above him in the branches: "Then he looked up and saw an old woman sitting in the tree" (da blickte er in die Höhe und sah ein altes Weib auf dem Baum sitzen). The witch's fate demonstrates how closely related the helplessness and vulnerability of isolation in, on, or under a tree is to summary execution, for this witch is bound and unceremoniously thrown onto the fire when she is encountered in a tree a second time, by a hunter. Only at the last minute, and sometimes even after the faggots have been ignited (for example, in "Our Lady's Child"), does something or someone intervene to distinguish the true princess from the witch.

When the elaborated image of female isolation in a forest includes fire, male hunter, and woman as prey, it leads inevitably to the pyre. It is tempting to conclude that the particular association of women with trees intentionally inverts the ancient belief in women's control over nature and attempts to eradicate it, for tree isolation in *Grimms' Tales* poses far greater dangers than tower isolation.

Men too climb trees in great forests. But the duration of their stay is notably brief in comparison to the years-long exiles of girls and women, and men's association with trees expresses not their egregious position with reference to society but their need to escape a clear and present danger. As in sentences of silence, only nonroyal males are forced to seek shelter in trees, while women of all social degrees are subject to this peculiar form of isolation. The skillful huntsman (no. 111) "found himself in a very large forest, which he could not get to the end of in one day. When evening came he seated himself in a high tree in order to escape from the wild beasts" (kam in einen sehr großen Wald, von dem konnte er in einem Tag das Ende nicht finden. Wie's Abend war, setzte er sich auf einen hohen Baum, damit er aus den wilden Tieren käme).

Likewise, the poor tailor in "The Glass Coffin" (no. 163) climbs a high oak because of his fear of wild animals. Robbers, too, drive frightened men to scale trees. When a poor man in "Simeli Mountain" (no. 142) sees twelve great, wild-looking men approaching, whom he believes to be robbers, he shoves his wheelbarrow into the bushes and hastily climbs a tree. And in a final joyous image, Hans the Hedgehog (no. 108) gets a rooster to carry him up into a tree, where he remains many years, watching his herds of swine and asses and playing beautiful music on his bagpipes. He is found, not accidentally by royal huntsmen, but by the king himself, who has lost his way in the forest and hears his music. Not forced from his hiding place like Allerleirauh or the poor maiden in "The Six Swans," Hans freely descends from the tree and offers to lead the king home in return for the first thing he meets on his return. Even

6. It synthesizes elements familiar from numerous other fairy tales.

though the king shows himself faithless, Hans eventually marries one of his daughters and inherits the kingdom.

A tree, if it is tall and well-situated, makes a good lookout, particularly for people lost in the woods. In three tales the protagonist climbs a tree to get his or her bearings. One of these is a female and the other two are males. After nine days without food in the forest, the princess in "The Iron Stove" (no. 127) climbs a small tree, since she is afraid of wild animals. At midnight, she sees a small light in the distance, climbs down and goes toward it, hoping to find help there. Whereas the princess climbs the tree impelled by fear and then finds her way serendipitously, the two men who find their way after climbing a tree begin not from fear but from a clear concern for getting their bearings. For example, the third brother in "The Knapsack, the Hat, and the Horn" (no. 54) "climbed up a high tree to find out if up there he could see the end of the forest, but so far as his eye could pierce he saw nothing but the tops of the trees" (Da stieg er auf einen hohen Baum, ob er da oben Waldes Ende sehen möchte, aber soweit sein Auge reichte, sah er nichts als die Gipfel der Bäume). Likewise the count seeking his beloved in "The Goose-Girl at the Well" (no. 179) strays from his companions and, stopping at nightfall, climbs a tree to spend the night, so that he won't lose his way by wandering in darkness. And, indeed, his perch provides him with distant perspective so that he discerns the enchanted goose-girl approaching the far-off moonlit well. These examples indicate that the woman finds her way fortuitously, while men purposefully exploit their environment. Even the trees available to fairy tale characters differ according to gender, for the princess climbs "a small tree," while the poor brother climbs "a high tree."

One possible explanation for the gender differences associated with men and women in trees might lie in popular Biblical tradition. There Zacchaeus climbs a tree to get a better view of Jesus entering Jerusalem (Luke 19:1–10), a subject often depicted in religious paintings and stained glass windows. Zacchaeus in the sycamore tree provides a ready-made category—a man in a tree as prelude to salvation—a complex theme that does not exist for women. Translated into nonreligious folk terms, "salvation" for men could easily be taken to mean earthly riches. Indeed, the poor tailor who climbs a tree in "The Glass Coffin" first witnesses an apocalyptic battle, in which a stag defeats a bull and then carries the tailor off to a magic mountain where he learns that "great good fortune awaits" him.

The duration of isolation, like the sentences of silence, differs for men and for women in forests. Whereas girls' and women's terms are generally measured in years, boys' and men's wanderings last only for days. Seeking to release the raven from her enchantment, for example, a man entered a dark forest and "walked for fourteen days and still could not find his way out" (ging vierzehn Tage darin fort und konnte sich nicht herausfinden). The count in "The Goose-Girl at the Well" has an even briefer sojourn in the wilderness, wandering there for three days, which the text suggests is a long time. How different are Marienkind's interminable years of forest exile, which are equalled or surpassed by the sisters' in "The Twelve Brothers" and "The Six Swans."

Outside the forest, isolation for a fairy tale boy or man seems antithetical to the basic terms of male existence but an integral part of female experience. In "The Three Green Twigs" a pious hermit heedlessly thinks and then carelessly expresses a condemnatory sentiment, for which he is punished by having to leave his isolation and to go among people. What a contrast to the many girls and women who are sent off in the opposite direction, into the forest, to expiate their own sins or to redeem others.

Isolation is so closely associated with women that a female figure expresses the generalized isolation of the human condition in another religious legend, "The Aged Mother" (leg. 8). Her loss of husband and children intensifies and defines her ultimate human isolation within society:

> In a large town there was an old woman who sat in the evening alone in her room thinking how she had lost first her husband, then both her children, then one by one all her relatives, and at length, that very day, her last friend, and now she was quite alone and desolate.
>
> Es war in einer großen Stadt ein altes Mütterchen, das saß abends allein in seiner Kammer: es dachte so darüber nach, wie es erst den Mann, dann die beiden Kinder, nach und nach alle Verwandte, endlich auch heute noch den letzten Freund verloren hätte und nun ganz allein und verlassen wäre.

But, from blaming God, she progresses to thanking him "for having dealt with her more kindly than she had been able to understand, and on the third day she lay down and died" (daß er es besser mit ihr gemacht hätte, als sie hätte begreifen können; und am dritten Tag legte sie sich und starb). This religious legend puts a female face on human isolation, affirming a close relationship between general female experience and isolation in *Grimms' Tales.*

Since women's isolation figures so prominently in *Grimms' Tales,* it is worth considering the outcome and fate of the one woman who chooses company. The king of the golden mountain (no. 92) violates his wife's command not to wish her away from her kingdom, and one day she wishes herself back to her realm, leaving her husband behind. Although she had never recriminated his trickery, he behaves very differently, for "he fell into a rage, and said: 'False woman, she betrayed me and deserted me whilst I was asleep' " (ward er zornig und sprach: "Die Falsche, sie hat mich betrogen und mich verlassen, als ich eingeschlafen war"). Numerous tales recount the patient rewinning of a lost lover by a jilted or forgotten maiden who uses her wiles or beauty to rekindle a passion or to reawaken a memory of her constancy.[7] This is not a reversible pattern. The abandoned husband in "The King of the Golden Mountain" (no.

---

7. "The True Bride" (no. 186), for example.

92) eschews gentle persuasion in favor of a violent, murderous rage. He arrives invisible at the wedding feast, takes his wife's meat and drink as she lifts them to her mouth and strikes her in the face, then makes himself visible, goes into the hall, and cries out to the kings, princes, and councilors assembled there, " 'Will you go away, or not?' " ("Wollt ihr hinaus oder nicht?"). When they refuse, he beheads them one and all with his magic sword, so that "all the heads rolled on the ground, and he alone was master, and once more King of the Golden Mountain" (damit rollten alle Köpfe zur Erde, und er war allein der Herr und war wieder König vom goldenen Berge.)[8] The king's violent response concludes the tale and seems to be regarded as appropriate given that a woman has chosen company over isolation or abandonment.

Nineteenth- and twentieth-century readers have become accustomed to Snow-White's glass coffin, but it was not always the young and beautiful heroine who was confined in it. In an eighteenth-century play, *Schneewittchen: Ein Märchen* (Snow-White: A Fairy Tale), Snow-White's association with glass is limited to her residence with the dwarves on a glass mountain, a motif familiar from other tales in the Grimms' collection, while imprisonment in a glass coffin for ninety-nine times ninety-nine years is reserved for the wicked Queen as punishment for her perfidy.[9]

Alterations made to the plot of "Rumpelstiltskin" (no. 55) clearly indicate Wilhelm Grimm's tendency to isolate the female protagonist within the plot. Aside from the fact that the heroine's problem in the earliest extant Grimm version revolves around her inability to spin anything but gold from her flax, the 1810 heroine is also accompanied by a faithful maidservant (getreue Dienerin) whom she sends into the woods and who learns the dwarf's name and reports this information to her mistress. By 1812 the hapless queen suffers alone, companionless, and learns the dwarf's name only fortuitously through her husband.

Grimm's marginal notes in his own copy of the First Edition (1812) clarify his intention to intensify and characterize his heroines' isolation. For example, "The Swan-Prince" begins, "There was once a girl in the middle of a great forest; then a swan came along . . ." (Es war ein Mädchen mitten in einem großen Wald, da kam ein Schwan . . .). In his personal copy, Wilhelm inserted the words "completely alone" (mutterseelig allein) after "in a great

---

8. This tale's conclusion hinges on the question of a broken promise in conjunction with the privileges associated with rightful kingship. Yet "kingship" here is problematic, for the king of the Golden Mountain is, after all, only a merchant's son who had assumed kingship through his wife, whose kingdom he had acquired by marriage after freeing her from enchantment.

9. In Wesselski, *Deutsche Märchen vor Grimm*, 74–125. Wilhelm Grimm's knowledge of this version, though highly likely, can only be conjectural. He was aware of enormous numbers of variants for well-known tales, but no record remains of those he chose not to include in his published commentary on the individual tales.

forest." Although this insertion functions literarily to focus the reader's attention on the girl, it also creates and stresses her aloneness. [10]

The marginalia for another tale in the First Edition, "About Spinning, Which Is Nasty" (no. 14), isolates a princess within society in conjunction with spinning. The tale includes the following lines:

> The princesses became sad and said: "If we are to spin all that, we have to sit here the whole day and mayn't get up even once.

> Die Prinzessinnen wurden betrübt und meinten: "wenn wir das alles spinnen sollen, müssen wir den ganzen Tag sitzen und dürfen nicht einmal aufstehen.

To this Wilhelm adds in the margin:

> + and look out the window; and we can't go into the garden at all.

> + und zum Fenster hinaus gucken; in den Garten aber können wir gar nicht gehen.

Beyond the social isolation this addition implies, Wilhelm also reduces women's control over their fate, for in this 1812 tale, as in the 1810 "Rumpelstiltskin," help still comes from women's efforts undertaken independently and on their own behalf. The princesses' mother, the queen, knows three ugly old women whom she calls on to help her daughters. However, in the next published version, 1819, Wilhelm has edited out the queen's maternal assistance and has reformulated her as the tacit instrument of the girl's (now singular and also no longer royal) misery, while the three old women do not come on request but wander into the tale by apparent accident. Thus at least four alterations have been made that emphasize the helpless isolation of the female protagonist(s): the textual notation about not being able to look out the window or go into the garden, the queen's shift from helper to threat, the change from two or more sisters suffering together to one girl suffering alone, and the loss of the autonomy involved in being able to call on supernatural assistance, which is reduced to waiting and hoping something might happen.

The third time a heroine appears deprived of female assistance confirms the existence of a predictable pattern of isolating women in a man's world in *Grimms' Tales.* "Bluebeard" appears only once (1812) in the publishing history of the collection. Thereafter Wilhelm dropped it because he considered it too French, like "Puss in Boots." Even within its brief history, the version Grimm prints differs from the French version in a few significant points, chief among which is the heroine's complete vulnerability to her bloodthirsty husband's attack. The Grimm maiden lives alone in Bluebeard's castle, while Perrault's version retains a loyal sister who climbs to the top of the tower and searches the horizon for the arrival of their brothers, a difference that Wilhelm noted in the appendix to volume 1. Grimm's predilection for isolating women is emphasized again by comparing his 1812 "Bluebeard" with Ludwig Bechstein's mid-

---

10. 1812 Handexemplar, Grimm Archiv, Kassel.

century "Märchen vom Ritter Blaubart" (Tale of the Knight Bluebeard), which also retains the wife's helpful sister watching in the tower.

Illustration History and Isolation

What Wilhelm wrote into the tales also emerges clearly in the illustrations he asked his brother, Ludwig Emil, to prepare for the 1825 Small Edition. Wherever one looks among Ludwig Emil's vast oeuvre, his drawings show happy groups: women boating together, families picnicking, mothers with their children. This spirit informed his first sketch for "Our Lady's Child," which illustrated the joyous moment when the poverty-stricken woodcutter hands his three-year-old daughter over to the Virgin Mary's care. [11] The reader knows that the child is now entering on a life of joy and plenty. Wilhelm rejected this illustration, however, and directed Ludwig Emil to draw one that captured what he considered the essential message of the tale. Ludwig Emil set to work and this time drew the adolescent girl, cast from heaven, clad only in her long hair and the remnants of her glorious clothing, sitting mute under a tree (whose branches became increasingly rotten and threatening as the illustration was redone for subsequent Small Editions), miserably alone in her thorny enclosure, with the king hacking his way through the brush toward her. The illustration and the text thus convey the same message of intensifying misery in isolating circumstances, confirming and elaborating each other.

The same process was at work in the illustration for Hansel and Gretel. Instead of Ludwig Emil's early version in which Gretel triumphed over the witch and released Hansel from his captivity, it was the tearful Gretel standing helplessly near Hansel's cage, under the baleful gaze of the old witch, that Wilhelm accepted for the Small Edition. In like manner, Snow-White was shown enclosed in her coffin, isolated by glass from the world around her; Ludwig Emil's final version of the illustration for "Little Briar-Rose" (no. 50) shows her chastely recumbent and quite alone on her tower bed, while Cinderella, banished to the scullery, watches the birds sorting seeds on the stone floor. It might be argued that Wilhelm Grimm has simply chosen to illustrate the dramatic moment that precedes recognition and restoration, but one must recognize that each of these fairy tales offers a multitude of possible illustratable moments, many of them sociable.

In illustrating the Small Edition in 1825, Grimm was limited by the financial constraints placed on him by his publisher. The first two editions (1812–1815, 1819) had sold slowly, and Georg Reimer was unwilling to undertake major illustration expenses. Thus, Wilhelm was restricted to a handful of illustrations for the collection's fifty tales. The tales and the

11. This, and the following illustrations alluded to, are reproduced in Dielmann, "Märchenillustrationen von Ludwig Emil Grimm."

moments he elected to illustrate play a particularly large role in how the individual tales were visualised, then and subsequently. The illustrations Wilhelm Grimm oversaw differ markedly from those his principal competitor, Ludwig Bechstein, included in his later popular volumes of fairy tales. Bechstein illustrated each tale with several drawings, so that a more balanced visualization of the narrative as a whole emerges. Bechstein's illustrator, Ludwig Richter, also tended to choose lighter, more sociable, less isolating moments for "Hansel and Gretel," "Snow-White," "Little Briar-Rose," and most other tales.

The direction set by Wilhelm Grimm in illustrating the isolation of fairy tale heroines has persisted and has come to inhere in the tradition of illustrating *Grimms' Tales*. Fairy tale figures rarely bridge their otherworldly separation by gazing directly from the page into the eyes of the reader. Boys and girls often look at each other or at something within the illustration. Girls, but not boys, are routinely shown with downcast eyes and demure demeanor, which effectively inhibits them from seeing their own surroundings and thus represents a form of personal isolation. Like the bad women who exercise their tongues, evil females show their faces. We often see the good heroine from the back while the witch bares her malevolent visage to the world at large.

Isolation in the Grimms' tales, like silence, has a female face, and it is most frequently seen in the forest. It was Wilhelm Grimm who edited specifically female isolation into many of the tales whose previous versions had reflected a different and far more sociable ethic for women. The illustration history of *Grimms' Tales* offers vivid visual confirmation both of the femaleness of isolation and its converse, the isolation of femaleness. In Ludwig Emil Grimm's illustrations, done under Wilhelm's careful supervision, a conscious pattern of isolating heroines emerges.

II

Spinning and Discontent

o single group of tales exemplifies the peculiarity of women's position in *Grimms' Tales* as well as those in which spinning plays a part.[1] The first signal that the spinning tales as a group differ from other tales lies in their opening phrases. Although occupational introductions abound—"There was once a miller . . ." (or a soldier, a farmer, a king, and so on)—neither the thirteen tales that concern spinning directly or indirectly nor any other of the more than two hundred tales begins: "There was once a spinner." "Spinning" (*Spinnen*) occasionally appears in the title, but the only tale initiator that includes it opens "The Three Spinners" (no. 14):

> There was once a girl who was idle and would not spin, and let her mother say what she would, she could not bring her to it.
>
> Es war ein Mädchen faul und wollte nicht spinnen, und die Mutter mochte sagen, was sie wollte, sie konnte es nicht dazu bringen.

The reason for this omission appears to lie in the work patterns of the eighteenth- and nineteenth-century tale-telling public, for whom spinning was a task performed by every woman, the task that awaited her when all other household work had been finished. In this context, one was not "a spinner"; one was a girl, a woman, a wife who spun—or who didn't want to spin. And whether a woman spun, and spun well, marked her in a particular way.

For twenty-five hundred years before the nineteenth century, hand spinning

---

1. For Jungian interpreters of fairy tales, spinning expresses the quintessential feminine condition. See Franz, *Problems of the Feminine in Fairy Tales,* 38: The spindle "was the sign of St. Gertrude in the Middle Ages, who took most of the qualities of the pre-Christian mother-goddesses such as Freja, Hulda, Perchta, and others. The spindle is also the symbol of the wise old woman and of witches. Flax was also regarded as having to do with feminine activities. In many countries women used to expose their genitals to the growing flax and say, 'Please grow as high as my genitals are now.' It was thought that the flax would grow better for that. In many countries flax is planted by the women, for it is linked up with their lives. Therefore, the sowing of the flax and spinning and weaving are the essence of feminine life with its fertility and sexual implications."

in Western Europe—whether with a drop spindle or with a spinning wheel—had been carried out exclusively by women.[2] Tale cycles about demiurges like Bertha report on frighteningly punitive consequences for any sort of inadequacy at spinning.[3] Spinning appears in constant association with women in Western literature and the visual arts, but its specific association with work itself takes a new tack with Wilhelm Grimm.

In the long tradition of European tale collections, work itself rarely obtrudes. Boccaccio did not admit it into the tales told by his ladies and gentlemen of Florence in the *Decameron,* except where spinning marks the lowest social level but does not form an employment or craft per se—"by dint of his work and the spinning she took in, they eked out a meager livelihood" (*Decameron* Day 7, no. 2).[4] This remains largely the case both in Straparola's *Piacevoli Notti* and Basile's *Pentamerone.* North of the Alps, different traditions obtained in the eighteenth and early nineteenth centuries. Women of both the middle and lower economic classes appear to have spun in England and Switzerland, whereas in France spinning was an occupation for the urban poor and for cottagers, and in the Germanies it was practiced mainly as a rural occupation. Beyond these differences in geographical and sociological locus, spinning in England, France, and Switzerland appears to have been integrated into general family employment,[5] whereas spinning in the Germanies appears to have been characterized as an occupation carried on *by* women primarily but not exclusively *among* women.[6]

2. There were individual exceptions, such as isolated shepherds.

3. For a complete discussion of this subject, see Rumpf, "Spinnstubenfrauen, Kinderschreckgestalten und Frau Perchta," 215–42.

4. This orientation may simply reflect the early industrialization of spinning in Italy, which began to take place in the thirteenth century, so that one may infer that in Italy only poor rural women tended to spin, whereas north of the Alps spinning was widespread among both urban and rural women until the eighteenth century. Spinning as a means of encouraging (or extracting) every possible source of female productive energy was introduced into Pestalozzi's schools in the nineteenth century, in which girls were taught to drive the spinning wheel while reading, as Rudolf Schenda points out in *Volk ohne Buch,* 86.

5. The spinning scenes in Goethe's *Wilhelm Meisters Wanderjahre* notwithstanding (Leonardo's Tagebuch, bk 3, chap. 5). They were based on an account taken in part verbatim by Goethe from his informant, a friend named Meyer, who recorded spinning as he found it on the shores of Lake Zurich.

6. Hans Medick describes ribald sixteenth- and seventeenth-century village gatherings as an occasional, or perhaps even frequent, variation on the theme of the staid all-female spinning-bee more familiar from nineteenth- and early twentieth-century research. In addition to the songs and tales attributed to *Spinnstube* culture, Medick sees the *Spinnstuben* as "places for the unfolding of sexuality, sensuality, and emotionality anchored outside the family, whose supporters were above all the age group of the unmarried in the villages" (324). Judging from the evidence Medick adduces, this behavior does not seem to have been part of the Protestant tradition but to have been expressed principally in Catholic peasant villages. See "Village Spinning Bees: Sexual Culture and Free Time among Rural Youth in Early Modern Germany," in Medick and Sabean, eds., *Interest and Emotion.*

In the German tradition, Jacob Grimm asserted that "the spindle is an essential characteristic of wise women."[7] The spindle is, as the tales themselves demonstrate, the identifying mark not only of wise women but of all women, and especially of diligent, well-ordered womanhood in the Germanies from the Middle Ages to the nineteenth century.

The Germany of Wilhelm Grimm's youth and manhood was saturated with contradictory images of spinning. Numerous poems in the literary canon, medieval and contemporaneous, associate spinning with peculiarly feminine misery. Hartmann von Aue's *Iwein* (ll. 6186–6220 and 6384–6406), Goethe's "Gretchens Spinnlied" in *Faust I* (ll. 3394–3413), as well as Brentano's "Der Spinnerin Lied," Novalis' "Klingsohrs Märchen" in *Heinrich von Ofterdingen* (sec. 1, chap. 9), and Tieck's "Die Spinnerin" all record and propagate the image of diligent but exhausted womanhood, which a poetaster, E. C. Bindemann, introduces into his *Neuer Berlinischer Musenalmanach für 1797*.

> Make haste, whirring wheel!
> Languishing, ailing girls
> Let you furtively stop;
> But, diligent little woman,
> I sit in my homey cap:
> Faster, ever faster you must go![8]

Popular literature like this fosters the image of spinning as diligence incarnate. Although it mixes images, the "Spinnerlied für Wilhelmina" delivers a straightforward message of hardworking womanhood awaiting her beloved.

Innumerable frontispieces and title pages of late eighteenth- and early nineteenth-century volumes of light literature (*Trivialliteratur*) directed at women and children show a woman spinning. Later in the century, the image embodied and expressed a well-ordered and contented household. A verse for the month of February in an 1850 *Jugendkalendar* sketches out such a domestic idyll:

> Father's smoking his pipe, mother's sitting and spinning,
> Grandma's telling about nixie and elfenkind,
> About Thumbling and Snow-White and about the magic bear,
> There're such scary stories and yet so wonderful to hear.
> It's so snug in the room . . .

This bourgeois image updates the nineteenth-century conception of the inevitable and intimate relationship of folk and fairy tales to spinning.[9]

---

7. Bolte-Polívka, *Anmerkungen*, 1:440.

8. Ed. Fr. Wm. Aug. Schmidt and Ernst Christoph Bindemann (Berlin, 1797), 106–07.

9. This notion captured the nineteenth-century European imagination so firmly that George Cruikshank, writing in *George Cruikshank's Magazine* (London, February 1854, 28–40) about

Unlike the tales produced for polite society, such as *Contes nouvelles ou les Fées à la mode* by Madame d'Aulnoy (1698), German folk tales have long been assumed to have originated in or in many cases to have passed through the spinning chamber (*Spinnstube*), where women gathered in the evening and told tales to keep themselves and their company awake as they spun. It was from female informants privy to, even if they were not an essential part of, this oral tradition that Wilhelm and Jacob Grimm gathered many of their folk tales.[10] Significant differences in plot and motivation separate the spinning tales that appear in the manuscript versions of 1810 from their published forms in 1812 and from other spinning tales that were published in 1819 and later, at which point Wilhelm Grimm's original bourgeois versions had been tempered by other tale variants. Despite that fact that tales like "Rumpelstiltskin" (no. 55) and "About Spinning, Which is Nasty" (no. 14) originated from bourgeois informants, their subsequent forms allow one to assume a personal relationship at a different level between tales about spinning and the spinners themselves. Two voices seem to be present in these tales: one expressing dissatisfaction toward this archetypically female employment, while another voice affirms and extols spinning as a worthwhile enterprise. The latter voice belongs to Wilhelm Grimm, through whom a nineteenth-century value system and its vocabulary entered the tales as we know them today.

"The Three Spinners" exemplifies most completely the characteristics of the spinning tales taken individually or as a group. Spinning itself is the subject of this tale, the German variant of a narrative tradition documented from Ireland in the west to Greece in the east and with an ancestry stretching back to the fifth century B.C. Moreover, the modernization of the ancient spindle to the spinning wheel, the direct agent of the girl's grief, implies the continued social relevance of the tale. Its largely female cast of characters suggests female-dominated narrative lineage: mother, daughter, queen, three crones, and only peripherally a prince. But he provides an additional modernization by mediating a typical eighteenth- and nineteenth-century happy ending—poor girl marries prince. Such a cast steps straight out of the spinning chamber of central Germany, predominantly populated by women. It is related to the oldest level of the German folk tale, in which women were considered intermediaries between men and natural forces, a theme evident in "The Goose-Girl" (no. 89) and in the figure of Mother Holle (no. 24). The tale further concerns the spinning of flax, the fiber prepared and worn by the

---

the young Shakespeare, says he imagines him sitting in the evening by the fireside listening to tales from an old woman plying her spindle, much like the frontispiece he drew for volume 2 of *German Popular Stories,* a translation of the Grimms' *Kinder- und Hausmärchen.*

10. This does not exclude the possibility that in the kitchen or in the nursery, informants like Marie Hassenpflug might have had access to tales from the spinning chamber, as Rölleke himself has suggested in *Die Märchen der Brüder Grimm,* 84.

broadest segment of the German population. Thus it makes a good choice for investigating basic assumptions about spinning tales.

Specific folk and fairy tale elements are fundamental to "The Three Spinners." Deceit steers the plot, first when the mother lies to the queen about why her daughter is crying, second when the daughter lies to the queen, and third when the crones imply to the prince that continued spinning, a deforming occupation, will transform his bride into their collectively hideous image. The number *three* appears prominently: three chambers full of flax to be spun, three crones who help, three days of futile contemplation of the task, three questions put to the three crones at the wedding feast. And finally, a promise the crones exact from the poor girl resolves her vexing problem at the tale's climax.

This tale recounts private preferences and public values. Private preferences inform the opening sentence: "There was a girl who was idle and would not spin" (Es war einmal ein Mädchen faul und wollte nicht spinnen). Public values contravene the girl's real habits and constitute a lie, when the mother declares to the credulous queen: "I cannot get her to leave off spinning. She insists on spinning for ever and ever, and I am poor, and cannot procure the flax" (Ich kann sie nicht vom Spinnen abbringen, sie will immer und ewig spinnen, und ich bin arm und kann den Flachs nicht herbeischaffen).

Even in her mother's absence the girl cannot confess the deceit she has been made party to. No threat, as in "Rumpelstiltskin," constrains the girl, for if she doesn't spin, she simply won't get to marry the prince (whereas the miller's daughter in "Rumpelstiltskin" must spin straw to gold or die). After three days have passed, deliverance appears magically. Three old women arrive, benevolently offering to spin in return for an invitation to her wedding feast, their acceptance of which results in the bride's being released forever from the hated spinning.

Thus, the private preferences of the poor protagonist are recognized, validated, and incorporated into her future by creatures who banish the work ethic publicly espoused by the mother, the queen, and—by his use of the adjective "lazy" (faul) in the opening sentence—Wilhelm Grimm himself. "Laziness" (Faulheit) has triumphed over "untiring industry" (unverdrossener Fleiß), and the "clever and industrious wife" (geschickte und fleißige Frau) remains an illusion created by magical forces that free the bride forever from "the nasty flax spinning" (das böse Flachsspinnen). [11]

The word "Hateful" or "odious" (garstig), which in other tales describes either a lazy woman who won't spin or the flax itself, here modifies the word

---

11. Diligence as an essential virtue for landing a husband pops up on every side in nineteenth-century popular literature. An example contemporary with Grimm is the following verse from the *Deutscher Jugend-Kalender* (Leipzig: Wigand, 1858). Adjuring Anne Marie to go about her predawn tasks merrily, the poem says: "Anne Marie,/Nur keine Gesichter zieh!/Kannst zum Fleiß dich nicht bequemen,/Wird dich ja kein Mann nehmen, . . ."

"friendship/friends" (Freundschaft) in the prince's question: "How do you come by these odious friends?" (Wie kommst du zu der garstigen Freundschaft?). With this in mind, the reader first understands that the prince's use of the adjective registers surprise at his beautiful bride's claiming such ugly relatives. But the survival of *odious* into the last edition of the *Tales* suggests an implicit commentary by the editor on how the "aunts'" actions have affected the entire tale: they've protected and confirmed idleness—odious indeed![12]

Each of the spinning tales can be similarly analyzed, using vocabulary and plot analysis in conjunction with motif and theme. The first, vocabulary analysis, leads directly into nineteenth-century German bourgeois attitudes as exemplified by Wilhelm Grimm. The second and third directions, plot and motif, take us into the oral tradition that preceded and produced the raw material for the collection.

Wilhelm Grimm altered his informants' formulation of the tales in many cases even before their first published appearance (1812), and he continued to make vocabulary and other changes in subsequent editions. Readers of these tales recognized and applauded a girl who took up the work appropriate to her and did it well, as specific words indicate. She was "clever" or "skillful" (*geschickt*), "diligent" (*fleißig*), "beautiful" (*schön*), "loyal" (*treu*), "nimble" (*flink*), "industrious" (*arbeitsam*), and "jolly" (*lustig*). She also distinguished herself by taking on additional household tasks like puffing up her mistress' down comforter, from which she gained great golden riches ("Mother Holle," no. 24).

The two tales "King Thrushbeard" (no. 52) and "Rumpelstiltskin" include young women who would spin if they could, but who either find the task impossible or haven't been bred to it. In this group a slightly different constellation of characteristics appears, which mingles positive with negative connotations: "beautiful" (*schön*), "proud" (*stolz*), "haughty" (*übermutig*), and golden riches. On the other hand the attributes of girls who don't want to spin indict them as reprehensible: "lazy" (*faul*), "laziness" (*Faulheit*), "to be lazy" (*faulenzen*), "hateful" (*garstig*), and "ugly/evil, nasty" (*bös*).

In terms of plot, four subgroups can be distinguished among the spinning tales. In the first, spinning itself forms the subject of the tale. In the second, spinning functions as an indicator of the character or characteristics of the female protagonist.[13] In the third group, spinning as an action merely

---

12. Feminist critics Sandra Gilbert and Susan Gubar understand this tale in a related but slightly different light. They interpret the marriage/spinning complex as a state of powerlessness from which grotesque older women help the girl to escape. See *The Madwoman in the Attic,* 521. Their emphasis on spinning and marriage as symbols for powerlessness certainly finds support, for example, in Johannes Reuchlin's 1497 play, *Henno,* where Else complains of her lot as a married woman, the fruits of whose spinning labor are dissipated by her drunkard husband (act I).

13. Grimm's predilection for equating beauty with inner goodness borders on the Calvinist

advances the plot, and in the last group, spinning symbolizes the female sex and/or onerous tasks per se.

Where spinning itself is the subject of the tale, the female protagonist detests it unequivocally and resorts to trickery, deceit, or supernatural powers to avoid it. Parallel tales from nearly every European country warn of the woeful consequences of spinning: hips that become too wide to pass through a doorway, lips licked away from constantly moistening the thread, a thumb that spreads—forms of ugliness incorporated into the outward appearance of the three "aunts" in "The Three Spinners." In this tale a female circle predominates: a mother who wants her lazy daughter to spin; a queen who wants an industrious wife for her son; a daughter who hates spinning; and three wise women who help her and whom she must publicly acknowledge as her relatives (Basen) as part of the bargain. Everything is presented from the woman's point of view, and it declares that flax-spinning is evil and nasty (bös) and the best one can do is to be quit of it![14]

Like "The Three Spinners," "The Lazy Spinner" (no. 128) was one of the earliest tales collected by Wilhelm Grimm.[15] No queen, no prince appear here, just a man and a woman. Hard necessity requires the woman to sustain her part of the domestic economy, but she resists. When she claims she can't wind her yarn because she has no reel, her husband goes to the woods to cut her one; but she climbs the tree and—hidden by its foliage—chants down at him:

> He who cuts wood for reels shall die,
> And he who winds, shall perish.
>
> Wer Haspelholz haut, der stirbt,
> wer da haspelt, der verdirbt.

Such trickery and deception are women's only defense in a generally unyielding environment ultimately controlled by men, because only men can promise the security which marriage offers, security that nowhere appears attainable outside of marriage, except in religious institutions. But the lazy woman does not escape without censure. Wilhelm Grimm's editorial voice is silent and the tale ends mildly enough in the 1812 and 1819 versions:

> Then he was quiet as a mouse and thought he had made a mistake and it was his fault and in the future he didn't bother his wife about yarn and spinning.

---

notion that wealth is a reliable indicator of God's grace. A Catholic Bavarian tale develops along very different lines when the *Holzfräulein* punishes a beautiful but vain girl but rewards her ugly but good sister. The Holzfräulein replaces the good girl's homeliness with her lazy sister's beauty, and in so doing, substitutes good works for visible grace as the narrative motor. See "Zweierlei Flachs," in Lukacs, ed., *Die goldene Spindel,* 17–18. For additional spinning tales, see Lukacs, ed., *Der silberne Faden.*

14. The original title for this tale, "About Flax-Spinning, Which Is Nasty," was dropped after 1812.

15. Collected from Dorothea Viehmann and first published in 1815.

Da schwieg er mäusechenstill, dachte, er hätt's versehen und wär Schuld daran und ließ in Zukunft die Frau mit Garn und Spinnen immer zufrieden.

But in later editions Wilhelm has the final word, concluding the tale with a stringent value judgment: "But you yourself must own she was an odious woman!" (Aber das mußt du selbst sagen, es war eine garstige Frau).

Among tales in which spinning functions as a character indicator, four females emerge as diligent and capable, but the tales describe three as either incompetent or lazy. Whereas diligence incarnate is fairly constant in its appearance, idleness can take the form of incapacity, sloth, or deceit. For instance, the proud princess in "King Thrushbeard" simply cannot spin flax, for the rough fibers flay her fine hands; and the industrious maid and her lazy mistress in "The Hurds" (no. 156) offer a familiar study in contrasts. On the other hand, the lazy ugly daughter in "Mother Holle" tries to make it appear that her diligent spinning has worn her fingers raw, when in truth she has simply thrust her hand into a thorn hedge trying to fool Mother Holle into believing that she, like her genuinely diligent sister, should also reap a rich reward. [16] Functionally, spinning in "Mother Holle" stands for female virtues, which are outlined in "The Three Little Men in the Wood" (no. 13) as selflessness and/or generosity, traits that in women are also associated with poverty. This complex—selflessness, generosity, women, poverty—appears especially clearly in "The Goose-Girl at the Well" (no. 179). Taken from *Kletke's Almanach* of 1840, it contains many familiar motifs and is more highly structured than the tales rendered by Wilhelm Grimm himself. Here spinning symbolizes and is the visible attribute of the penury and personal degradation into which a princess is plunged when she is deprived of male protection. The same poverty-generosity-spinning complex emerges in "The Spindle, the Shuttle, and the Needle" (no. 188) with its naive and ingenuously moralistic pro-spinning ethic. In this tale, the spinning, weaving, and sewing tools seem to operate on their own:

> It seemed as if the flax in the room increased of its own accord, and whenever she wove a piece of cloth or carpet, or had made a shirt, she at once found a buyer who paid her amply for it, so that she was in want of nothing, and even had something to share with others.

> Es war, als ob sich der Flachs in der Kammer von selbst mehrte, und wenn sie ein Stück Tuch oder einen Teppich gewebt oder ein Hemd genäht hatte, so fand sich gleich ein Käufer, der es reichlich bezahlte, so daß sie kein Not empfand und andern noch etwas mitteilen konnte.

16. That spinning itself is peripheral to this tale emerges in several ways. Although Mother Holle appears in other contexts as the special protectress of spinners, the 1812 version of this tale contains no reference to a bloodied spindle; this derives apparently from a later informant. In addition, the main idea of rewarding stepsisters differentially according to their merits also appears in "The Three Little Men in the Wood" (no. 13), which contains reference not to spinning but to each girl's willingness to share her food with the dwarves.

This bourgeois mirage of picturesque and carefree cottage labor rewarded by rich patrons first appeared in Auerbacher's *Büchlein für die Jugend* in 1834 and was taken directly into the next edition of *Grimms' Tales*, where it remained as a sentimental evocation of a past age symbolized by the spinning maiden. It contrasts starkly with social conditions at the time for Prussian spinners, for example, whose very occupation certified them as mendicants, or for Swiss or South German spinners, whose labor was paid for at so low a rate that a day's wages did not cover the daily cost of bread.[17]

In the third group of tales, spinning is also peripheral to the central theme and serves principally to advance the plot. A characteristically female occupation—either spinning or sewing—is essential to "Little Briar-Rose" (no. 50) in all its European and Near Eastern variants. In Catalonia a princess pricks her finger on a flax fiber; in the late French medieval prose novel, *Perceforest*, a tiny splinter in the first fiber pulled from the distaff causes a deep sleep; while in the Arabian story of Sittukan, a flax filament under the heroine's fingernail sends her to sleep. In eastern European variants a needle replaces fibers and spindles as a sleeping agent and characterizes women's occupations much as the spindle does elsewhere. Here spinning represents a neutral value, a mere hinge on which the tale turns.

The other tale in this group, "Rumpelstiltskin," amalgamates several traditions in its historical development into the form in which we know it.[18] Polívka sees a relationship between it and "The Three Spinners," finding "the origin of both (tales) among the Germanic peoples, according to whose beliefs elves and dwarves spin and weave, which is fostered by Frau Holde and Frikke . . . the Swedish version is the original one, in which the girl receives from the dwarf a pair of gloves with which she can spin straw to gold."[19] If Polívka is correct in this assumption, then one must posit the incorporation of another tradition that appears in many tales: offering help and/or riches in return for something young, as in "The Nixie in the Mill-Pond" (no. 181), or for the first thing that greets the returning husband or father, as in "The Girl without Hands" (no. 31), or for something craved, as in "Rapunzel" (no. 12). This by no means exhausts the list, but it serves to indicate the variety and frequency with which this theme recurs in the collection. Even if the historical basis for "Rumpelstiltskin" is to be found in the associates of a Mother Holle

17. Historically, spinning was also poorly paid. Robert W. Scribner points out that "another issue which the reader in 1523 would hardly have overlooked . . . was the common grievance against the economic activity of nuns, whose spinning and weaving provided competition for town weavers, often the poorer element of urban society." See *For the Sake of Simple Folk*, 41.

18. Lutz Röhrich acknowledges the validity of the process of collating tale variants to arrive at a standard version, but in connection with "Rumpelstiltskin" he notes that this method is "bei kaum einem anderen allerdings mit gleicher philologischer Skrupellosigkeit [praktiziert]." See *Sage und Märchen: Erzählforsachung heute*, 280–81.

19. Bolte-Polívka, *Anmerkungen*, 1:438.

figure, Rumpelstiltskin's antagonistic mien toward the miller's daughter removes this tale from the tradition of the mild and gracious Mother Holle. By the time Wilhelm Grimm had recorded it from Dortchen Wild in 1811, an earlier plot in which elves freely offered help to enable a girl to spin straw into gold had changed to one in which a girl's father's false pride precipitates her into the greedy hands of a king from whose threat of death (if she does not spin a roomful of straw into gold) she can be saved only by pledging her firstborn to the dwarf who saves her life. Mother Holle and related figures function quite differently: they reward demonstrated good will and diligence, whereas the dwarf, as one of the men who enter or share her life (the others are her father and her sovereign), casts the miller's daughter into great peril. Awareness of shifts in narrative traditions like these sharpens readers' perceptions of the tales' current form. The benevolent assistance of a Mother Holle or of the three crones in the spinning chamber in the older tale is here displaced and replaced by a fearful tributary relationship to men in general.

In the fourth and last group of tales, "Allerleirauh" (no. 65), "The Water-Nixie" (no. 79), "Tales of the Paddock" (no. 105), "Eve's Various Children" (no. 180), and "The Nixie in the Mill-Pond," spinning occupies a clearly symbolic position representing either the work appropriate to the woman or girl in the tale or the onerous toil of a captive or poverty-stricken female.

The importance to Wilhelm Grimm of spinning for plot development emerges from a comparison of the Ölenberg MS of 1810 with the first edition of 1812. In reworking the material for publication, Grimm added spinning as an indication of hardship to several tales. For instance, the princess' sufferings are increased by the addition of spinning in "King Thrushbeard." In "The Water-Nixie," Grimm expands the idea of two impossible tasks—filling a leaky water-bucket and hewing a tree with a blunt axe—by interpolating flax spinning in the 1812 edition. Furthermore, although spinning exists in both early versions of "Rumpelstiltskin," Wilhelm Grimm inverted the motivation for the tale between 1810 and 1812. The MS version begins:

> There was once a little girl who was given a hank of flax to spin, but everything she spun was golden thread and not flax at all. She got very sad and sat on the rooftop and started spinning, and for three days she spun nothing but gold. Then a dwarf came along and said: I will help you . . .

> Es war einmal ein kleines Mädchen, dem war ein Flachs knoten gegeben, Flachs daraus zu spinnen, was es aber spann war immer Goldfaden und kein Flachs konnte herauskommen. Es ward sehr traurig und setzte sich auf das Dach und fing an zu spinnen, und spann drei Tage aber immer nichts als Gold. Da trat ein kleines Männchen [sic] herzu, das sprach: ich will dir helfen aus all deiner Noth . . .

The motivation for the entire tale shifts from the girl's being released from spinning gold (1810) to her being forced to spin gold at the risk of her life (1812):

Then the king had the miller's daughter come and commanded her to change the whole room full of straw into gold in one night, and if she couldn't do it, then she'd have to die.

Da ließ der König die Müllerstochter alsogleich kommen, und befahl ihr, eine ganze Kammer voll Stroh in einer Nacht in Gold zu verwandeln, und könne sie es nicht, so müsse sie sterben.

Spinning as an activity is characterized only once in the final Large Edition (1857) of *Grimms' Tales*. In "The Three Spinners", it is termed "ugly" and "nasty" (bös), the adjective "nasty" a remnant of the tale's 1812 title, "About Flax-Spinning, Which Is Nasty" (Von dem bösen Flachsspinnen). In other tales the fibers themselves are represented as "hateful" (garstig) and "rough" or "hard" (*hart*), a limited though consistent sample of evaluations of this work.

Throughout the tales the act of spinning emerges as highly undesireable despite the surface message that it will lead to riches. It identifies subjugated womanhood in "Allerleirauh"; it is an occupation to be escaped in "The Lazy Spinner"; it is also a punishment in "The Water-Nixie", a deforming occupation in "The Three Spinners," "Mother Holle," and "King Thrushbeard"; and at its worst, it is an agent of death or a curse in "Little Briar-Rose." Although many tales declare that spinning mediates wealth in the form of gold, it is primarily associated with poverty in "Tales from the Paddock" and "The Goose-Girl at the Well." Above all, it is the archetypal employment of domesticated, poverty-stricken womanhood in "Eve's Various Children."

As though to confirm the mean station occupied by spinning women in the Germanies, a Nuremberg woodcut of 1490 adjuring women to stay in their place and spin depicts the spinners not in human form at all but as swine.[20] And in a traditional French tale two fairies each carry two immense boulders, one on their heads and one in their aprons, while spinning with their free hand. If they didn't have to spin, they say, they could each carry two more boulders, thus equating spinning with the enormous burden of two boulders apiece.[21]

Despite the good face that Wilhelm Grimm tried to put on spinning as a female occupation, incontrovertible internal evidence appears on every side to contradict him. The spinning tales send a double message. In plot the tales generally convey the conventional morality of hard work rewarded, while on the lexical and narrative level the subjects of these tales themselves communicate the grim reality of generations of spinning girls' and womens' lives. In reformulating earlier folk material, Wilhelm Grimm perhaps unwittingly buried a message within these tales. Uncovering the manner and direction in which the material has been reshaped reveals not only his patriarchal and conservative social interest, but also his informants' narrative of misery and exploitation.

20. *History of Technology*, ed. Charles Singer et al., 2:208.
21. Jacob Grimm, *Deutsche Mythologie*, 1:342.

12

Work, Money, and Anti-Semitism

I stole it, I stole it!" cried he; "but you have honestly earned it." So the judge
had the Jew taken to the gallows and hanged as a thief.

"The Jew among Thorns"

ork, money, and anti-Semitism are bound together in a
knotty and contradictory set of assumptions that emerges
from a close reading of *Grimms' Tales*. But to understand the
place of Jews in the tales, one must first examine the explicit
and implicit ethic in the collection regarding work and
money.[1] No one in these tales is able to earn money by
working for it, although various characters acquire wealth serendipitously or
as a reward for acknowledged virtues, such as diligence, goodness, or loyalty.
Actively trying to acquire or amass wealth generally meets censure and often
earns punishment; reward is often bestowed freely, but payment rarely arrives
on time or in the proper amount.[2] Work and money, censure and punishment
join in the figure of the Jew in all three tales which have a Jewish protagonist,
particularly in "The Jew among Thorns" (no. 110).[3] The text assumes that the
Jew desires wealth, proceeds in the belief that he has acquired money, and
provides evidence of his greed, for all of which he must be punished. The
reason offered for punishing him is that he has not earned his money, like the
candid and honorable apprentice, but has stolen it (du hast's verdient; ich hab's
gestohlen), which in this case can only refer to usury. Yet in tale after tale,
honest physical labor, a generally acknowledged virtue, is a demonstrably
unproductive route to financial reward.

1. For some recent historical perspectives on anti-Semitism in Germany, see Tal, *Christians
and Jews in Germany;* and Katz, *From Prejudice to Destruction.*

2. Max Lüthi distinguishes reward (*Belohnung*) from payment (*Lohn*) in "Belohnung, Lohn,"
EM.

3. These three are "The Good Bargain" (no. 37), "The Jew Among Thorns" (no. 110), and
"The Bright Sun Brings It to Light" (no. 115).

Work itself makes an excellent starting point for exploring how these three themes are related.[4] An inner dynamic turning on the definition and consequences of work unites these three apparently disparate topics. As an activity, work is far more prominent in *Grimms' Tales* than in earlier European collections. Protagonists are introduced more often by their occupation than by any other characteristic.[5] Moreover, the work performed is generally hard physical labor, which differentiates it radically from either Perrault's or d'Aulnoy's tales in France or Boccaccio's *Decameron* in Italy, where physical labor barely intrudes in the occupations alluded to.[6]

Crushing physical labor was a major component of the lives of the vast majority of adults and children in nineteenth-century Germany. The Stein-Hardenberg reforms in early nineteenth-century Prussia lifted traditional restrictions imposed by the guild system but led to untrammeled exploitation of laborers, especially of children. When both Jacob and Wilhelm lived in Berlin in the 1840s, over 40 percent of all school-age children worked in factories and mills.[7]

Work in *Grimms' Tales* exists in both male and female modes. My conclusions about women's work and women working in chapter 11 can be taken to stand for all the tales in which diligent womanhood appears. They delineate a relationship between spinning and reward that is ambiguous at best and in general highly problematic. Numerous tales promise and deliver gold as a

---

4. The points I make here have been ignored or overlooked until now. In his summary of the scholarship on work ("Arbeit"), Josef K. Klíma distinguishes attitudes toward work by genre. He finds the Märchen well disposed to those who labor ("dem schwer Arbeitenden freundlich gegenüber"), and claims that industry is highly valued ("Arbeitsamkeit ist hochgeschätzt"), which reflects surface ethic in the tales but not the embedded message.

5. Introductory designations in tales 1–55: woodcutter (nos. 3, 8, 15), sexton (4), servant (6, 16, 17), peasant (7), butcher (7), sentry (7), musician (8), spinner (14), skipper (16), tailor (20, 35, 36, 45), innkeeper (22), miller (31, 36, 40, 55), joiner (36), turner (36), shoemaker (39), poor man (42, 46), rich man (47), farmer (48), forester (51), charcoal burner (54), king (1, 3, 4, 6, 9, 11, 13, 16, 17, 20, 21, 49, 51), queen (14, 53).

6. See Thelander, "Mother Goose and Her Goslings," which makes the point that work never appears and the king is never busy (493). The first quarter of Boccaccio's tales contain the following descriptions: Usurer (1–1), monk, friar, abbot (1–1, 4, 6; 3–4), merchant (1–2; 2–2, 9; 3–3), moneylender (1–3), king, etc. (1–3, 5, 9; 2–7, 9; 3–2), marquise (1–5; 2–3; 3–2), pretty girl (1–4; 2–10), gentleman (1–7, 8; 2–3), minstrel (1–8), lady (1–9, 10; 2–4, 6, 9; 3–3, 4), physician (1–10), actors (2–1), robbers (2–2, 5), widow (1–10; 2–2), pope (2–3), military (2–4), horse purchaser (2–5), prostitute (2–5), lord's daughter (2–6, 7), outcast (2–6), count (2–8), silk embroiderer (2–9), judge (2–10), gardener (3–1), nuns (3–1), groom (3–2).

7. Ernst Dronke, writing in 1846, points out that 29,000 of the 66,000 children supposed to be in schools had been sacrificed to total ignorance through factory work, a situation which continued until 1891 when factory work was strictly forbidden to children of legal school age. Quoted in *Die gesellschaftliche Wirklichkeit der Kinder in der bildenden Kunst*, catalogue for an exhibit of the same name in Berlin in 1979. See esp. the chapter by Bodo Rollka, "Kinderarbeit, Öffentlichkeit und Gesetzgebung im 19. Jahrhundert in Preußen" (105–17).

reward for female diligence, after it has been recognized by a supernatural agency, such as Mother Holle. But for every Cinderella who arises before daybreak, carries water, lights fires, cooks and washes, smudged and unseen but ultimately rewarded, there is a lean Lisa (no. 168) who, together with her husband, "slaved away from morning til evening" but "all to no purpose, for they had nothing and came to nothing" (äscherte sich ab von Morgen bis Abend . . . es war aber alles umsonst, sie hatten nichts und kamen zu nichts).

Work encompasses people's lives, giving rise to the dream of an automated world where work performs itself, as in "The Spindle, the Shuttle, and the Needle" (no. 188). Alternatively, arduous tasks fall to an enchanted agent, like the flower in "Sweetheart Roland" (no. 56), which magically cleans the house, sweeps, polishes, lights the fire, carries water, sets the table, and cooks the meals. The giants and countless hands of "The True Bride" (no. 186) are required to make any headway at all against the endless requirements of daily work.

As in "Lean Lisa," whose work all came to nothing, men's work is also demonstrated to be without genuine payment in tale after tale. Seven years' faithful service brings Hans a clump of gold in "Hans in Luck" (no. 83), while the diligent servant in "The Jew among Thorns" works for three years for a paltry three hellers. Work as a futile effort, even when a prince performs it, is recorded once again in "The Golden Bird" (no. 57):

> The King's son began, and dug and shoveled without stopping, but when after seven days he saw how little he had done, and how all his work was as good as nothing, he fell into a great sorrow and gave up all hope.

> Der Königssohn fing an, grub und schaufelte, ohne abzulassen, als er aber nach sieben Tagen sah, wie wenig er ausgerichtet hatte und alle seine Arbeit so gut wie nichts war, so fiel er in große Traurigkeit und gab alle Hoffnung auf.

The impossible task for all social levels in German tales involves work that cannot be accomplished by human agency and contrasts with impossible tasks as they appear in other national tale traditions. Finnish tales, for example, often revolve around guessing a mindbending riddle. Unending labor forms so central a motif in *Grimms' Tales* that it provides the metaphor for the meaning of the span of life for earth's creatures, including human beings:

> So man lives seventy years. The first thirty are his human years, which are soon gone; then he is healthy, merry, works with pleasure and is glad of his life. Then follow the ass' eighteen years, when one burden after another is laid on him, he has to carry the grain [RBB] which feeds others, and blows and kicks are the reward of his faithful services. ("The Duration of Life," no. 176)

> Also lebt der Mensch siebenzig [sic] Jahr. Die ersten dreißig sind seine menschlichen Jahre, die gehen schnell dahin, da ist er gesund, heiter, arbeitet mit Lust und freut sich seines Daseins. Hierauf folgen die achtzehn Jahre des Esels, da wird

ihm eine Last nach der andern aufgelegt: er muß das Korn tragen, das andere nährt, und Schläge und Tritte sind der Lohn seiner treuen Dienste.

In *Grimms' Tales* work generally bears no measurable or logical relationship to the success that follows. "The Two Travelers" (no. 107) expresses with rare clarity how other attributes—in this case charming looks—lead to success. Note in particular how the German makes use of a circumlocution, "gab ihm jeder gerne" (everyone gave gladly to him), and thus avoids associating work with success:

> Because the tailor looked so lively and merry, and had such fine red cheeks, every one gave him work willingly, and when luck was good the master's daughter gave him a kiss beneath the porch, as well.
>
> . . . und weil das Schneiderlein so frisch und munter aussah und so hübsche rote Backen hatte, so gab ihm jeder gerne, und wenn das Glück gut war, so gab ihm die Meistertochter unter der Haustüre auch noch einen Kuß auf den Weg.[8]

Work inhibits and atrophies fantasy and freewheeling thought processes that might release the laborer from his bondage, as the reader learns from "The Cunning Little Tailor" (no. 114), who was "a little, useless harum-scarum, who did not even know his trade" (ein kleiner unnützer Springinsfeld, der nicht einmal sein Handwerk verstand). His diligent brothers are so anchored in their trade that they can't escape its confines to solve the princess' riddle, but the third brother, the ne'er-do-well, slips past his trade, guesses correctly, and wins a royal bride.

Wealth often rewards hard workers, but only after they accidentally but luckily encounter a magical being who recognizes their special qualities and confers heaps of gold, as in "The Elves" (no. 39). Sudden and unanticipated reward after ceaseless labor seems to represent a constant dream at least among Western laborers, and probably among laboring people worldwide, a dream of eternal release from endless grinding toil. It recurs too often to be attributed to consciously bourgeois reformulations intended to foster cynical exploitation of labor by capitalism.[9] That this wish could be exploited and used as a form of worker control by the bourgeoisie is true, but it is doubtful that these tales consciously or unconsciously intend such manipulation. On the contrary, they seem part of a centuries-long one-sided discourse of the laboring poor with their unyielding fate.

Wealth forms as integral a part of the fairy tale world as work. Where princesses dwell, there grow trees of silver, gold, and diamonds ("The Shoes

---

8. A single exception to this pattern, discussed in chap. 13, is provided by "The Three Brothers" (no. 124), who love each other and whose diligence leads to wealth, as is explicitly stated: "and as they had learnt [their trades] so well and were so clever, they earned a great deal of money" (und da sie [ihr Handwerk] so gut ausgelernt hatten und so geschickt waren, verdienten sie viel Geld).

9. See Zipes, *Fairy Tales and the Art of Subversion,* esp. 61ff.

That Were Danced to Pieces," no. 133). In peasant parlance, wealth is particularized in the coin of the realm. Hellers, pennies, and farthings signify a pittance, but thalers and louis d'or mean wealth. Greed infects monarchs, too, as when the king in "The Griffin" (no. 165) learns that the griffin can confer gold, silver, cows, sheep, and goats and sets out to increase his own wealth.

The Grimms' tales of sudden reversals in fortune share a European origin with medieval tales of the wheel of fortune, whose turns produce death and destruction as well as sudden affluence and esteem. However, the nineteenth-century motivation for telling such tales differs. Whereas medieval tales of reversal stress the uncertain tenure of earthly goods and success, the Grimms' tales grow out of the straightforward wish for improving one's own situation. [10]

The utter absence of wealth in any form provides the starting point for numerous tales. Masters notoriously cheat apprentices and servants of their just wages, though the odd and unaccustomed form their payment takes often masks pure gold. The ass in "The Wishing-Table, the Gold-Ass, and the Cudgel in the Sack" (no. 36) produces gold pieces fore and aft, and a knapsack full of sweepings turns to gold on the journey home in "The Devil's Sooty Brother" (no. 100).

Kings equal cheating masters in their niggardliness. They unjustly discharge old soldiers with a few pennies or turn them out when they can no longer bear arms, but the soldiers' derisory severance pay opens the door to later enrichment. Three farthings is all a brave man receives for his service in "How Six Men Got on in the World" (no. 71); Brother Lustig (no. 81) receives four kreuzers; a discharged soldier in "The Devil's Sooty Brother" has no pension at all. Bearskin (no. 101), dismissed when peace is concluded, must go begging, and the king in "The Blue Light" (no. 116) tells his faithful old soldier:

> I need you no longer, and you will not receive any more money, for he only receives wages who renders me service for them.

> Ich brauch dich nicht mehr; Geld bekommst du weiter nicht, denn Lohn erhält nur der, welcher mir Dienste dafür leistet.

Heads of household work fruitlessly, as "The Spirit in the Bottle" (no. 99) clearly indicates when a woodcutter tries to insure his old age by investing what little he's earned in his son's education. The old man assumes that if his son learns an honest trade, he'll be able to support his aged father. But it is neither from his own work nor from his son's learning that money pours in, but

---

10. Like a fingerprint, characteristic sets of motivations inhere in each collection of tales. Boccaccio's narrators, for instance, assume an amused distance toward the turns of fortune precipitated by quick-witted ripostes, physical beauty, accident, or canny exploitation of a situation.

from a chance encounter with a genie in a bottle whom the son outwits. Nor can the shoemaker, who "by no fault of his own, had become so poor that at last he had nothing left but leather for one pair of shoes" (ohne seine Schuld so arm geworden, daß ihm endlich nichts mehr übrigblieb als Leder zu einem einzigen Paar Schuhe) hope for a comfortable old age on what he has set aside.

Laboriously acquired skills rarely lead to material success. When the locksmith's father gives him money to go out into the world to seek his fortune, he has no inkling that his son will apprentice himself instead to a huntsman. His scant reward is an air gun, which however always hits its mark. The skillful huntsman (no. 111) then makes his fortune with his sharpshooting, with no further reference to his lengthy apprenticeship in locksmithing. The same is true of the son in "The Spirit in the Bottle." Two years of hard study exhaust his father's savings so that he too has to go into the forest to earn his keep.

Whether the protagonist is poor or rich, a hot desire for wealth or money regularly and speedily subverts any possibility of reward. Every culture seems to produce at least one tale like those in the Grimms' collection in which greed is somehow paid out in false coin. The goldsmith in "The Little Folks' Presents" (no. 182), who returns on a second night for more of the elves' coal that magically turns to gold, ends up with pockets full of coal as well as losing the first night's gold. "Then he recognized the punishment of his greediness" (Da erkannte er die Strafe seiner Habgier).

A transgression, no matter how unwitting, can destroy the goose that lays the golden egg, even when the "goose" is a toad wearing a gold filigree crown that a little girl unthinkingly removes in "Tales of the Paddock" (no. 105).[11] Indeed, wanting more wealth seems the surest way of losing what one has already acquired.[12] One might lose life as well, as does the rich brother whose

11. One tale contradicts the foregoing material: "Doctor Knowall" (no. 98). A burlesque, it recounts how a peasant named Crabb accidentally sees the interior of a doctor's house and decides that he would like to live that well himself. His wife tutors him in what he must do to attain this level of comfort, and with a new suit of clothes and his own native stupidity, he unmasks thieves and is richly rewarded, receiving "from both sides so much money in reward" that he "became a renowned man" (von beiden Seiten viel Geld zur Belohnung und ward ein reicher berühmter Mann). The burlesque genre always has the option of turning values topsy-turvy, although with this definition one may be tempted to declare any tale that turns the rules inside out to be a burlesque, thereby discounting the possibility of alternative readings of social values. In this case, other evidence shows this tale to be a burlesque, for example, the man's stupidity and the absence of a supernatural helper.

12. Katalin Horn refers to this aspect of fairy tale heroes' lives in *Der aktive und der passive Märchenheld* when she says simply: "Während der Vater die Verarmung unerträglich findet, bedeutet dem Sohn Kaufmannsreichtum meistens nichts. Im Gegenteil: Fleiß und Vermögen sind ihm in seinen Abenteuern eher hinderlich, er ist auf höheres aus" ("While the father finds impoverishment unbearable, wealth derived from commerce generally means nothing to the son. On the contrary: diligence and property are rather hindrances for him, since he is set on higher [goals]").

greed propels him to Simeli Mountain (no. 142) to get the jewels his kind and generous brother left behind. The robbers whose booty he covets waste no time in cutting off his head. Biblical reasoning about how hard it is for a rich man to get into heaven clearly imputes sinfulness to the rich (who therefore deserve punishment) and contrasts both with Calvinist ethics concerning wealth as a sign of grace and with wealth as a goal for the poverty-stricken. For if the rich man generally suffers because his possessions mark him in an inauspicious manner, why then should anyone wish to don his sinful mantle? The answer seems to be that the ideas about wealth that inhere in tales concerning work belong to the experience of the laboring poor, for whom the Calvinist system of values was both alien and irrelevant. It is grace, rather than the principle of good works, that permeates these tales, for it has already been shown that one cannot earn a reward; it can only be conferred. In any case, in several tales the rich who strive to increase their wealth gain nothing but "vexation, trouble, and abuse" (Ärger, Mühe und Scheltworte), as in "The Poor Man and the Rich Man" (no. 87), while the greedy king in "The Devil and the Three Golden Hairs" (no. 29) gains perpetual drudgery instead of the gold he sought.

If, through supernatural agency (Godfather Death or a fish, for example), an impoverished man has attained some degree of wealth, nothing endangers it as quickly as a woman. Through her avarice and ambition a palace becomes a hut, as in the well-known tale "The Fisherman and His Wife" (no. 19), or else her curiosity endangers the wealth conferred ("The Gold-Children," no. 85). A man's love for a woman also exposes him to danger. In "Godfather Death" (no. 44), death shows his godson how to predict the outcome of an illness and presents him with a life-giving herb but explicitly prohibits him from using "the herb against my will" (das Kraut gegen meinen Willen).[13] His supernatural knowledge soon enriches the godson. On one occasion the godson contravenes Godfather Death's prohibition and is pardoned, but when he falls in love with a princess doomed to death and tries to deceive his godfather by giving her the magic herb, he must die. Godfather Death seizes him, a victim of love for woman, with his icy hand and shows him the guttering candle of his own life-span, which flickers out as he watches in fear and horror.

Even in those tales in which the conclusion seems to contradict the idea that women pose danger to wealth, internal evidence suggests a certain antipathy to women's controlling or possessing wealth. The fact that the king commends all his goods into the care of his wife, the peasant's wise daughter (no. 94), seems to contradict this idea. However, he subsequently rejects her, and when he restores her as his wife, her control of or access to the king's wealth is

---

13. This tale provides a pithy, iconoclastic summary of God's injustice when the poor man rejects God as godfather, saying, "I do not desire to have you for a godfather . . . you give to the rich, and leave the poor to hunger" ("So begehr ich dich nicht zu Gevatter . . . du gibst dem Reichen und lässest den Armen hungern").

mentioned no further. How ill it becomes a woman to have sway over vast wealth is suggested in "The True Bride":

> And now the magnificent castle belonged to the girl alone. At first she did not know how to reconcile herself to her good fortune.

> gehörte das prächtige Schloß dem Mädchen ganz allein. Es wußte sich in der ersten Zeit gar nicht in seinem Glück zu finden.

Indeed, her newfound fortune initiates misfortune, and although she emerges from her trials married, her own riches are silently relegated to obscurity. [14] Even "The Goose-Girl" (no. 89), which communicates strong independent womanhood, loses sight of the wealth that has been packed up for her wedding journey. Although she sets out with "costly vessels of silver and gold, and trinkets also of gold and silver; and cups and jewels, in short, everything which appertained to a royal dowry" (viel köstliches Gerät und Geschmeide . . . Gold und Silber, Becher und Kleinode, kurz, alles, was nur zu einem königlichen Brautschatz gehörte), and although she and her husband ultimately rule their realm together in peace and happiness, her own wealth silently fades from view.

Wherever Wilhelm Grimm explicitly addresses the question of women and wealth, the two appear antithetical to one another. This differs vastly from what Wilhelm knew from the Danish ballad and tale tradition, where it is abundantly clear that women are considered legitimate possessors of wealth. "Stolz Ingerlild" bears this out:

> Now proud Ingerlild rules over her house[hold],
> Now proud Ingerlild rules over her gold so great. [15]

Children, too, are anathema to wealth, and so is wealth to children, a curious perception. *Grimms' Tales* here inserts another internal contradiction similar to that concerning the sinful nature of the rich. The wealth a protagonist wants to acquire would apparently thrust the newly enriched hero into a category of voluntary childlessness, but since all of the tales which also appear in the Small Edition were meant specifically for children's eyes, a different explanation must be sought. Could Grimm have meant to imply that children were worth more than gold? That along with Cornelia he held children to be the true jewels? And that as a corollary, children were the jewels and gold of poor folk? Or did he intend to suggest that not the new rich but only the old

---

14. This represents a shift in Wilhelm Grimm's thought. Two early tales, "Bluebeard" and "The Castle of Death" both of which appeared in the 1812 edition, end with women happily in charge of their former husbands' worldly goods. In 1819, "Bluebeard" was replaced by "The Robber-Bridegroom" (no. 40) and "The Castle" with "Fitcher's Bird," (no. 46), both of which conclude with no mention of women's control of wealth.

15. *Altdänische Heldensagen,* no. 84.

rich embodied the sinfulness that characterizes so many of the misers in his tales?

Whatever the mental route by which Wilhelm Grimm arrived at his final formulations (or his informants may have furnished them in their raw material), the childless wealthy couple and, conversely, the poor family with more children than it can feed provide consistent and recurring motifs.[16] As long as the couple in "Ferdinand the Faithful and Ferdinand the Unfaithful" (no. 126) were rich, they had no children, but when they were poor they got a little boy. Similarly, the rich farmer had no children, and when his wife brought forth a child they had to name it "Hans the Hedgehog" (no. 108), for it was a hedgehog above and a boy below, confirming the antipathy between wealth and proper progeny. Royalty, too, can share this difficulty, as in "The Little [RBB] Donkey" (no. 144), which introduces us to "a King and a Queen, who were rich, and had everything they wanted, but no children" (ein König und eine Königin, die waren reich und hatten alles, was sie sich wünschten, nur keine Kinder). The queen laments that she is a barren field in which nothing grows, but when God at last heeds her, she bears not a human child but an ass.

The best-known of Grimms' tales dealing with the childlessness of the rich and powerful is "Little Briar-Rose" (no. 50). Every day the king and queen say: "Ah, if only we had a child!" (Ach, wenn wir doch ein Kind hätten!). But when the child is finally born, an affronted guest curses her with an early death, though a gentle wise woman subsequently softens the prophecy to a century's slumber. Raising the question of wealth and children to a quasi-theological level, Grimm includes this theme in a religious legend, "God's Food" (leg. 5), which begins:

> There were once upon a time two sisters, one of whom had no children and was rich, and the other had five and was a widow and was so poor that she no longer had food enough to satisfy herself and her children.

> Es waren einmal zwei Schwestern, die eine hatte keine Kinder und war reich, die andere hatte fünf Kinder und war so arm, daß sie nicht mehr Brot genug hatte, sich und ihre Kinder zu sättigen.

This tale links the childless rich with the "child-rich" poor and introduces all those tales in which impoverished parents send their children out into the world. Usually the number of children is limited to the fairy tale triad of three brothers or three sisters, although the best-known tale of all, "Hansel and Gretel" (no. 15), has just a brother and a sister pitted against their parents and poverty alike. All the foregoing characteristics unite in this tale. Poor parents have children but not money; wealth belongs to the (wicked) witch; the

---

16. In this respect it is interesting to note the difference between French and German expressions for a large family: *famille nombreuse* as opposed to *kinderreich*, the latter incorporating "rich" into the compound word.

children arrogate the witch's pearls and jewels to themselves, dutifully turning them over to their (good) father at the end, and the text notes that "all anxiety was at an end" (alle Sorgen [hatten] ein Ende) but specifically avoids mentioning the words *money* or *rich*.

Still another internal contradiction appears in connection with the inherent value of children, for parents often inadvertently exchange a child for great wealth. The devil, a little black mannikin, and a nixie all enrich fathers who unwittingly agree to accept great wealth for something specified by their mysterious companion. The most complex of these tales is "The Girl without Hands" (no. 31), in which an old man approaches an impoverished miller and says:

> "Why do you plague yourself with cutting wood, I will make you rich, if you will promise me what is standing behind your mill." "What can that be but my apple-tree?" thought the miller, and said: "Yes," and gave a written promise to the stranger.

> "Was quälst du dich mit Holzhacken, ich will dich reich machen, wenn du mir versprichst, was hinter deiner Mühle steht." "Was kann das anders sein als mein Apfelbaum?" dachte der Müller, sagte ja und verschrieb es dem fremden Mann.

It is not the apple tree, however, but the miller's daughter, who is sweeping the yard behind the house.

Another tale, "The King of the Golden Mountain" (no. 92), introduces "a certain merchant who had two children, a boy and a girl." The text, interestingly enough, avoids stating that the merchant is wealthy, which would contradict the implicit premise that children and wealth are incompatible; instead, upon meeting him, the reader learns:

> . . . two richly-laden ships of his sailed forth to sea with all his property on board, and just as he was expecting to win much money by them, news came that they had gone to the bottom, and now instead of being a rich man he was a poor one, and had nothing left but one field outside the town.

> Es gingen aber zwei reichbeladene Schiffe von ihm auf dem Meer, und sein ganzes Vermögen war darin, und wie er meinte, dadurch viel Geld zu gewinnen, kam die Nachricht, sie wären gesunken. Da war er nun statt eines reichen Mannes ein armer Mann und hatte nichts mehr übrig als einen Acker vor der Stadt.

At that point a black mannikin approaches him and promises him as much money as he wants in return for the first thing that rubs itself against his leg when he returns home. The merchant thinks of his dog and writes and seals his promise to the little man, thus signing away his son. In like manner, a siren-like nixie in the millpond (no. 181) emerges from the water to offer an impoverished miller all his former riches and happiness in return for the young thing that had just been born in his house. Thinking that she means a kitten or a puppy, he promises what she asks and is thunderstruck when he returns home to learn that his wife has just borne a baby boy.

Each of these tales speedily quits the arena of the enriched parents and moves toward its conclusion through a series of tests and trials of the jeopardized child. This introduces the final internal contradiction about children and wealth: the parents, disappearing from the tale, are left in undisturbed enjoyment of their accidentally gained wealth, but the victimized children must disentangle themselves from the forces that have enriched their parents and have endangered their own lives. If the family appeared as an indissoluble unit, so that enriching one segment of it benefited all members, then amelioration of the parents' condition at the immediate expense of their children might be seen as a source of ultimate benefit to the children. But families are generally treated as a dispensable irrelevance, a mere springboard to catapult the young protagonist onto center stage. Having served its purpose, the family then disappears presumably in complete and secure enjoyment of its newly won wealth. On the other hand, each of these enriched families ultimately loses the child who has been the instrument of its enrichment, confirming the conclusion that wealth and parenthood are in some essential sense incompatible in *Grimms' Tales*.

There are, however, acceptable—though surprisingly amoral or non-moral—ways of acquiring money or wealth that do not precipitate punishment or danger. Serendipity, stupidity, guile, and revenge head the list in curious tales of vice rewarded. Another far smaller group rewards virtue. Serendipitous acquisition of wealth looms large in the fairy tale world, even when a logical inner dynamic guides the course of events. When the two brothers (no. 60) unwittingly eat the heart and liver of a golden bird that the greedy (and childless) goldsmith had earmarked for himself, it is the hunger resulting from their uncle's lean and miserly table that drives them to snatch the heart and liver from the broiling pan. Eating them incorporates the wealth-spawning qualities of the golden bird from whose body they come, and from this point forward, the two boys each find a gold piece under their pillows every morning. Driven away from their home by the enraged uncle, the boys find their way to a solitary, childless huntsman, who welcomes them, saying that finding gold under your pillow is not "so very bad, if at the same time you remain honest, and are not idle" (wenn ihr . . . rechtschaffen . . . bleibt und euch nicht auf die faule Haut legt).[17] He brings them up, saving for their future use the gold pieces he finds under their pillows every day.

"The Turnip" (no. 146) begins on the same serendipitous note. The poorer of two brothers finds a gigantic turnip in his fields, which he presents to his king as a mark of his respect (ihm eine Verehrung machen). The king sympathizes with his poverty and rewards him with gold, farmland, meadows,

17. This interpolation seems to function as a release from the caveat against the prior possession of money for those who are good at heart. Significantly the huntsman avoids urging the boys to be "diligent" (fleißig), which traditionally does not immediately result in acquiring wealth, as this chapter has shown.

and herds. It is patently absurd to gain riches in return for a worthless turnip whose only distinction is its size. This becomes all too apparent when the king passes the turnip on to the rich brother, as a special recognition for the gifts of gold and horses he has offered in the hope of receiving an even greater reward than his brother has received for his humble gift.

Like serendipity, stupidity can also propel the hero to fame and fortune. The youngest of three sons, incapable of learning anything, gains enormous wealth and the papal throne itself in "The Three Languages" (no. 33).[18] The count, his father, had sent him to one famous master after another, but all the boy had learned was the language of dogs, birds, and frogs. Disgusted and angry, the count commands his retainers to carry the boy into the forest and kill him, but like the hunters in "Snow-White" (no. 53) they cannot commit the deed. Instead, the stupid son comprehends the wild howling of dogs, which reveals the location of an enormous treasure; his wanderings subsequently take him to Rome at the moment the college of cardinals is to choose a new pope, a position the boy gains with the help of a dove perched on his shoulder. In another tale, "The Good Bargain," a peasant's mistaken belief that he understands the language of frogs reveals how utterly stupid he is, but he retains enough canniness to trade the five hundred (blows!) his king promises him to an extortionate soldier and a grasping Jew in exchange for two hundred groschen, a coat, the king's exoneration from the five hundred blows he was to have received, and a reward of all the money he can stuff into his pockets. The peasant's apparent greed, which in other tales would have met with instant penury, has become acceptable because the peasant showed himself witless about money in the opening lines of the tale.[19] "The Poor Miller's Boy and the Cat" (no. 106) formulates the special relationship between stupidity and money with great clarity in its concluding sentence:

> . . . and he was rich, so rich that he had enough for all the rest of his life. After this let no one ever say that anyone who is foolish [RBB] can never become a person of importance.

> . . . und war er reich, so reich, daß er für sein Lebtag genug hatte. Darum soll keiner sagen, daß wer albern ist, deshalb nichts Rechtes werden könne.

Guile and stealth can also lead to wealth. In "The Three Sons of Fortune" (no. 70), a father bequeaths laughably common articles to his three sons, but advises them sagely, "Only seek out a country where such things are still unknown, and your fortune is made" (sucht euch nur ein Land, wo dergleichen

---

18. Maria Tatar discusses numskulls and simpletons in "Born Yesterday: The Spear Side," *The Hard Facts of the Grimms' Fairy Tales.*

19. Both "The Three Languages" and "The Good Bargain" display transparently parochial sectarian sentiments, for the first openly ridicules Catholicism, while the second espouses a clear anti-Semitism.

Dinge noch unbekannt sind, so ist euer Glück gemacht). The three brothers turn their worldly goods—a clock, a scythe, and a cat—into wealth beyond measure by locating a land without clocks, a country that harvests its wheat by firing cannons through the stalks, and—like Dick Whittington—a country infested with mice. On the one hand, cheap and often useless objects of everyday existence that propel the poor man to fortune are a stock-in-trade of the fairy tale and burlesque. On the other hand, the popularity of this theme from one century to the next bespeaks its continuing relevance among an impoverished audience clinging to whatever promises the tales they read and hear offer for a better future.

Simple guile can turn into criminal stealth. The little peasant (no. 61) embodies this sequence when he induces an innocent shepherd to take his place in the executionary barrel and then returns to the village with the shepherd's flocks, saying he has gotten them from the enchanted land on the riverbed. Led by the mayor, the town's citizens vie with one another to be first to jump into the river until "the entire village was dead, and the small peasant, as sole heir, became a rich man" (Da war das Dorf ausgestorben, und Bürle als der einzige Erbe ward ein reicher Mann). Likewise, the dirt-poor peasant Hans marries richly (no. 84) by tricking his intended bride's miserly father into believing that the fields, vineyards, and meadows they pass belong to him. Similar to "Puss in Boots" in motif and theme, this tale celebrates the wily and amoral trickster who cleverly plays on his listeners' desires to gain his own ends.

Revenge for crimes against the community also provides an acceptable avenue for arrogating outlaw riches to the protagonist. The implicit definition of these crimes results in an odd lineup. In Grimms' Tales justifiable extortion is presented in conjunction with the following victims: an innkeeper whom three army surgeons (no. 118) hold responsible for his maidservant's carelessness, a robber, a dwarf, a giant, and a Jew. The three army surgeons threaten the innkeeper with arson unless he coughs up a great deal of money; strong Hans (no. 166) first beats some robbers unconscious and then packs a gunny-sack with all the gold and silver he can carry. The enchanted prince requites the ungrateful red-eyed and mean-minded dwarf in "Snow-White and Rose-Red" (no. 161) with a single fatal blow and divides the dead creature's treasure with his brother, much as the king executes Old Rinkrank (no. 196) and expropriates his gold and silver. At the other end of the scale, the youth who went forth to learn what fear was (no. 4) beats an old man with an iron bar until he offers the boy great riches. The text excuses the lad's behavior by labelling the bearded old man a fiend (Unhold), just as the text of "The Jew among Thorns" in later versions overlays the designation of the Jew as an "old man" with a description of his "goat's beard." Removing the elderly Jew from the realm of the aged where reverence is due exposes him to the treachery of completely unjustified attack, first in the thornbush and later on the scaffold.

Lest one conclude that amorality reigns uncontested in Grimms' Tales, I should point out that the collection also offers moral means of gaining great wealth. Quite often wealth rewards perceived virtue: a boy shows himself to be good-hearted or loyal or a girl distinguishes herself by her industry or kindness.[20] This represents a twilight zone between grace and good works. Good deeds cannot be consciously undertaken to earn a reward, for such efforts fail regularly and predictably, as in "Mother Holle" (no. 24). To elicit reward, good deeds must proceed from the goodness of the individual, and it is, further, the individual's goodness, rather than the good works, that supernatural creatures reward with great and unexpected wealth. The pear tree bows before the good sister but refuses its golden fruit to the bad sisters in "One-Eye, Two-Eyes, and Three-Eyes" (no. 130). The prohibition against actually desiring gold continues in these moral tales; rather than being explicitly stated, it inheres in the way in which rewards are offered. When Hans sets out to find the griffin (no. 165) on a journey which leads eventually to rich reward, he is requested "to be so kind as to ask the Griffin what would make their daughter healthy again. Hans said he would willingly do that, and went onwards" (er söll doch so guet si und der Vogelgrif froge, was die Tochter wieder chön gsund mache. Der Hans säit, das weller gärn tue, und goht witer). Absolutely no mention is made of potential reward when the sick girl's parents request his help, so that when they present Hans with gifts of "gold and of silver, and whatsoever else he wished for," the reader is left with the distinct impression that Hans had neither wished for nor earned the gold and silver, but that it had been freely conferred in recognition of his inherent merit. In like manner the stepdaughter's goodness is triply rewarded in "The Three Little Men in the Wood" (no. 13): she will become more and more beautiful, gold coins will fall from her mouth, and a king shall marry her. Similarly, a shower of gold completely covers the good, beautiful, industrious daughter when she leaves Mother Holle's service, and St. Joseph heaps money on the virtuous youngest sister in "St. Joseph in the Forest" (leg. 1). A more overtly pious version of this occurs in "The White Bride and the Black Bride" (no. 135). Because of their incivility,

> God was angry with the mother and daughter, and turned his back on them, and wished that they should become as black as night and as ugly as sin. To the poor step-daughter, however, God was gracious, and went with her, and when they were near the village said a blessing over her, and spoke: "Choose three things for yourself, and I will grant them to you." Then said the maiden: "I should like to be as beautiful and fair as the sun," and instantly she was white and fair as day. "Then I should like to have a purse of money which would never grow empty." That the Lord gave her also, but he said: "Do not forget what is best of all." Said she: "For my third wish, I desire, after my death, to inhabit the eternal kingdom of Heaven." That also was granted unto her, and then the Lord left her.

20. See Kurt Ranke's discussion of individual characteristics and tests of them in "Charaktereigenschaften und -proben," *EM.*

Da zürnte der liebe Gott über die Mutter und Tochter, wendete ihnen den Rücken zu und verwünschte sie, daß sie sollten schwarz werden wie die Nacht und häßlich wie die Sünde. Der armen Stieftochter aber war Gott gnädig und ging mit ihr, und als sie nahe am Dorf waren, sprach er einen Segen über sie und sagte: "Wähle dir drei Sachen aus, die will ich dir gewähren." Da sprach das Mädchen: "Ich möchte gern so schön und rein werden wie die Sonne;" alsbald war sie weiß und schön wie der Tag. "Dann möchte ich einen Geldbeutel haben, der nie leer würde," den gab ihr der liebe Gott auch, sprach aber: "Vergiß das Beste nicht." Sagte sie: "Ich wünsche mir zum dritten das ewige Himmelreich nach meinem Tode." Das ward ihr auch gewährt, und also schied der liebe Gott von ihr.

The magic sack, whether filled with food or money or possessing the ability to fulfill wishes, is an established fairy and folk tale motif, so that its introduction here not only allows the narrator to avoid having the girl wish for money itself, which is prohibited to the good, but also utilizes a standard fairy tale prop, the ever-full purse. Thus she is enriched bit by bit, not by a set amount of gold or coin, but by the unending capacity to spend.

Men as well as women receive their reward for distinguishing qualities rather than for actual performance. The conversation between a dismissed soldier and the devil ("The Devil's Sooty Brother") shows that heaven and hell both follow the same rules:

. . . when he looked round, a strange man stood before him, who wore a green coat and looked right stately, but had a hideous cloven foot. "I know already what you are in need of," said the man; "gold and possessions shall you have, as much as you can make away with, do what you will, but first I must know if you are fearless, that I may not bestow my money in vain."

. . . wie er sich umblickte, stand ein unbekannter Mann vor ihm, der einen grünen Rock trug, recht stattlich aussah, aber einen garstigen Pferdefuß hatte. "Ich weiß schon, was dir fehlt," sagte der Mann, "Geld und Gut sollst du haben, soviel du mit aller Gewalt durchbringen kannst, aber ich muß zuvor wissen, ob du dich nicht fürchtest, damit ich mein Geld nicht umsonst ausgebe."

Thereupon a great bear rushes to the attack, but the soldier coolly raises his gun and shoots, jesting as he does so. His subsequent enrichment is based not on having shot the bear, but on his presence of mind in confronting this fearsome spectacle (daß dir's an Mut nicht fehlt), reward for characteristics not for accomplishment. Thus, in *Grimms' Tales*, it is not what people *do*, but what they *are* that justifies their good fortune.

Paradoxically, but in complete accord with the logic of fairy tales, ignoring or refusing wealth also precipitates its sudden acquisition. In "The Water of Life" (no. 97), a princess constructs a broad golden road to her castle. Only he who heedlessly rides along its center shall win her, for only he will be thinking of the princess "so incessantly that he never noticed the golden road at all" (dachte immer an [die Königstochter] und wäre gerne schon bei ihr gewesen und sah die goldene Straße gar nicht). Likewise, the third brother in "The

Knapsack, the Hat, and the Horn" (no. 54) states explicitly: "Silver and gold do not move me" (Silber und Gold, das rührt mich nicht). Even the young giant (no. 90) refuses wages both for his work and for ridding a mill of spirits, saying: "Money I will not have, I have enough of it" (Geld will ich nicht, ich habe doch genug). These statements validate the ultimate transfer of wealth to deserving recipients, who demonstrate their worthiness by not overtly wanting the wealth they eventually receive.

The question of who deserves money and who does not underlies the plot development in the anti-Semitic tales, while the twin concepts of service (Dienst) and earning (verdienen) money provide a probe for analyzing "The Jew among Thorns."[21] The tale itself avoids rational causation and obfuscates responsibility for actions, perhaps to dim the reader's perception of its purposefully unjust conclusion. An outline of the plot follows:

For three years' hard work a miserly master pays his faithful servant three farthings. After he departs, the servant meets a little man with whom he shares his pittance. As a reward the man grants him three wishes. The servant wishes for a gun that will hit everything he aims at; a fiddle that will compel its hearers to dance; and the ability to have whatever favor he requests granted. Further down the road he encounters a Jew admiring a songbird and wishing it were his. The servant shoots it down and urges the Jew to fetch the bird from the thorn thicket. As soon as the Jew is fast among the thorns, the "good servant's humor so tempted him that he took up his fiddle and began to play." Wounded and with his clothes torn to bits, the Jew begs the servant to stop, but the fiddler continues, justifying his ill treatment by asserting that the Jew has fleeced others in the past. To stop his fiddling, the Jew offers him a purse full of gold, and when the servant has left, the Jew finds a judge to whom he complains that he has been abused and robbed of his money. When caught, the servant claims that the Jew had given "it to [him] of his own free will, that [he] might leave off fiddling because he could not bear [his] music." The judge does not believe the servant and condemns him to be hanged, but on the scaffold the servant asks to play his fiddle a final time. His music forces everyone to dance to the point of shrieking with exhaustion, until the judge offers the servant his life in return for stopping. The servant demands that the Jew confess where he got the money in his purse, or else he will resume his fiddling. "I stole it, I stole it!" cries the Jew; "but you have honestly earned it." The judge orders the Jew taken to the gallows and hanged as a thief.

Like many of the tales in the Grimms' collection, this one is rife with

---

21. The question of racism arises in conjunction with anti-Semitism, since many tales characterize the evil that must be eradicated, or at least punished, as metaphorically or actually black, e.g., in "The King's Son Who Feared Nothing" (no. 121) or "The White Bride and the Black Bride" (no. 135). This blackness forms part of the European fairy tale vocabulary and is not integrally related to work and money.

internal inconsistencies and contradictions. The demonstrably miserly master who cheats his servant escapes reproach; it is malice pure and simple that induces the servant to tempt the Jew into the thorns and then to torment him by making him dance; the servant characterized as "honest" (redlich) thinks factually that "You have fleeced people often enough, now the thorn-bushes shall do the same to you," although he actually knows nothing of the Jew or of his past; the "honest servant" lies, reformulating his account of what occurred when he met the Jew in order to incriminate him, and finally the "honest servant" extorts a confession to justify the Jew's hanging.

These characterizations of the servant and the Jew did not fall into place accidentally but resulted from careful editing throughout the tale's history, from its first appearance in volume 2 of the First Edition of 1815 to its final version. In 1815, the servant was called "faithful" and "diligent" (getreu, fleißig); this was intensified in 1819 to "really faithful" (gar getreu). By 1839 he had become "diligent" and "honest" (fleißig, redlich), which remained his sobriquet through the final edition. The Jew first appears in 1815 as "an old Jew" (ein alter Jude). Old age, however, requires respect in the fairy tale world, and thus he subsequently becomes "a Jew with a long goat's beard" (ein Jude mit langem Ziegenbart), which links him both to the devil, according to hallowed iconographic traditions, and to scapegoat figures. On their first encounter in the 1815 version, the servant thinks to himself that the Jew has cheated enough people and the narrative adds that the 100 gulden the Jew offered the servant to stop playing the fiddle had just been squeezed out of a Christian. The final sentence (1815) reads, "Then my servant let his fiddle rest and the scoundrel was hanged on the gallows in his place" (Da ließ mein Knecht die Geige ruhen und der Schuft wurde für ihn am Galgen gehängt).

One could contend that Grimm actually softened rabidly anti-Semitic statements, like "squeezed out of a Christian," by tainting another character, the master, with miserliness (he is called a skinflint, or *Geizhals*), but this does not alter the outrageous outcome. As the servant's star rises and he is called "the good servant" in 1839, the figure of the Jew is increasingly jeopardized by caricature. In 1815 the Jew complains to the judge that he's been robbed of his money (seines Geldes beraubt), whereas by 1839 he is made to embroider his complaint in what is clearly meant to be a characteristic Jewish manner, adding that the gold together with the purse have been taken and they were all ducats, one more beautiful than the last. The Jew is also shown as increasingly cowardly, with the 1839 version stressing that he waited until the servant was safely beyond earshot before beginning to curse him.

Wilhelm's notes to this tale in 1815 emphasize that the tale is "dramatically lively" (dramatisch lebendig), with further discussion centering on the motifs of dancing in the thorns, the final wish, and the tale's source. Commenting on the source, Albrecht Dieterich's *Historia von einem Bauernknecht und München, welcher in der Dornhecke hat müssen tanzen* (1618), Wilhelm remains firmly literary, skirting any analysis of how the figure of the Jew came to be substituted for that of the monk two hundred years before and also omitting entirely discussion of the fact that in some versions with a monk instead of a Jew, the monk escapes punishment altogether with no question of his swinging in the servant's stead.[22]

The opening and closing scenes that parenthetically enclose the narrative are central to understanding this tale in the context of work, money, and anti-Semitism. The honest servant has worked and has been cheated of his just wages; the Jew bears ill-gotten money, the product of no labor on his part and the cause of his harsh punishment. Historically barred from most occupations, excluded from guilds, and confined to moneylending, the Jew becomes the target for the servant's frustrated anger, which cannot and does not vent itself on the immediate exploiter, the "skinflint" who has just cheated him of three years' wages.

A more profound question poses itself, however. Why does this tale appear at all in the Grimms' collection? Berthold Auerbach, the nineteenth-century novelist, himself Jewish, was outraged that the Grimms included "The Jew among Thorns" in the *Tales*. Nothing like it exists in Ludwig Bechstein's four volumes of folk tales or in Simrock's *Märchen* (1864). Münchener Bilderbogen (Munich posters) at the mid-nineteenth century show no. 122: Frieder mit der Geige, whose victim is not a Jew, but the monk of earlier versions.[23] Furthermore, some versions of the tale in which the monk is a victim end far less violently and destructively, with the monk being taken home by the bailiff to talk it over rather than being hanged as a thief.[24] Even between 1933 and 1945 several publishers brave enough to set their own direction published collections of tales from Grimm that pointedly omitted "The Jew among Thorns."

In this exposition of the publishing history of anti-Semitic tales in Grimms' collection, it is noteworthy that Wilhelm placed both overtly anti-Semitic tales, "The Good Bargain" and "The Jew among Thorns," not only in the Large Edition but also in the Small Edition, where they would and did get maximum exposure among particularly impressionable young readers, while confining the one tale with a positively portrayed Jewish protagonist, "The Bright Sun Brings It to Light," to the Large Edition.[25] Wilhelm's decision to

22. See, e.g., Ayrer, *Ein Fassnachtspil von Fritz Dölla mit seiner gewünschten Geigen.*

23. Moreover, this tale appears in a twentieth-century collection from Upper Austria as "Der Pfarrer im Dorn," retaining the late medieval dramatis personae and depicting the fiddler as an unredeemed scoundrel rather than as victim. See Karl Haiding, *Märchen und Schwänke aus Oberösterreich,* 181–82.

24. See Ayrer, *Fassnachtspil.*

25. The Grimms' *Deutsche Sagen* also include three legends about Jews. "Der ewige Jude auf dem Matterhorn" (no. 343) credits the formation of that peak to the third passage of the wandering Jew, and the other two, "Der Judenstein" (no. 352) and "Das von den Juden

include these tales in their anti-Semitic forms may have been related to his friendship with members of the Christlich-Deutsche Tischgesellschaft (Christian-German Society), a reactionary group of hereditary nobles, higher bureaucratic functionaries, and a few scholars and artists. Formed in Berlin as part of conservative resistence to Hardenberg's reforms, its program was anti-Philistine, anti-Semitic, and anti-woman, as evidenced by Clemens Brentano's address, "The Philistine before, in, and after History." It may be significant for Wilhelm's attitudes that the society's membership included his revered mentor, Karl Friedrich von Savigny, as well as Fichte, Kleist, Clausewitz, and Brentano.[26]

Although it has often been stated that Wilhelm Grimm gives no indication in his own writings that he heard fairy tales (*Märchen*) as a child, a dream he had in 1810, well before he is assumed to have come into possession of "The Jew among Thorns," consists of several motifs familiar from the published tale and thus suggests, first, that Wilhelm Grimm had heard something like this tale in a form like the one he transcribed, and second, that its anti-Semitic cast at least paralleled similar unselfconsciously recorded feelings of his own.[27]

Taken as a group, the three themes—work, money, and anti-Semitism—illustrate basic values in the society from which these tales emerge.[28] Caught

---

getödtete Mägdlein" (no. 353), record tales of nameless victims of bloodthirsty Jews analogous to the hagiography of St. William of Norwich, Little St. Hugh of Lincoln, and St. Simon of Trent.

26. For a brief but useful (and classic) discussion, see Bramsted, *Aristocracy and the Middle Classes in Germany,* 40.

27. The dream as Wilhelm wrote it down reads as follows: "ich saß mit dem Jacob in einem Cabinet vor einem weißem Bett worin jemand lag, und erzählte ihm, daß sich der Procurator Pfeiffer nun auch mit altdeutschen Sachen abgebe. Auf einmal kam ein Jude herein, reich gekleidet mit einer Perucke und einem kleinen dreieckigen Hut, etwa wie der Abraham Susman. Ich sagte, wir müßten den verfluchten Juden ärgern, und wir wüßten, daß er eine Sklavin hatte, die wollten wir ihm nehmen. Sie kam bald herein, schneeweiß angezogen und sehr schön und zierlich. Ich fing eine Komödie an zu spielen, und hielt mit dem Jacob einen Dialog, der Jude saß und ärgerte sich stark, das Ende war daß wir drei anfangen mußten zu tanzen, so brachte das Stück mit sich. Der Jude konnte nichts dagegen haben und ärgerte sich schwer. Wir fingen endlich an zu tanzen. Jedes drehte sich im Kreis herum, ohne den andern anzurühren, und so tanzten wir der Reihe nach und aus der Stube, und hatten das Mädchen in der Mitte. Es waren auf einmal drei Hochzeiten von allen Nachbarn—" Numerous points of agreement identify elements of this dream with "The Jew Among Thorns": the desire to annoy the Jew, the Jew's powerlessness against the intention, and the dancing. Indeed, Wilhelm's instigation of the tormenting identifies him with the servant in the tale, which may explain why the servant is referred to in the earliest (1815) version as "my" servant (Da ließ mein Knecht die Geige ruhen und der Schuft wurde für ihm am Galgen gehängt). The dream was recorded on 19 June 1810 and was published for the first time by Heinz Rölleke in *Brüder Grimm Gedenken* (1981), 32.

28. Alan Dundes has argued in *Life is like a Chicken Coop Ladder* that anti-Semitism in Germany arose from a collective anality in German culture, a provocative but problematic viewpoint.

in a social web that offered limited resources and in which their own labor could not be expected to bring meaningful reward, workers had to restrain whatever socially disruptive desire for wealth they might feel. Unable to vent their frustration on the immediate sources of their grinding poverty (like the miserly master in "The Jew among Thorns"), they invented scapegoat figures like the Jew, who in the words of the text even has a goat's beard to identify him with the scapegoat (*Sündenbock*).[29] Attacking the egregious Jew whom numerous regulations kept outside the social fabric not only diverted disruptive feelings from socially related figures like the servant's master, but it also united the poor in hatred of a common enemy for whom no epithet was bad enough. Forbidden to practice the same trades as his peasant and artisan compatriots, the Jew was accused of idleness.

Another clue to the scapegoat nature of the Jew in *Grimms' Tales* is his singular appearance. Neither Jewish mother, Jewish child, nor Jewish grandparent appears. Jewish aunts and uncles are equally absent. The Jewish fool, the Jewish sage, the Jewish stutterer, and the Jewish Demosthenes fade before the single image of the Jewish usurer whom anyone may bait, deceive, or defraud. Given the hopeless poverty delineated in these tales and the futility of gainful employment, virulent hatred seems almost inevitable. The tales' fatal focus on Jews, the outsiders who replaced monks in the collective resentment of the poor, fit neatly into preexisting Romantic anti-Semitic sentiments and meshed with subsequent anti-Semitic sentiments growing out of nationalistic resentment against a French conqueror who had enfranchised Germany's Jewish population.

29. The problems inherent in choosing the Jew as scapegoat appear in the third tale with a Jewist protagonist, "The Bright Sun Brings It to Light," where the Jew is nearly as poor as his murderer. This tale, which shows the poor preying upon one another, has never appeared in the Small Edition.

13

Christian Values and Christian Narratives

istorically, the question of Christian values is highly problematic. In the case of gender-specific propriety, the individualistic message of the Gospels is frequently at odds with Paul's epistles. Out of this disparity has grown a tension in Christian religious practice that is reflected in canonical literature as well as within the minor genres of oral and written folk narrative, where this tension gives way to ambivalence. Eugen Weber concludes that "Christian motifs in real folktales seem ambiguous,"[1] and speaking specifically of the Grimms' collection in a recent essay, Heinz Rölleke writes that "God seems to be nothing more than an idiomatic embellishment."[2] Discussing narrative development, Rölleke continues that in most of the tales in which God is called upon, he is in no sense important and is dispensable from nearly every point of view. In this sense Rölleke's views fit comfortably within the belief that a thoroughly non-Christian mentality underlies folk narrative.[3]

That Rölleke's approach should appear iconoclastic must be understood with reference to the fact that the German readership has been primed more recently with Christian interpretations of *Grimms' Tales.* In Germany, Christian exegesis of the Grimms' collection is far more popular than any similar undertaking in non-German-speaking countries.[4] In insisting on the presence

1. "Fairies and Hard Facts," 110.
2. "Das Bild Gottes in den Märchen der Brüder Grimm," in *"Wo das Wünschen noch geholfen hat,"* 211.
3. Ibid., 212. This attitude was expressed in "Christliche Motive im deutschen Volksmärchen," in Mackensen, ed., *Handwörterbuch des deutschen Märchens.* Dietz-Rüdiger Moser represents the antipodal position in "Christlich Erzählstoffe," which claims that the extent of Christian material in oral narrative has been underestimated in the past, citing the Catholic Church's active role in disseminating Christian tales that then entered the oral tradition, especially during the Counterreformation. The final word on this subject is not yet in.
4. The Christian, anthroposophist interpreter most familiar to English-speaking audiences, Rudolf Steiner, is himself of German origin. Christian interpreters are unparalleled in their exploitative manipulation of *Grimms' Tales.*

143

of Christian values in the tales, twentieth-century interpreters may simply be reacting against late nineteenth- and early twentieth-century readings of *Grimms' Tales* as an integral part of indigenous Germanic mythology, which above all had the virtue, as they said, of not being "foreign" like the Bible. Thus, one Christian commentator finds it possible to understand tales of sudden reversal—rags to riches—as an expression of Christian love for all creatures who are abandoned and cast aside, their release from suffering implicitly identified with the resurrection and the life, *caritas* in a fairy tale setting.[5] Far more widespread among the general public are writings whose superficially persuasive interpretations consist largely of restatements of the text in symbolic language so that the interpreter can evoke meanings that he or she has assigned to specific passages.[6]

The Christian exegetic school has been so pervasive that it has influenced Freudian interpreters like Bruno Bettelheim, who assumes that many of the Grimms' tales express Christian values.[7] But "important and fascinating" as he finds "these religious aspects of fairy stories," they often occur, apparently paradoxically, in connection with brutality, threat, and extortion, a fact Bettelheim either overlooks or chooses to ignore.

Despite evident interest in *Grimms' Tales* as a Christian text, a complete catalogue and analysis of Christian elements in the *Tales* and the contexts in which they appear have not yet been attempted. Interpreters have either restricted their consideration to a few carefully selected tales that neatly prove specific points or they have directed their gaze toward essentially superficial and insignificant Christian components, for example, exclamations like "Oh, God" (Ach Gott). Although these utterances definitely flavor the tales, they do little to Christianize them. Rather, they form part of a national emotive metaphor, the nonreligious nature of which Antonio Gramsci recognized when he translated them into Italian as *per carità, ahimè,* or *per Bacco.*[8]

German and *Christian* are two concepts that have been inextricably linked in Germany for centuries. Innumerable religious sentiments grace exterior portals and lintels, mottos like "He whom God wishes well no one can harm", which appears on a Marburg house dated to ca. 1600; the 1884 motto on the house facing it proclaims, "German house, German land, may God protect it with a powerful hand". Richly embroidered samplers hung on parlor walls offer sentiments like "May God's strong fatherland protect your married state."[9]

In folk literature before the Grimms, on the other hand, Christianity and

5. Silvia Bürgler, quoted in Lukacs, ed., *Die goldene Spindel,* 58.
6. See especially Geiger, *Mit Märchen im Gespräch.*
7. See *The Uses of Enchantment,* 13ff., 219, 228ff.
8. Rölleke, *"Wo das Wünschen noch geholfen hat,"* 211.
9. Late nineteenth-century sampler, Amtshaus, Steinau.

Christian elements are more notable for their absence, though humorous chapbooks of the seventeenth and eighteenth centuries contain virulently sectarian anticlerical jokes and anecdotes.[10] Moreover, a close look at the editorial history of *Grimms' Tales* clearly shows that it was Wilhelm Grimm himself who iced the cake, so to speak, with Christian exclamations, very few of which existed in the 1812 or 1819 versions of the tales.

Despite their hermeneutical insignificance, these exclamations and expressions set the stage for understanding *Grimms' Tales* in a Christian context, and it is therefore useful to display their nature and the extent of their occurrence, because the interpolation of Christian admonitions, reminders, and exclamations, no matter how automatic and formulaic, results in a "philosophical alteration" to the text as a whole.[11]

Christian Interpolations, Locations, and Representatives

Christian interjections and exclamations include references to the entire Christian pantheon as well as to Christian liturgical functions. The narrative voice assures the reader that a character "thanked God" (dankte Gott, no. 163), that the characters were happy as long "as it pleased God" (solange es Gott gefiel, no. 129), that "the husband selected from on high" (der vom Himmel bestimmte Gemahl, no. 163) had appeared, that something was "the divine sign" (den Wink Gottes, no. 121), and that it was "as if an angel came from heaven" (als ob ein Engel vom Himmel käme, no. 178). The Christian devil occasionally takes center stage, too (nos. 59, 60), and innumerable characters are cloaked in church language when they are "saved" (erlöst), particularly those who are "pious" (fromm), but never those who are "godless" (gottlos).

God is invoked in colorful variety: "Good God" (lieber Gott, no. 127), "Lord God" (Herr Gott, nos. 6, 192), "God!" (Gott, no. 119), "My God" (Mien [sic] Gott, no. 187), "Oh, God" (Ach Gott, nos. 16, 53, 59, 89, 94, 106), "For Heaven's sake" (um Himmels willen, no. 64), "God forbid" (Gott bewahr, nos. 94, 110), "God knows" (weiß Gott, no. 96), "May God reward you" (Gott lohne euch, no. 150), "May God protect us" (Gott behüte uns, no. 166), "May God take pity" (daß Gott erbarm, no. 11), and "Help, Lord God" (hilf, Herr Gott, no. 171). Hansel is certain that "God won't abandon us" (Gott wird uns nicht verlassen, no. 15) and also that "God will help us" (Gott wird uns schon helfen).

Christian architecture sets the stage with chapels and churches for several of the tales (nos. 20, 51, 68, 79, 114, 138; leg. 9) and then peoples them with

---

10. For a recent discussion of humorous chapbooks in the seventeenth and eighteenth centuries see Moser-Rath, *"Lustige Gesellschaft,"* 7–36.

11. See Heinz Rölleke's discussion, "Zu den Veränderungen in den Einzeltexten," in *Kinder- und Hausmärchen,* (1982), 2:575.

sextons (nos. 4, 68), godparents (nos. 12, 95, 188), pastors and priests (nos. 37, 52, 59, 61, 64, 66, 92, 95, 138, 139, leg. 9), and even the pope (no. 33). Christian liturgical practice also looms large, with church bells ringing (no. 4), a christening (no. 3), a baptism (no. 25), prayer (nos. 39, 53, 86, 65, 101, 109, 119, 123, 130, 169), blessing (nos. 77, 92, 141, 146, 153, 188), and care for salvation (nos. 101, 120, 135). Christian folk tradition surfaces within this context with a goat-bearded Jew, reminiscent of one of Lucifer's attributes (no. 110), and a chalk circle drawn to exclude the devil (nos. 31, 92), as well as a Christian proverb (no. 107).

In and of itself, this catalog—which is undoubtedly incomplete—proves only the extent to which Christian vocabulary, references, and imagery have penetrated *Grimms' Tales*. For instance, "Hansel and Gretel" (no. 15) does not become a Christian tale simply by the addition of Hansel's assurances that God will protect the two of them, nor does the nixie's going to church (no. 79) mean that this arch personification of pagan water-nymphdom has absorbed or expressed a single Christian value. On the contrary, the Christian tales that are meaningful to this inquiry are those that operate within a Christian framework and that include explicitly stated Christian intentions. The simplest of these are the Christian etiological tales.

Etiological Tales

As a group, the Christian etiological tales explain the divine origin of, and thereby justify, particular creatures or familiar social structure. [12] A handful of tales in the Grimms' collection explain how God has ordered society's various levels, agricultural fruitfulness, the length of life, and the creation of animals. On the surface this list seems neutral enough, yet it cloaks an unexpected ordering of gender. These etiologies offer a vision of a predominantly male world. In forming a social structure from Eve's various children (no. 180), the handsome ones are made ruler, merchant, and scholar, while the ugly ones people the lower rungs of society's ladder: tiller of the soil, baker, tailor, potter, messenger, and servant. The duration of life (no. 176) is likewise measured against grammatically masculine creatures, the ass, dog, ape, and human.

Though man grumbles at his fate, everything proceeds peaceably in this male world. Even the account of God's unpaid debt to his arch rival, the devil, for loosing his wolves on the devil's goat is settled without much fuss in "The Lord's Animals and the Devil's" (no. 148). But the appearance of women in these tales, aside from Eve's necessary maternity in "Eve's Various Children," precipitates a punitive and violent mood. When a mother cleans her daughter's dress with an ear of grain (no. 180) in what passes for the Golden Age of

12. Wayland D. Hand categorizes etiological tales as legends rather than as Märchen. See "Status of European and American Legend Study."

Plenty, her wastefulness incenses God, who withdraws the grain's wonted fruitfulness. Only pity for chickens leads God to restore some of the grain's former plentifulness. The tale is intended to clarify the inadequate level of production that grain "now" has. [13]

The comic origins of the race of apes are accounted for in "The Old Man Made Young Again" (no. 147), a narrative with clear connections to seventeenth- and eighteenth-century chapbooks' humorous accounts of wife-beating. By tacking on an etiological conclusion, however, the narrator seems to attempt to socialize the story's violence. In this tale, God and St. Peter, moved to compassion by the physical torments of an old beggar bowed by age and infirmity, hammer him to health on a smithy's anvil. The smithy's mother-in-law, herself aged and half-blind, asks the beggar if it had hurt. Since he replies that he had never felt more comfortable, she assents to her son-in-law's suggestion that she too be rejuvenated. Since he lacks divine knowledge, however, his efforts produce disfigurement and an agony of pain that so terrifies the old woman's daughter and her maid that they are both delivered of misshapen boys—from whom the race of apes sprang.

Gender should be inconsequential in this tale, for the central point—as in "Brother Lustig" (no. 81)—is that divine powers far exceed those to which any human might aspire. Whether this tenet is proved on a male or a female body should be immaterial. The fact is, however, that a female body was chosen and that her torments were described in chilling detail:

> . . . the smith . . . thrust the old woman into [the great fire], and she writhed about this way and that, and uttered terrible cries of murder. "Sit still; why are you screaming and jumping about so?" cried he, and as he spoke he blew the bellows again until all her rags were burnt. The old woman cried without ceasing, and the smith thought to himself: "I have not quite the right art," and took her out and threw her into the cooling-tub. Then she screamed so loudly that the smith's wife upstairs and her daughter-in-law heard it, and they both ran downstairs, and saw the old woman lying in a heap in the quenching-tub, howling and screaming, with her face wrinkled and shriveled and all out of shape.

> . . . der Schmied . . . stieß die Alte hinein, die sich hin und wieder bog und grausames Mordgeschrei anstimmte. "Sitz still, was schreist und hüpftst du, ich will erst weidlich zublasen." Zog damit die Bälge von neuem, bis ihr alle Haderlumpen brannten. Das alte Weib schrie ohne Ruhe, und der Schmied dachte: "Kunst geht nicht recht zu," nahm sie heraus und warf sie in den Löschtrog. Da schrie sie ganz überlaut, daß es droben im Haus die Schmiedin und ihre Schnur hörten: die liefen beide die Stiegen herab und sahen die Alte heulend und maulend ganz zusammengeschnurrt im Trog liegen, das Angesicht gerunzelt, gefaltet und ungeschaffen. [14]

---

13. This tale is discussed at greater length in chap. 8.

14. Wilhelm Grimm transcribed this tale from Hans Sachs' 1562 *Ursprung der Affen*, not from oral folk tradition.

Other Christian tales confirm the status quo. In a paraphrase of the Gospel parable about the difficulty a rich man experiences getting into heaven, the peasant in heaven (no. 167) watches disconsolately when a rich arrival is received with music and song, although his own entry was barely noticed. "You are just as dear to us as anyone else," the peasant is told, "and will enjoy every heavenly delight that the rich man enjoys, but poor fellows like you come to heaven every day, but a rich man like this does not come more than once in a hundred years" (Du bisch is so lieb wie alle andere und muesch alle himmlische Freud gnieße wie de rich Herr, aber lueg, so arme Bürle, wie du äis bisch, chömme alle Tag e Himmel, so ne riche Herr aber chunt nume alle hundert Johr öppe äine).

More innovative is "The Moon" (no. 175), one of the last additions Wilhelm Grimm made to the collection.[15] "The Moon," which appeared for the first time in 1857, is a tale of the restoration of natural and moral order. It begins with a theft, continues with the anarchic resurrection of the dead, and ends with St. Peter's first calling the heavenly hosts (Heerscharen) together and then mounting his steed and riding to the underworld to bring the dead to order. As a sign of control reestablished, he hangs the moon high up in the firmament to light the underworld, inaccessible to those who would or might steal it. It is a tale whose genre is artificially determined by the outcome: the moon, which had formerly hung in an oak tree, now swings aloft in heaven, and the tale becomes thereby an etiology. This tale situates heavenly order within the most basic human context—life and death—with the apostle of order not God or Jesus, but Peter, God's representative agent. In this way, "The Moon," like several other tales, reiterates a male heavenly bureaucracy empowered to oversee the regularization of vital processes. On a scale measuring the Christianization of fairy and folk tale content, etiological tales represent a higher level than tales that merely include exclamations and mentions of churches or of liturgical functioning. Furthermore, in calling the heavenly hosts together to restore order, St. Peter unites Germany's epic heroic past to the Christian present. In "The Moon," Peter, a central figure in the Christian pantheon, effectively Christianizes an essentially nonreligious folk structure.

Tales with protagonists from the Christian pantheon frequently superimpose Christianized ideas onto narratives that are not necessarily Christian in their origins. Jesus is remarkably absent from this catalog of Christian folk. God himself appears (nos. 44, 82, 87, 135, 147, 176, 180), as does St. Peter (nos. 35, 81, 82, 147, 175). Together their appearances are nearly balanced by those of the Devil (nos. 4, 29, 31, 43, 92, 101, 120, 125, 189, 195). The Virgin Mary's three appearances are mostly in the legends (legs. 7, 10), while her problematic behavior in "Our Lady's Child" (no. 3) relates her more closely

---

15. It replaced "The Misfortune," a tale of peasant labor requited by fear, mortal danger, flight, apparent rescue, and mindlessly accidental death, all orchestrated by a malevolent fate.

to amoral or pagan figures than to a religious precursor. Angels, on the other hand, offer straightforward images of goodness (no. 76, legs. 7, 10), as do the apostles (no. 3, leg. 2). But as far as saints are concerned, any magic image could just as well stand in for St. Christopher (no. 113) or St. Anne (no. 139), and any other fairy tale figure at all could represent "the Christian" in "The Griffin" (no. 165). St. Joseph (leg. 1) and the Christ child (leg. 10), however, appear as thoroughly Christian figures in Christian tales extolling Christian virtues.

Beyond explaining how life came to be ordered as it is, the tales occasionally offer Christian reminders about how to live it. When, for instance, the king explains that he must marry his own daughter, Allerleirauh (no. 65), his shocked counselors gather and figuratively shake their fingers, saying: "God has forbidden a father to marry his daughter. No good can come from such a crime, and the kingdom will be involved in the ruin" (Gott hat verboten, daß der Vater seine Tochter heirate, aus der Sünde kann nichts Gutes entspringen, und das Reich wird mit ins Verderben gezogen). But none of these tales, no matter how highly colored with Christian virtues, approaches the level of Christian sentiment in the most Christian of the tales. The Christian message of the animal tale "The Sparrow and His Four Children" (no. 157) purports to be a mere recasting of what the fourth, silliest, and weakest nestling has heard while perched on the church windowsill. [16] The narrative voice tells the reader, and none too subtly, that Christian reward is for the humblest—and here doubly so, since the Bible identifies sparrows as the least of God's creation and this fellow is the least even among his brothers. Whereas Perrault proffered worldly wisdom with each of his *contes*, Father Sparrow's moral verse that closes the tale recasts, reformulates, and Christianizes the preceding narrative:

He who to God commits his ways,
In silence suffers, waits, and prays,
Preserves his faith and conscience pure,
He is of God's protection sure.

Denn wer dem Herrn befiehlt seine Sach,
schweigt, leidet, wartet, betet, braucht Glimpf, tut gemach,
bewahrt Glaub und gut Gewissen rein,
dem will Gott Schutz und Helfer sein.

Christian tales with female protagonists end on a far different note. Not reward but punishment sets the tone. It signals Ilsebill's end when she is thrust back into the pisspot poverty of her beginnings in "The Fisherman and His Wife" (no. 19). Her pride, which drove her onward to wish she could be like God, must be reduced by an angry deity who dashes her dreams. In "The Girl

---

16. This tale offers confirmation even in the animal world of Maria Tatar's assertion that ultimate success falls not to the strong and brave but to the lowest and most compassionate. See "Born Yesterday" in *The Hard Facts of the Grimms' Fairy Tales*.

without Hands" (no. 31), a putatively loving God rewards the maiden queen with restoration: her severed hands are replaced and she regains her rightful place in her husband's kingdom. But restoration for a woman requires suffering and persecution—here mutilation, exile, and isolation—in contrast to the restoration of male royalty, which follows not sufferings but adventures, as in "The King of the Golden Mountain" (no. 92).

Another problem remains to be resolved. Numerous internal contradictions are cleared up if one posits that it is sex, not sin, that causes suffering in *Grimms' Tales*. For example, in "Our Lady's Child" a girl's sufferings grow out of the opposite state, her recalcitrance, a sinful quality that must be expunged, but in "The Girl without Hands," the queen's sufferings result from her goodness. [17] Contrasting the heroine's sufferings in "The Girl without Hands" with the experiences of the humble compassionate little girl in "The Star Money" (no. 153), we can draw a further conclusion. For girls and women personal goodness alone is not sufficient to avert extreme suffering; only when immaculate and unassailable virtue is coupled with extreme isolation and penury can a female figure finally qualify for reward. The child—orphaned, homeless, poverty-stricken, pious, and good—who gives away her last stitch of clothing to the poor exemplifies childlike, unquestioning trust in God. God rewards her with a shower of gold and her picture has graced the frontispiece of countless editions of *Grimms' Tales* since the brothers' death.

The Children's Legends

The religious Children's Legends which are appended to *Grimms' Tales* offer special gender-specific conclusions. Here, too, male protagonists uniformly gain a heavenly reward, while female protagonists more frequently experience punishment. The reward promised in the little verse in "The Sparrow and His Four Children" is gained in the five legends with male protagonists. Whether it is twelve impoverished, starving brothers, waiting in a crystalline cave for their resurrection as Jesus' twelve apostles (leg. 2: "The Twelve Apostles"), a spurned and scorned princely hermit (leg. 4: "Poverty and Humility Lead to Heaven"), or a quite ordinary hermit (leg. 6: "The Three Green Twigs") who dies, each receives his reward for a life well lived. Our Lady rewards a wine merchant more immediately and in a far more secular manner when she frees his cart from the mud in return for a glass of wine (leg. 7: "Our Lady's Little

---

17. In another Christian tale, God curses a willful child (no. 117) with sickness and death, but still the child's willfulness holds sway. The child's mother beats the corpse until it retracts its defiant little arm into the grave. In the German, the child's gender is not identified, but in English translation the neutral German *es* becomes the English *she*. This occurs in the Margaret Hunt and James Stern translation of the Pantheon edition of *Grimms' Tales* but not in the Ralph Manheim translation.

Glass"). At the other end of the scale, a holy idiot's fervent belief gains him entry into heaven (leg. 9: "The Heavenly Wedding"). Reward characterizes all of the Christian tales with male protagonists, not just the Legends. Reward is attenuated in the case of "The Peasant in Heaven," unmerited in the case of "Brother Lustig," or arrogated viciously in the final paragraph of "The King of the Golden Mountain," but it is nonetheless granted.

The Children's Legends offer a concentrated version of the religious values inhering in the collection as a whole. "St. Joseph in the Forest" (leg. 1) tells the story of three daughters, the youngest pious and good, the eldest badly behaved. The good one is rewarded with money, like the lass in "The Star Money," but, consistent with the propensity to stress punishment for heroines, the tale trains its lens not on the good girl but on her naughty sister. Snakes and lizards are sent to bite her to death. There is no escape for her or for her mother, who is bitten painfully (though not fatally) because she has brought her oldest daughter up so badly. No similar tale details the ethical execution of one of several brothers. "The Rose" (leg. 3) crowns a life of starvation and labor with death, a "reward" also granted to the mother of five in "God's Food" (leg. 5). Death likewise releases and thus rewards an aged and desolate widow whose husband and children have all preceded her to the grave.

With their strong Christian ethic, the Children's Legends appear at first to tell the same tale for male and female protagonists. A closer look shows that the medieval inquiry with regard to whether girls and women were human and possessed souls survives in these legends, though in a veiled manner. Whereas the legends with male protagonists press forward teleologically past St. Peter and enter heaven either actually or symbolically, those with female protagonists end abruptly at the grave. Death for males is only a way station: an angel leads twelve brothers to a sepulchral sleep to await Jesus' coming three hundred years hence, when they will awaken to walk the earth with their savior. In another legend, the visible and symbolic signs of the princely hermit's salvation are the rose and the lily; first he holds them in his hand, and then they flank his grave, living plants that grow from the soil. A similar metaphor borrowed from the New Testament promises continuing life for the hermit of legend 6. Robbers he has converted find him dead in the morning, but three green twigs grow out of the dry block of wood on which his head lies, a sign that the Lord has received him into his grace with consequent everlasting life. Even the wine merchant whose cart the Virgin Mary dislodges continues forward on his earthly journey, while the holy idiot who longs to go to the wedding with the Virgin, dies "and was at the eternal wedding" (und war zur ewigen Hochzeit), that is, passed through the grave to a new life.

Legends with female protagonists, however, end abruptly with death and are devoid of the symbols of continuing existence that characterize male legends. One assumes that the good girl in "St. Joseph in the Forest" gains some ultimate reward beyond the sack of money St. Joseph has given her, but the conclusion of the tale speaks only of the snakes and lizards stinging the wicked child to death and stinging her mother "in the foot, because she had not brought her up better" (in den Fuß, weil sie es nicht besser erzogen hatte). The rose that blooms after the death of the genderless child in "The Rose" is not a living plant like that by the grave of the princely hermit; instead, this cut flower exists in a symbolic neither/nor world consistent with the gender ambiguity of the child (das Kind): the cut flower blossoms but, separated from the living plant, it must shortly wither and die, like the young life it stands for. What sort of promise of immortality can one extract from this image? In like manner, the mother of five sinks "down dead" and that's the end of it, just like the aged widow, whose tale ends on this note: "and on the third day she lay down and died" (und am dritten Tag legte sie sich und starb). The language of these tales, together with the abbreviated and abrupt death scenes of the women, contrast clearly with the symbolically elaborated death scenes of male protagonists.

Men's elaborated death scenes parallel in turn the dramatis personae of the Children's Legends. Variety characterizes the male-oriented legends. In the five legends with male protagonists, we encounter a mother and her twelve sons, a prince and his brother, a hermit, a wine merchant, and a holy idiot. But on the distaff side there is predictable sameness: mothers and their children, though in all fairness it must be said that one set ("The Twelve Apostles") consists of a divine dyad, the Virgin Mary and Jesus.[18] Above all, these casts of characters suggest, not too surprisingly, that boys may anticipate choice and differentiation in their adult life, whereas girls and women can look forward only to motherhood. The male legends look backward to a set of male possibilities that existed as categories of experience in Germany's medieval past—princes, hermits, and holy idiots—but any possibilities beyond motherhood have been erased in the female legends.

This account of Christian tales in the Grimms' collection differs significantly from other commentators' analyses. First of all, the basic categorizations form a different analytic base. Rölleke distinguishes among tales with Christian expressions and exclamations, after which he sets into a single group tales with a Christian–Biedermeier spirit of the times, like "Hansel and Gretel," "Brother and Sister" (no. 11) and the beginning of "Cinderella" (no. 21). His final and most Christian category comprises "The Goose-Girl" (no. 89), which he understands as one in which the Christian world view has penetrated deeply into its structure, while I understand it as a tale embodying non-Christian female attributes in a barely changed form.[19]

18. Properly speaking this legend (10) is an etiological tale accounting for the properties of hazel-bush twigs.

19. "Das Bild Gottes in den Märchen der Brüder Grimm," 212ff. in "Wo das Wünschen noch geholfen hat." Compare with Bottigheimer, "Iconographic Continuity."

Wilhelm Grimm's Christian vision required, coincided with, and presupposed a mute or muted suffering female constituency, in whom the medieval theological quandary about salvation appears not to have been resolved. This jarringly revisionist conclusion can be tested by a close reading of non-Christian tales bare of Christian language, imagery, and belief.

Non-Christian Tales

Given the pervasiveness of the Christian exclamations and expletives, Christian explanations and justifications, Christian violence and Christian bigotry that occasionally keep company with gentler Christian attributes, it is remarkable to find tales with reference neither to God and heaven nor to death and resurrection. They do exist, however, and they tell us something about the composition of the tales themselves. By choosing tales according to their Christian or non-Christian content, one ignores and avoids other categories that should be reviewed quickly in order to throw the qualities associated with the Christian world into high relief. The jest tale (*Schwank*) can be either Christian or not, as can etiologies and tales of the fantastic. Whereas Christian etiologies in *Grimms' Tales* deal with social structure, non-Christian etiologies in the collection attempt to explain problems of the individual human condition, such as death.

God's absence becomes as significant as his presence in non-Christian tales. "The Three Brothers" (no. 124) provides a telling example. This tale of affection and amity hinges on the problem that only one brother can inherit his father's house. Their father, however, loves his sons equally, and the three brothers admire each others' skills. No strife divides them, and their competition ends with all of them victorious, because each son has become uncannily skilled at his respective trade—barbering, horseshoeing, and swordsmanship—and they agree to live together under one roof.

This story defies fairy tale convention. In Christian tales, two children are typically necessary to provide polar opposites of good and evil, white and black, beautiful and ugly, to match the heavenly and hellish possibilities offered by God and the devil. In other Christian tales, the magical triadic constellation pits the youngest and humblest against his or her older, cannier, but fatally flawed siblings. But this tale retains the triad without the dissension. May one conclude that God's absence allows amity?

A second characteristic of Christian tales lies in the pattern of role assignment: bad is played by girls, bold by boys. Certain malevolent motifs and themes are fobbed off on women more often than they are on men, with the result that women end up in nail-studded barrels or on pyres while men quite literally walk away from their misdeeds with clear consciences and unthreatened bodies. In non-Christian tales, on the other hand, pervasive punishment for women disappears magically, and often unjustifiably. "Ferdinand the Faithful and Ferdinand the Unfaithful" (no. 126) contains among its constituent parts a vignette of a wife who fancies Ferdinand the Faithful and contrives to dispose of her husband gently but murderously so that she may consort with the more attractive courtier:

> The Queen, however, did not love the King because he had no nose, but would have much liked to love Ferdinand the Faithful. Once, therefore, when the lords of the court were together, the Queen said she could do feats of magic, that she could cut off anyone's head and put it on again, and that one of them ought just to try it. But none of them would be the first, so Ferdinand the Faithful, again at the instigation of Ferdinand the Unfaithful, undertook it and she hewed off his head, and put it on again for him, and it healed together directly, so that it looked as if he had a red thread round his throat. Then the King said to her: "My child, and where have you learnt that?" "Oh," she said, "I understand the art; shall I just try it on you also?" "Oh, yes," said he. So she cut off his head, but did not put it on again; and pretended that she could not get it on, and that it would not stay. Then the King was buried, but she married Ferdinand the Faithful.

> De Künigin mogte awerst den Künig nig lien, weil he keine Nese hadde, sonnern se mogte den Ferenand getrü geren lien. Wie nu mal alle Herens vom Hove tosammen sied, so segd de Künigin, se könne auck Kunststücke macken, se künne einen den Kopp afhoggen un wier upsetten, et sull nur mant einer versöcken. Da wull awerst kener de eiste sien, da mott Ferenand getrü daran, wier up Anstifften von Ferenand ungetrü, den hogget se den Kopp af un sett 'n ünn auck wier up, et is auck glick wier tau heilt, dat et ut sach, ase hädde he 'n roen Faen [Faden] üm 'n Hals. Da segd de Künig to ehr: "Mein Kind, wo hast du denn das gelernt?" "Ja", segd se, "die Kunst versteh ich, soll ich es an dir auch einmal versuchen?" "O ja", segd he. Do hogget se en awerst den Kopp af un sett 'n en nig wier up, se doet, as ob se 'n nig darup kriegen künne, un as ob he nig fest sitten wulle. Da werd de Künig begrawen, se awerst frigget den Ferend getrü.

Aside from the covertly sexual aversion the queen feels for the king, which is remarkably similar to Mrs. Fox's basis for choosing a new husband ("The Wedding of Mrs. Fox," no. 38), her "understanding the art," as she says, puts her firmly beyond the Christian domain and inside her own, in which she clearly can voluntarily manipulate the forces of life and death.

Several explanations present themselves for this remarkable tale. It is, first of all, a dialect tale, a type that Wilhelm Grimm rarely altered. We may infer various reasons for his not doing so—perhaps, for example, he was not sufficiently in control of various German dialects to manipulate them as he could the high German tales or those of his native Hesse. This must remain a surmise, however. One might also suggest that such a dialect tale, which came through the Haxthausens, perhaps from someone on their estate in the Paderborn vicinity, displays archaic folk characteristics, such as the general absence of Christian elements. The principle and salient fact in this case is that a woman acknowledges occult powers, exercises them, gains her own, amoral, ends, and escapes either censure or punishment, and that this rarity occurs significantly in conjunction with another rarity in the Grimms' collection: a tale completely uncolored by Christian language, characters, or values.

What seems evident is that Christian values seem to form part of a conscious socializing process that is unambiguously gender specific. Each of these assertions has been made previously, but the nature of gender specificity has not been scrutinized. Far from tending to develop individuals, as has been asserted so often, Christianized tales in the Grimms' collection separate the characters not so much into good and evil as into male and female, their fates determined and defined not according to the ethical and moral quality of their lives, but according to their sex.

14
Eroticism in Tradition, Text, and Image

Tradition

 asy eroticism, jocular sex, domestic trickery, and adultery run through the traditional European collections of tales of which *Grimms' Tales* forms a part.[1] Boccaccio's saucy maids and randy lads speak openly of sexual attraction and escapades, explicitly praising the pleasures of love, and in Chaucer's *Canterbury Tales* the stories range from the nun's priest's delicately phrased allusions to carnal pleasure to the miller's lewd and vulgar tavern stories. Straparola's naughty storytellers titillate their listeners with risqué double-entendres in the "enigma" that closes each tale.

How different the thundering voice of Johann Brantius in his sixteenth century Pauline tract, which warns that the omnipresent devil tempts Christians with drunkenness and illicit sex. Jacob Grimm must have believed in the efficacy of such hellfire and damnation tracts, for he accepted the idea of folk innocence, at least in sexual matters. But even a cursory reading of nineteenth-century folk literature contradicts his position very quickly,[2] while Max Lüthi's study of the origins of the Rapunzel fairy tale provides a detailed view of one tale's journey from the worldly chambers of Charlotte de la Force

---

1. Nothing could better illustrate shifting attitudes toward this subject than a comparison of the entries under "Erotik" in Mackensen's *Handwörterbuch des deutschen Märchens* (1930–40) and in the *Enzyklopädie des Märchens* (1977–). Even granting the more limited scope of Mackensen's reference work, the entry is remarkable for its brevity and its insistent crossreference to love. It reads: "s. Liebe, ferner Belle et Bete, Betrüger überführt I, 2 Busch 7, Charaktermotive."! It is unbelievable that Mackensen did not know of publications like *Anthropophyteia* or *Kryptadia*, turn-of-the-century repositories of erotic or eroticized folklore. In contrast to Mackensen's article, Lutz Röhrich's "Erotik, Sexualität" (4:234–78) is one of the longest articles in the *EM*.

2. See "Violenz im populären Roman," in Schenda, *Die Lesestoffe der kleinen Leute.*

through early translations into German which the Grimms scrubbed clean for a readership they had come to perceive as youthful rather than scholarly.[3]

Text

Exploring eroticism is not without its problems for the scholar. How is one to know how individuals respond to particular stimuli? In one culture, the curve of a lip may ignite passion while in another it would go quite unnoticed. The same is true of ankles, shoulders, hair, and thighs. But of all sexual stimuli, removing articles of clothing one at a time and nakedness enjoy a long erotic history in the best of company: think only of Salome's dance.

Stripping is where we shall begin in considering eroticism in *Grimms' Tales:* not, however, with a nubile young woman, but with her simple cousin, the miller's boy in "The Poor Miller's Boy and the Cat" (no. 106). The tale begins with a hopeless quest and ends with a brilliant marriage. This pattern provides the alpha and omega for many a tale; what happens in between distinguishes "The Poor Miller's Boy and the Cat" from closely related variants and shines the spotlight on sexy females in this little drama of sweet subjection. In other tales a gray mannekin or an old woman materializes as supernatural helper. But here we encounter a seductive cat who invites Hans to the dance, and when he refuses to "dance with a pussy cat" (mit einer Miezekatze tanze ich nicht), the tabby cat orders her feline maids-in-waiting to take him to bed.

> So one of them lighted him to his bed-room, one pulled his shoes off, one his stockings, and at last one of them blew out the candle.

> Da leuchtete ihm eins in sein Schlafkammer, eins zog ihm die Schuhe aus, eins die Strümpfe, und zuletzt blies eins das Licht aus.

With darkness the curtain falls and we are left to our imaginations. But the following morning the game proceeds:

> . . . they returned and helped him out of bed, one put his stockings on for him, one tied his garters, one brought his shoes, one washed him, and one dried his face with her tail. "That feels very soft!" said Hans.

> . . . kamen sie wieder und halfen ihm aus dem Bett: eins zog ihm die Strümpfe an, eins band ihm die Strumpfbänder, eins holte die Schuhe, eins wusch ihn, und eins trocknete ihm mit dem Schwanz das Gesicht ab. "Das tut recht sanft," sagte Hans.

Filled with erotic possibility and metaphor, one can imagine this tale told, not in the nursery, but with leers and snickers to friends of the narrator. Even the vocabulary carries on a German tradition as old as medieval courtly lyric, when

---

3. "Über den Ursprung des Rapunzelmärchens (AaTh 310)." See also Rölleke, *Grimms Kinder- und Hausmärchen* (1982), 2:573–74.

Hans asks the princess if she might not finally give him his reward (ob sie ihm noch nicht seinen Lohn geben wollte). But his seven years' service results in continuing postponement, for the cat sends Hans ahead, promising to follow with his "reward," the horse he needs to win the competition set by his master, the miller. But when the cat arrives, Hans is in no condition to receive her, for he's wearing his old worn-out smock which has gotten too short for him—everywhere—as we are explicitly told (das ihm in den sieben Jahren überall zu kurz geworden war). And when the miller sends people to haul Hans out of the goose-stall where he is lying, "he had to hold his little smock together to cover himself" (er mußte sein Kittelchen zusammenpacken, um sich zu bedecken). In this moment the competition for the mill is overlooked, for Hans is about to get his reward. The horse, for which he has worked for seven years, is delivered, and the miller awards the mill to Hans, who has produced the best steed. The next moment makes it clear that this story is not really about winning a mill, for it is returned to the miller as his own, and the tabby cat assumes her true shape as a magnificent princess and marries Hans, enriching him so that he has enough for the rest of his life.

Once an erotic context has been set, nearly every image and metaphor in "The Poor Miller's Boy and the Cat" can be read erotically. Other forms of erotic tension inhere not in the words themselves, but in the situation, for which "Our Lady's Child" (no. 3), traditionally considered an arch-Christian tale, unexpectedly provides an excellent example.

Literary nakedness has not usually been male, as in the preceding example, but female, consistent with the male imagination that has so often produced printed text and painted canvas. The highly Christianized tale "Our Lady's Child" includes a detailed description of the protagonist's nakedness, which forms part of her social degradation and personal humbling and establishes a distinctly erotic tension when the king's clothed power confronts her naked helplessness. In part, this contrast borrows its meaning from the entire corpus of *Grimms' Tales,* where clothing the destitute body represents both an investiture with real clothing and a symbolic accession to power. Its opposite, nakedness, clearly stands for the divestiture of individual as well as regal prerogative. Therefore, we know how completely Marienkind is exposed both literally and figuratively when we read: "Before long her clothes were all torn, and one bit of them after another fell off her" (Nicht lange, so zerrissen seine Kleider und fiel ein Stück nach dem andern vom Leib herab). And in this condition the king finds her:

One day . . . the King of the country was hunting in the forest, and followed a roe, and as it had fled into the thicket which shut in this part of the forest, he got off his horse, tore the bushes asunder, and cut himself a path with his sword. When he had at last forced his way through, he saw a wonderfully beautiful maiden sitting under the tree; and she sat there and was entirely covered with her golden hair down to her very feet. He stood still and looked at her full of surprise . . .

Einmal . . . jagte der König des Landes in dem Wald und verfolgte ein Reh, und weil es in das Gebüsch geflohen war, das den Waldplatz einschloß, stieg er vom Pferd, riß das Gestrüppe auseinander und hieb sich mit seinem Schwert einen Weg. Als er endlich hindurchgedrungen war, sah er unter dem Baum ein wunderschönes Mädchen sitzen, das saß da und war von seinem goldenen Haar bis zu den Fußzehen bedeckt. Er stand still und betrachtete es voll Erstaunen . . .

We know, however, that under her golden hair Marienkind hasn't a stitch on. Her sexual vulnerability must form part of a conscious design, for Grimm generally expunged sexuality wherever he recognized it. Here, however, he gradually and consistently heightens his own and the reader's awareness of her nakedness by removing the crimson velvet gown she had worn in heaven (1808 letter to Savigny and 1810 Ölenberg MS), first turning it to rags (1812 edition), and subsequently leaving her only with her own hair and fallen leaves to cover her. The violent language and traditional metaphor of this paragraph embed the imagery of nakedness in the language of rape; given the fact that we know Marienkind covers herself with leaves, the King's tearing the bushes asunder and then cutting himself a path with his sword suggest not so much an attack on her surroundings as on Marienkind herself.

"The Six Swans" (no. 49) disrobes the heroine far more dramatically. Treed by the kings' hunters, she tries to drive them off, first by throwing down her necklace, then her sash, her garters, and bit by bit everything she has on and can do without until she is down to her shift. What an extraordinary striptease! Even if stripping produces shaming in a variety of cultures, as one anthropologist has observed,[4] it is less likely to shame the hunters than to puzzle a child and titillate an adult, and narratively it does not work as a shaming device:

> The huntsmen, however, did not let themselves be turned aside by that, but climbed the tree and fetched the maiden down and led her before the King.
>
> Die Jäger ließen sich aber damit nicht abweisen, stiegen auf den Baum, hoben das Mädchen herab und führten es vor den König.

If simple nakedness provides fortuitously erotic opportunity and occasions, loving and choosing a mate introduces volition and often violent action. The sorcerer who wants a wife first ingratiates himself with his hosts and with his intended bride, and then bursts into her chamber through two locked doors to demand that she submit to his desire (seinem Wunsche fügen), a desire that can be read as either marriage or rape. This all takes place in "The Glass Coffin" (no. 163), where the sorcerer subsequently miniaturizes and imprisons not only the woman to whom he wants to offer heart and hand, but also her castle, retainers, and friends. That she is ultimately saved, by a poor little tailor whom she marries, almost goes without saying, and the plot ends satisfactorily in an expected fairy tale mode.

---

4. See Ardener: "Sexual Insult and Female Militancy," in *Perceiving Women*, 29–53.

The pattern is reversed in "Ferdinand the Faithful and Ferdinand the Unfaithful" (no. 126), with amoral intention and erotic satisfaction. Here the queen takes the most direct route to eradicate the difficulties obstructing her union with the handsome man who saves her, and whom she fancies because her own husband, the king, has no nose.[5] She simply demonstrates her occult arts first on Ferdinand, thus persuading her husband that she can with the greatest of ease cut off a head and set it back on again, leaving nothing more than a red threadlike mark on the neck. He consents to his own decapitation . . . and her magic suddenly "fails" her:

> So she cut off his head, but did not put it on again; and pretended that she could not get it on, and that it would not stay. Then the King was buried and she married Ferdinand the Faithful.

> Do hogget se en awerst den Kopp af un sett 'n en nig wier up, se doet, as ob se 'n nig darup kriegen künne, un as ob he nig fest sitten wulle. Da werd de Künig begrawen, se awerst frigget den Ferenand getrü.

The king is missing something important, perhaps central, and the Queen can't say what it is. But what she can't utter, Mrs. Fox can. In "The Wedding of Mrs. Fox" (no. 38) she rejects all of her suitors until one arrives who has nine tails just like her "deceased" husband. Here we face the unambiguous double entendre that Jacob Grimm denied, for in German *tail* (*Schwanz*) also means *cock* or *prick*.[6] The sexual inadequacy of Mrs. Fox's suitors offers us a clue to the meaning of the otherwise incomprehensible lack of a "nose" from which the King suffers in "Ferdinand the Faithful." Other fairy tale heroines' love for their monstrous husbands disenchants the beasts, erasing deformity and restoring their good looks, but the king's missing part seems to be something inadmissible, at least in the narrative circumstances in which this tale was in all likelihood collected.

As veiled and easily denied as the hidden meaning of *nose* was and is, Wilhelm Grimm had no problem in accepting "Ferdinand the Faithful and Ferdinand the Unfaithful" for his collection in 1819. But where the erotic import of an activity rose up palpably from the text, Wilhelm lost no time in suppressing it. In the earliest version of "The Frog King" (no. 1) the princess is altogether too eager to jump into bed with the frog once he is shown to be a handsome prince, and so the Ölenberg MS is swiftly and inexorably altered. Instead of her outright alacrity in 1810, we are told:

> When he hit the wall, he fell down into the bed and lay there, a handsome young prince, then the princess lay down with him.

5. One can only imagine how the informant telling this tale to one of the Haxthausen young women might have changed this word, emasculating the text rather than the king.

6. See Achim von Arnim's correspondence with Jacob Grimm on this subject, discussed by Rölleke in *Kinder- und Hausmärchen* (1982), 2:538.

Wie er aber an die Wand kam, so fiel er herunter in das Bett and lag darin als ein junger schöner Prinz, da legte sich die Königstochter zu ihm.

He becomes "her dear companion" (ihr lieber Geselle) in 1812, with whom she falls asleep contentedly (sie schliefen vergnügt zusammen ein), a formula which was still too racy and which was eventually replaced by unexceptionable and far more sedate wording. In its final form the bed becomes the place from which the frog is banished; only afterward does the prince become her companion and husband according to her father's wish (Der war nun ihres Vaters Willen nach ihr lieber Geselle und Gemahl). Since one consistent direction of development in the editorial history of *Grimms' Tales* is the subversion and eradication of feminine will (see chapter 7), it becomes clear that feminine desire should also disappear, which this cameo clearly shows.

In some tales, retiring together to the bedchamber, if not to the bed itself, neither should nor can be ignored in terms of the narrative's overall development. When this occurs, this problematic action is cloaked with virtue, as in "The Hut in the Forest" (no. 169). Here a girl goes into the woods (danger, isolation, often speechlessness, sometimes murder, rarely salvation) and sees lights in the distance (generally in a witch's hut, generally malevolent, on rare occasions helpful). In this tale, however, the girl, the first of three sisters to make this journey, encounters an old, ice-gray man with a floor-length white beard. She asks for shelter, cooks a common meal, eats, and is told to prepare the beds in his room, for he, too, wishes to retire. When the old man himself climbs the stairs and finds her asleep, he regards her with disappointment and dumps her summarily through a trap door. The text does not make a single mention at this point of her lack of compassion for his three animals, the ostensible reason for her punishment, but says simply the following:

> The girl went up, and when she had shaken the beds and put clean sheets on, she lay down in one of them without waiting any longer for the old man. After some time the gray-haired man came, held his candle over the girl and shook his head. When he saw that she had fallen into a sound sleep, he opened a trap-door, and let her down into the cellar.

> Das Mädchen stieg hinauf, und als es die Betten geschüttelt und frisch gedeckt hatte, legte es sich in das eine, ohne weiter auf den Alten zu warten. Nach einiger Zeit aber kam der graue Mann, beleuchtete das Mädchen mit dem Licht und schüttelte mit dem Kopf. Und als er sah, daß es fest eingeschlafen war, öffnetete er eine Falltür und ließ es in den Keller sinken.

What is raised in high relief here is the girl's ignoring the old man, offending him because she has not waited for him, an insult that has nothing at all to do with the reason stated later for her imprisonment and subsequent punishment, that is, her lack of attention to and compassion for his three animals. One sees here a sexual slight rather than an organic relationship between her treatment of the animals and her fate.[7]

It is instructive to compare this little tale of domestic competence with "Mother Holle" (no. 24). Here a girl's character test results depend on her demonstrating compassion (for an apple tree and for bread in an oven) and diligence (principally in cooking and above all in shaking out the bedding and making it up again neatly), but neither sister is expected to sleep with her host(ess), as each of the three sisters in "The Hut in the Forest" is supposed to do. In "The Hut," the fairy tale theme of compassion for animals, which determines the course of so many other tales, seems laid on to cloak the true (sexual) offense and to conceal a watered-down "Fitcher's Bird" (no. 46) or "Bluebeard" narrative. Nonetheless, the tale's sexuality shimmers palely and unmistakeably through the veil behind which the unsatisfactory girls have been dumped. This masquerade is kept up when the third, good, compassionate sister waits for the old man, then says her prayers and falls asleep. The religious interjection seems altogether too purposefully included in order to confirm the absence of hanky-panky, especially since the bearded ancient turns into a handsome young prince the next morning.

If we imagine such a tale being told to a group of listeners well-versed in folk material, every stage of the narrative development emerges, not naively, but as a contrast to and comparison with widely known folk narratives. The contrast would sometimes be tinged with irony and would always slip into and out of ambiguity, for the widespread tale, "Fitcher's Bird," a Teutonic variant on "Bluebeard," also centers around an unknown man with a house in the woods to which three sisters come one after the other to be married and murdered in a passion of (erotically inspired?) violence.

I don't for a moment assert that the erotic content I find in the tales inheres in the material itself if it is read naively and in isolation. However, the tales as they are published do not now exist in isolation, nor did they in the past.[8] Although bourgeois girls might have been kept ignorant of the erotic and violent popular literature that permeated nineteenth-century society, it is highly unlikely that their brothers, with their greater freedom of movement, could have remained ignorant for long.[9] Knowing snickers were thus likely to have accompanied the reading of this tale to a mixed adolescent group.

As a youth and young man, Jacob Grimm moved in a far more varied society than his younger brother Wilhelm ever did. The sophisticated and wicked capital cities of Paris and Vienna, neither of which he liked, were his home for

---

7. The fact that this tale was collected by a man, perhaps less prim than the Grimms themselves, rather than by or from a woman of the educated class, lends credence to this reading.

8. The eroticizations collected by Wolfgang Mieder and included in *Grimms Märchen–Modern: Prosa, Gedichte, Karikaturen* confirm the potential for eroticized readings which I offer here.

9. See Schenda, *Die Lesestoffe der kleinen Leute.*

months at a time on several occasions. If he could affirm that the folk were pure and naive and believe that Mrs. Fox was interested in fur rather than fornication when she counted the tails of her suitors, then it is even more likely that sickly Wilhelm, who lived a protected and retiring life surrounded first by his siblings and later by his adoring wife and children, should have remained remarkably innocent. All contemporary accounts attest to both brothers' exceptional unworldliness.

What Wilhelm recognized was what he could see, and when he saw pregnancy in fairy tales he would have none of it. He erased Rapunzel's tightening garments (no. 12) and her inquiry about her changing shape in favor of more discreet references to her "friendship" with the prince who daily clambered into her tower.[10] This kind of editorial change preserved a text fit for children's as well as scholars' eyes. But nothing could prevent or prohibit illustrators from locating and illustrating potentially erotic scenes based on Wilhelm's final text.

Image

Illustrations serve text at many levels and with several functions; within the limited context of this inquiry into eroticism in *Grimms' Tales,* illustrations reveal latent erotic content, develop potential erotic content, and sometimes impute erotic content where none can be reasonably thought to exist. In looking at illustrations either from another generation or another century, my eyes undoubtedly "see" differently from the eyes of the illustrators themselves or their audiences. I thus attempt to limit my perceptions to unequivocally erotic visual content in order to avoid interpretive bias. It would be useful to retrace our steps through the texts that have become familiar from the preceding discussion, but in doing so we encounter a curious phenomenon. Aside from "Our Lady's Child," the eroticized illustrations adorn different tales altogether. In part this is due to the fact that illustrators until very recently have principally addressed those of the Grimms' tales that Wilhelm singled out for inclusion in the Small Edition, especially for children. From this little volume he excised all talk of going to bed with strange men.

"Our Lady's Child" offers illustrators great latitude in exploring female nudity in conjunction with a clothed male, the same charged subject that electrified the Paris public at the later (1863) *Salon des Refusés,* when the exhibition of Manet's *Déjeuner sur l'herbe* ultimately led to its closing. Numerous illustrators linger over the moment of discovery and sneak a look at the king carrying Marienkind off. Most leave her covered by her long hair; but some part it to show her nakedness beneath. The tale's final violent scene, in which Marienkind is tied to the stake with flames rising, offers several

10. Rölleke, *Kinder- und Hausmärchen* (1982), 2:573–74.

illustrators the opportunity of pulling her gown off her shoulder to expose her swelling breast and plump arm (Thekla Brauer, 1895) in a complex of violence, eroticism, and Christian sentiment.

Both "Little Briar-Rose" (no. 50) and "Snow-White" (no. 53) conclude with a prince coming upon a sleeping young woman, a subject that has been a magnet for discussions of gender roles in passivity and sexuality. The two differ considerably, since Briar-Rose's prince arrives just as she is ordained to awaken, a literary fact more often overlooked than understood. When the prince arrives in this strange country,

> [he] heard an old man talking about the thorn-hedge, and that a castle was said to stand behind it in which a wonderfully beautiful princess, named Briar-Rose, had been asleep for a hundred years. . . . But by this time the hundred years had just passed, and the day had come when Briar-Rose was to awake again.

> [er] hörte, wie ein alter Mann von der Dornhecke erzählte, es sollte ein Schloß dahinter stehen, in welchem eine wunderschöne Königstochter, Dornröschen genannt, schon seit hundert Jahren schliefe . . . Nun waren aber gerade die hundert Jahre verflossen, und der Tag war gekommen, wo Dornröschen wieder erwachen sollte.

The prince's kiss coincides with the last moment of her slumber.

Briar-Rose's pose in her chaste sleep determines the reader's initial response to her as a sexual being. The bed she lies on is a relatively late acquisition in the editorial history of the tale, for she is simply said to fall down in a deep sleep in the tale's early appearances. But by the end of the collection's history, illustrators were completely justified in laying Briar-Rose out on a bed. But how? Prone? Or supine?

Supine is standard, and since this indoor bower needs no blankets, Briar-Rose's dress can be shown hugging her limbs, outlining her torso and legs (Thekla Brauer, 1895). Or else, wielding a phallic sword, the prince can burst in (Anon. 1941). Her legs may part slightly, her sexual maturity perfectly evident from her rounded bosom (Willy Werner 1899). Or she lies apparently waiting, plump and delectable (Paul Meyerheim 1893). It is Ludwig Emil Grimm's chaste depiction of Briar-Rose resting on her side that shocks the viewer into a sudden recognition of how she has been made to look sexually available in her supine pose by generations of illustrators.

Snow-White's sexuality, on the other hand, is stressed by the illustrator's reading backward from the tale's conclusion. The prince's bride must be ipso facto nubile, and so it is that she appears, not only in the glass coffin but serving the dwarves at table and also fleeing into the forest. Rare the illustrator who pays heed to the fact that Snow-White is only seven when her beauty first arouses her stepmother's wrath. It is worth quoting for emphasis:

> . . . and when she was seven years old she was as beautiful as the day, and more beautiful than the Queen herself. And once when the Queen asked her looking-glass:

Looking-Glass, Looking-glass, on the wall,
Who in this land is the fairest of all?
it answered:
Thou art fairer than all who are here, Lady Queen.
But more beautiful still is Snow-White, as I ween.
The Queen was shocked, and turned yellow and green with envy. From that hour, whenever she looked at Snow-White, her heart heaved in her breast, she hated the girl so much.

. . . und als es sieben Jahre alt war, war es so schön wie der klare Tag und schöner als die Königin selbst. Als diese einmal ihren Spiegel fragte:
Spieglein, Spieglein an der Wand,
wer ist die schönste im ganzen Land?
so antwortete er:
Frau Königin, Ihr seid die schönste hier,
aber Sneewittchen ist tausendmal schöner als Ihr.
Da erschrak die Königin und ward gelb und grün vor Neid. Von Stund an, wenn sie Sneewittchen erblickte, kehrte sich ihr das Herz im Leibe herum, so haßte sie das Mädchen.

Despite the fact that the text implies the passage of time by saying the Queen's heart knew no peace "day or night," and even if we take German usage of "child" (Kind) into consideration, Snow-White must still have been very young when she was taken to the forest. But the obligatory prince offering his hand has accelerated the seven-year old's maturation, so that she appears bosomy and decolleté at the table (Meyerheim 1893 and others). On occasion an individual illustrator eroticizes the text to imply sexuality. Maurice Sendak does this when he undresses the countess in "The Master-Thief" (no. 192) (1973); Leopold von Kalckreuth displays the queen's nipple in "The Pink" (no. 76) (1918); and the goose-girl (no. 89) is sketched nude when her maid forces her to change garments with her (n.d.).

Just as tale illustrations can be made to imply events that haven't taken place in the text, so cover illustrations can promise contents that don't materialize, as did the unidentified designer of the Dümmler edition of the *Kinder- und Hausmärchen* in 1873. His fairyland cover exhibited a bare-breasted fairy whom the publishing house clothed ten years later.

The opposite intention can be expressed by stripping a tale of erotic content when the illustrator asserts a particular age or appearance for the protagonist. This modest pattern is particularly well developed in the German Democratic Republic, where two editions may stand for much of that country's fairy tale illustration tradition. Karl Fischer (1958) sets Briar-Rose in an arm chair and avoids illustrating the prince's kiss, while Erika Klein (1966) shows all her fairy tale characters as very young children.

Despite the evident effort Wilhelm Grimm made to suit the text of these tales to a young and innocent readership, with eyes of that blue translucence of early childhood he so treasured,[11] both the text and its illustrators existed as part of a broader tradition in German society, within which erotic elements might be denied, but could certainly not be expunged as easily as Wilhelm had done, or attempted to do, within the text of the *Kinder- und Hausmärchen*. Resonances and echoes of other tales heard, of other scenes played out in other places, found their way into the text as well as into the images that accompanied the tales.

11. See his Preface to the 1819 edition.

15

The Moral and Social Vision
of *Grimms' Tales*

hroughout this study of the moral and social vision of *Grimms' Tales,* I have stressed the importance of viewing an individual motif within the context of the tale in which it is embedded, as well as of interpreting an individual tale within the corpus of the entire collection. Max Lüthi early pointed out that European fairy and folk tales—their characters, situations, and episodes—typically appear before us sublimated and emptied of meaning. This condition makes them susceptible to "filling" and coloring by interpreters in Christian, psychological, nationalist, feminist, Marxist, or anthropological hues. To avoid this as far as possible, I have tried to consider the events, motifs, and themes of several tales together as a corrective for what might be mistakenly concluded from an individual tale.

One of the most influential approaches to folk narrative, that of the Finnish research school, collates and compares variants of a single narrative, based on their underlying assumption that variants represent alternative tellings of specific tales or tale types. The special significance of alternative tellings for my work revolves around the interplay between culture and narrative. In this light the simple narratives of folk and fairy tales can be seen to make sense within the society that tells—or publishes—them. Reordering symbols, images, and motifs in tale variants produces changes in meaning, often profound, which can turn a tale on its head; furthermore, such reorderings may tell us something about the society that produced a particular variant. As readers and interpreters, we cannot simply note the existence, for example, of the motif of a woman in a tree; we also have to look at the motif in terms of how it functions in the narrative as a whole.

In subject after subject, I have found a tension, if not an outright contradiction, between the surface presentation of many subjects—language use, Jews, money, women, and religious values, for example—and the language, associations, and imagery with which they are communicated, which suggests a deep ambivalence about these subjects. For instance, both men's and women's work is shown in a negative light in terms of language, associations, and imagery, but in a positive light in the editorial asides that embellish the tales. Another case of ambiguous, even contradictory, imagery involves women and nature. Chapter 3 pulls together evidence of a belief in female chthonic powers involving water, and chapters 7 and 10 delineate the special suffering reserved for women in woods. In *Grimms' Tales* women's power over nature is more than balanced by nature's and society's power over women. The emergence of this revealingly unequal division suggests the special contribution that a literary investigation of *Grimms' Tales*—a collection not generally considered in literary terms—can make.

How can the textual tensions found here be reconciled—or understood? There are at least three contending traditions in *Grimms' Tales*. The first is an enlightened educated tradition contemporary with Wilhelm's and Jacob's early collecting, which is evident in the Ölenberg MS and volume 1 of the First Edition (1812). The tales of these two texts, many of which came from the Grimms' Cassel informants, evince a generally sociable outlook and a higher degree of social equality between women and men, especially in the realm of the spoken word. The second tradition is a rude, unlettered folk tradition. And the third is a two-pronged tradition emanating from the Grimms themselves: on the one hand, the continuing influx of texts from earlier ages—chapbooks, manuscripts, and story collections of the sixteenth, seventeenth, and eighteenth centuries—and, on the other hand, Wilhelm Grimm's imposition of a Christian overlay based on the late medieval and early modern value system that permeates many of the tales the Grimms, especially Jacob, unearthed in archives.

The collection as a whole presents a consistent vision of gender differences which does not support many of the psychological interpretations that have been made up to now. Bruno Bettelheim asserts that *girl* and *boy* in *Grimms' Tales* can be and are read, without gender distinction, as *child* by youthful readers. Instead, we have seen that there emerges from the tales a pattern of radically different moral expectations for girls and for boys. Whenever and wherever psychological interpretations of *Grimms' Tales* use the deceptively generalizing vocabulary *man, one,* or *the child,* we must look behind those formulations to the gender message implicit in the tales; there we find a consistent vision of gender-specific and gender-appropriate behavior that includes kindred values revived and incorporated from preceding centuries.

The values evident in *Grimms' Tales* have been neither universal nor enduring in Europe, yet they were—and continue to be—frequently cited as valid paradigms for childhood development. Wilhelm Grimm himself knew that the tradition he was editing differed even from that of Germany's nearest neighbors to the north, for he had published *Altdänische Heldenlieder, Balladen und Märchen* in 1811, a year before *Grimms' Tales* first appeared in print. Many of the heroines in the Danish ballads and tales demonstrate an independence utterly alien to the women in later editions of the *Tales*. If we look only at the subject of pride, we see dramatic differences between the two collections. Where female pride appears in the Grimms' collection, it must be promptly humbled. In "King Thrushbeard" (no. 52) the proud princess haughtily refuses all suitors until her father bestows her hand on an apparent beggar, who humiliates her day after day until she is made to see her abject worthlessness, even as a market vendor of cheap pottery. Humbling a woman plays no part in the Danish ballads and tales. Indeed, these narratives show pride and initiative as positive feminine attributes. It is tempting to speculate about whether the independent and articulate "Maid Maleen" (no. 198) of Danish origin, added to *Grimms' Tales* in 1850, would have undergone the same weakening and isolating process that so many other Grimm heroines suffered, had Wilhelm Grimm lived to produce subsequent editions of the collection.

Submission is equally alien to Danish heroines' personalities. When Herr Ebbe's daughters are dishonored, they themselves murder their rapists—in church, no less![1] And when—at the other end of the social spectrum—the king murders little Christel's beloved so that he can marry her himself, she sleeps with him only to get close enough to drive the dagger home.[2] In another narrative, a sexually playful version of the taming of the shrew, a skilled chess-playing princess confidently pledges her body to her apparently humble opponent should she lose the game. When he surprises her by winning, she indulges in verbal striptease, offering one garment after another to avoid paying off the bet. But unlike the punitive royal suitor of "King Thrushbeard," he immediately identifies himself as "the best prince who happens to live on earth" (des besten Königs Sohn, der auf Erden leben mag), and she freely offers him both her honor and her fidelity (so sollst du haben meine Ehre, darzu auch meine Treu). It is apparently unthinkable that a Danish princess should be socially or spiritually humbled. *She*, not her father, sets the conditions for disposing of her body. Unlike King Thrushbeard, her husband doesn't force her into a humiliating union, nor does he continue humbling her after marriage. The Danish princess proudly enters a union with a royal competitor who has beaten her at her own game.

The persistent denial of female voice in *Grimms' Tales* culminates in the act of speaking (sprechen), which is often made to herald female viciousness. This characteristic, at odds with fairy and folk tales in the contemporaneous French and English traditions, continues the rough misogyny of early modern German chapbooks, which regularly belittled and castigated women's speech: "for exactly like unto the wicked way of women [you] make a lot of dumb chit-chat" (dann ganz nach schlechter weibischer art [du] viel einfeltigenn sprach und red gestellest).[3] Wherever one looks—in crude misogynistic tracts, in handbooks of proper behavior, on printed kerchiefs, and in memoirs—finger-

---

1. No. 45, Herr Ebbes Töchter im Kämmerlein.
2. No. 59: Frauen Rache.
3. "Der bösen weiber / Zuchtschul."

shaking prohibitions dovetail neatly with Wilhelm Grimm's own clear awareness that speech is allowed only to those who dominate their world.[4]

Can we locate an image to tie together the bewildering and occasionally incomprehensible prohibitions and punishments that women and girls in *Grimms' Tales* suffer?[5] One powerful image recurs in both pictures and words: the fall from grace as it is interpreted in the late Middle Ages. The 1497 tract "Vom heilgen swygenhaltten" (On the Holy Maintenance of Silence), by Heinrich Vigilis von Weissenburg, succinctly explains why women should maintain silence by reference to Eve's original sin: her guilt in paradise disqualifies her sex from further speech.

> But why women should be silent and in subjection . . . the first woman incurred guilt in Paradise, she was the first to be deceived and led astray and not the man. . . . But Adam was not deceived by the same [creature], but he is overcome by one who was his nature and body and life and his half part, to whom he was bound so closely with natural love, that he does not grieve her.[6]

Was ever woman so wanton in her sinning as Eve, and was ever man so sinned against as Adam? Given God's nature and Adam's nurture, Heinrich Vigilis von Weissenburg implies, Eve should never have listened to the devil's base suggestions; his tract is but one of many late medieval and early modern descriptions of the fall from grace suggesting that Eve's misuse of her voice in speaking with the serpent was the primary cause of sin in the world. In illustrations of the fall from grace, the serpent that coils its plump body around the limbs of the tree of the knowledge of good and evil more often than not has a woman's head. Eve is both under the tree and in it. The tree, so central to Germanic tradition—the great oak of justice, as well as the associations with women's power over nature—is reformulated as the locus of *mulier loquax,* the she who must be silenced.

Eve's sin led directly to expulsion from Paradise and to the further curse of woman's giving birth in pain and man's laboring with an unyielding soil. One of the reasons that work cannot be rewarded metaphorically or actually in *Grimms' Tales* may be because of its long association with the fall from grace. Work, after all, is defined by Genesis as the consequence for men of Adam's eating from the tree of knowledge. It makes primitive sense that Adam's work—defined as punishment—should prove fruitless, for beyond the penitential nature of the act must lie the laborer's awareness of the futility of his efforts.

Vigilis' text, like so many others, stresses the fact that Eve brought suffering on Adam. Its use of the present tense ("she has no relationship . . .

---

4. Letter to Savigny, 7 February 1838, quoted in Seitz, *Die Brüder Grimm,* 161.

5. See also Schwarz, "Eva: Die neue Eva."

6. Ruberg, *Beredtes Schweigen in lehrhafter und erzählender deutscher Literatur des Mittelalters,* 276.

he is overcome . . . he does not grieve her") makes the sin contemporary. Everywoman as Eve and Everyman as Adam, the sinner and the sinned against, she who must be punished and he who must be exculpated—these images are also central to the view of woman in *Grimms' Tales.*

Not all women in *Grimms' Tales* are or can be Eves who offend by their speech, because many of them have already lost their voices or have been silenced in one manner or another. But even if not all women are Eves threatening a clear and present danger, the notion that all women share in Eve's sin may account for the necessity to punish female characters in *Grimms' Tales.* Men, in comparison, are usually excused from the imputation of sinning by the removal of specific prohibitions, or else they are forgiven for actual transgression and are freely offered a second or even a third chance.

One could also say that "all women as Eve" makes it particularly easy to see some women as witches. The associations remain constant. It is those who speak who must be silenced; forests and trees, the site of original sin, become a *locus poenitentialis* to a much greater extent than towers; and witches, who are believed to derive their powers from their association with the devil, as does Vigilis' Eve, must be punished.

The medieval revival that swept through Europe in the eighteenth and nineteenth centuries expressed itself most visibly in England and France in clothing, architectural, and literary fashions. Germany had all this and more, for there a set of images and associated values were resuscitated from archives and libraries and were amalgamated with a tradition which had lived on among the common people. The images of Eve as the first sinner who must be punished and as *mulier loquax* who must be silenced superseded an educated and enlightened tradition; these images were also elevated to national significance when Eve came to stand for all women. This notion is implicit in *Grimms' Tales,* a volume that became the nation's primer. Thus was a weighty and consequential element of modern German culture forged.

I am reserving for a later study the question of why and precisely how *Grimms' Tales* came to have the particular constellation of characteristics that have emerged in this study, but I will make a few suggestions here. The Grimms' early archival work put them in touch with a past that seemed both simpler and more unified than Germany's troubled nineteenth-century disunity. The past has a perennial way of seeming simpler, a consequence perhaps of the evanescence of contextual detail.

Alternative Eves had existed in Germany's past, however. Some social and religious traditions in the seventeenth and eighteenth centuries had denied a sexist view of the fall from grace and had replaced it with more enlightened egalitarian ideals. The Grimms themselves came from a long line of families imbued with these ideals, and so did most of their peers in Cassel. Powerful emotional and political forces were necessary to overcome these deeply ingrained values growing out of this past, values that found expression in the earliest versions of many of the tales in their collection, and to replace them with the moral and social vision that emerges from the final Large Edition of 1857. Napoleon's national humiliation of the German-speaking peoples may have provided that force. We still know little—beyond truisms—about the social consequences of victory and defeat. But the codification of the moral and social values found in *Grimms' Tales* points to a politically activated moral upheaval of prodigious importance for nineteenth-century Germany, and for all who felt, or still feel, its power.

Appendix A
Tales Discussed

39. The Elves	Die Wichtelmänner
40. The Robber-Bridegroom	Der Räuberbräutigam
41. Herr Korbes	Herr Korbes
43. Frau Trude	Frau Trude
44. Godfather Death	Der Gevatter Tod
45. Thumbling's Travels	Daumerlings Wanderschaft
46. Fitcher's Bird	Fitchers Vogel
47. The Juniper Tree	Von dem Machandelboom
48. Old Sultan	Der alte Sultan
49. The Six Swans	Die sechs Schwäne
50. Little Briar-Rose (Sleeping Beauty)	Dornröschen
51. Fundevogel	Fundevogel
52. King Thrushbeard	König Drosselbart
53. Snow-White	Sneewittchen
54. The Knapsack, the Hat, and the Horn	Der Ranzen, das Hütlein und das Hörnlein
55. Rumpelstiltskin	Rumpelstilzchen
56. Sweetheart Roland	Der Liebste Roland
57. The Golden Bird	Der goldene Vogel
60. The Two Brothers	Die zwei Brüder
61. The Little Peasant	Das Bürle
68. The Thief and his Master	De Gaudeif un sien Meester
69. Jorinda and Joringel	Jorinde und Joringel
70. The Three Sons of Fortune	Die drei Glückskinder
71. How Six Got On in the World	Sechse kommen durch die ganze Welt
76. The Pink	Die Nelke
79. The Water-Nixie	Die Wassernixe
81. Brother Lustig	Bruder Lustig
82. Gambling Hansel	De Spielhansl
83. Hans in Luck	Hans im Glück
84. Hans Marries	Hans Heiratet
85. The Gold-Children	Die Goldkinder
87. The Poor Man and the Rich Man	Der Arme und der Reiche
89. The Goose-Girl	Die Gänsemagd
90. The Young Giant	Der junge Riese
91. The Gnome	Dat Erdmänneken
92. The King of the Golden Mountain	Der König vom goldenen Berge
93. The Raven	Die Rabe
94. The Peasant's Wise Daughter	Die kluge Bauerntochter
96. The Three Little Birds	De drei Vügelkens
97. The Water of Life	Das Wasser des Lebens
98. Doctor Knowall	Doktor Allwissend
99. The Spirit in the Bottle	Der Geist im Glas
100. The Devil's Sooty Brother	Des Teufels rußiger Bruder
101. Bearskin	Der Bärenhäuter
103. Sweet Porridge	Der süße Brei
104. Wise Folks	Die klugen Leute

105.	Tales of the Paddock	Märchen von der Unke
106.	The Poor Miller's Boy and the Cat	Der arme Müllersbursch und das Kätzchen
107.	The Two Travelers	Die beiden Wanderer
108.	Hans the Hedgehog	Hans mein Igel
109.	The Shroud	Das Totenhemdchen
110.	The Jew among Thorns	Der Jude im Dorn
111.	The Skillful Huntsman	Der gelernte Jäger
113.	The Two King's Children	De beiden Künigeskinner
114.	The Cunning Little Tailor	Vom klugen Schneiderlein
115.	The Bright Sun Brings It To Light	Die klare Sonne bringt's an den Tag
116.	The Blue Light	Das blaue Licht
117.	The Willful Child	Das eigensinnige Kind
118.	The Three Army-Surgeons	Die drei Feldscherer
120.	The Three Apprentices	Die drei Handwerksburschen
121.	The King's Son Who Feared Nothing	Der Königssohn, der sich vor nichts fürchtet
122.	Donkey Salad	Der Krautesel
123.	The Old Woman in the Wood	Die Alte im Wald
125.	The Devil and His Grandmother	Der Teufel und seine Großmutter
126.	Ferdinand the Faithful and Ferdinand the Unfaithful	Ferenand getrü un Ferenand ungetrü
127.	The Iron Stove	Der Eisenofen
128.	The Lazy Spinner	Die faule Spinnerin
130.	One-Eye, Two-Eyes, and Three-Eyes	Einäuglein, Zweiäuglein und Dreiäuglein
132.	The Fox and the Horse	Der Fuchs und das Pferd
133.	The Shoes That Were Danced to Pieces	Die zertanzten Schuhe
134.	The Six Servants	Die sechs Diener
135.	The White Bride and the Black Bride	Die weiße und die schwarze Braut
136.	Iron Hans	Der Eisenhans
137.	The Three Black Princesses	De drei schwatten Prinzessinnen
142.	Simeli Mountain	Simeliberg
144.	The Little Donkey	Das Eselein
146.	The Turnip	Die Rübe
147.	The Old Man Made Young Again	Das junggeglühte Männlein
148.	The Lord's Animals and the Devil's	Des Herrn und des Teufels Getier
149.	The Beam	Der Hahnenbalken
153.	The Star Money	Die Sterntaler
156.	The Hurds	Die Schlickerlinge
157.	The Sparrow and his Four Children	Der Sperling und seine vier Kinder
161.	Snow-White and Rose-Red	Schneeweißchen und Rosenrot
163.	The Glass Coffin	Der gläserne Sarg
164.	Lazy Harry	Der faule Heinz
165.	The Griffin	Der Vogel Greif

The Children's Legends

Appendix B
Patterns of Speech

Herein I attempt to measure the incidence, distribution, and presentation of direct speech in several different tale groupings. I begin with an analysis of "Cinderella" (no. 21), comparing the occurrence of direct speech in the Final Edition of 1857 (Ausgabe letzter Hand) with that in the First Edition.[1] The other tale groupings include popular tales, by which I mean the most frequently published texts; Christian tales; animal tales; less frequently published tales; and jest (*Schwank*) tales. This organization mixes categories: the second and fifth use publishing history as the basis for tale choice; the third, Christian tales, refers to a thematic category; while the fourth and sixth are based on genre—animal and jest tales. Mixing categories does not vitiate the results, in my opinion, since each category represents a valid grouping for purposes of comparison, despite the fact that their individual origins lie in various quarters.

Because the 1857 version served as the source for most further publications of *Grimms' Tales,* I have used it rather than any other edition as the base that reflects the content of the tales in modern German editions and in translations, with which people are most likely to come into contact.

1: "Cinderella" (no. 21), 1812

The frequency of direct speech basically defines the opposition of good and evil figures on table A.1. Cinderella has six introduced utterances. Her single use of *sprach* precedes an incantation. Her familial opponents balance and/or overwhelm her with a total of twelve utterances. The bad older sister also speaks six times introduced by roughly the same verbs (principally *sagte*) but with a revelatory *fragte,* which suggests that she does not conform to norms for young female propriety. The stepmother speaks only four times (four times as often as Cinderella's good but dead mother), overwhelming both the silent father and the prince with his three direct speeches.

---

1. The number of utterances recorded in table 6.1 may not correspond to totals given in the following tables, because it tabulates *all* direct speech whether introduced or not, while these record only direct speech introduced by one of the five most frequent verbs: *fragten, antworteten, riefen, sagten* and *sprachen.* Rölleke details plot and some stylistic changes in "Zur Biographie der Grimmschen Märchen," in *Kinder- und Hausmärchen* (1982), 2:521–78. His discussion does not, however, touch on the incidence and distribution of verbs introducing direct speech.

Table A.1. "Cinderella" (no. 21) 1812

Good Girl	fragen				
	antworten	x			
	rufen				
	sagen	xxxx			
	sprechen	x			
Mother	fragen				
	antworten				
	rufen				
	sagen	x			
	sprechen				
Witch Figure	fragen		x		x
	antworten				
	rufen		x		xx
	sagen	xxxx	xxxx	xx	xx
	sprechen	A	B	C	D
Father		(no direct speeches)			
Suitor	fragen				
	antworten				
	rufen	x			
	sagen	xx			
	sprechen				

A = Stepmother
B = Older Stepsister
C = Younger Stepsister
D = Both Stepsisters

"Cinderella," 1857

Table A.2 indicates the radical shift that had already become apparent in the Second Edition of 1819. The verbs introducing Cinderella's speeches have shifted away from *antwortete* and *sagte* to *rief* and *sprach;* each of the verbs introduces an incantation. The stepsisters, no matter how bad they are, no longer use *fragte;* their one actual question is introduced by *sprachen* and punctuated by an exclamation point rather than a question mark. An increase in the number of her utterances signals the stepmother's evil nature. Her verbs of introduction confirm her malevolence: seven instances of *sprach.* Relatively speaking, the father remains unheard with only two introduced utterances, while his thoughts are noted with quotation marks in the text but introduced with "thought" (*dachte*). He alone is allowed to pose a question (*fragte*), but only in indirect speech. The prince now balances the stepmother with a total of eight utterances, six of which begin with *sprach,* one with *rief,* and one with *sagte.*

A comparison of the instances of *sprach* offers some insight into the unconscious

Table A.2. "Cinderella" (no. 21): 1857

		A	B	C	D
Good Girl	fragen				
	antworten				
	rufen	xxx			
	sagen				
	sprechen	xx			
Mother	fragen				
	antworten				
	rufen		xxx		
	sagen				
	sprechen	x			
Witch Figure	fragen				
	antworten	x			
	rufen				xx
	sagen				x
	sprechen			xxxxxxx	xx
Father	fragen				
	antworten				
	rufen				
	sagen	x			
	sprechen	x			
Suitor	fragen				
	antworten				
	rufen	x			
	sagen	x			
	sprechen	xxxxxx			

A = Mother
B = Birds
C = Stepmother
D = Stepsisters

mental processes that must have dictated Wilhelm Grimm's choices. Both the stepsisters and Cinderella are given two instances of *sprach*. Both of Cinderella's are accounted for by their use in introducing incantations, an example of formal speech that seems to require the more ceremonial *sprach*. One of the stepsisters' *sprach*s is used to introduce a question, which neutralizes it as an indicator of evil, but they are left with one *sprach* to introduce a perfectly ordinary statement, which drops a clue to their bad nature.

The stepmother offers another avenue of approach to Grimm's thoughts on the subject. Only one female's discourse is regularly introduced by *sprach* without prejudice to her character in *Grimms' Tales:* that of the Virgin Mary, an acknowledged figure of apparently unimpeachable authority. Thus the presence of seven *sprach*s in conjunction with the stepmother's speech alerts the reader to an unfavorable estimation of her character, which the plot bears out.

Six instances of *sprach* in connection with the prince's speech, however, establish an authority within the text which is also borne out by the plot. The father also enjoys the prerogative of *sprach*.

Familiar Tales

Unlike the seven-member dramatis personae Vladimir Propp postulates for the more elaborate Russian fairy tale, most of the popular, frequently published tales in the

Table A.3. Familiar Tales

Good Girl	fragen	x
	antworten	xxxxxxx
	rufen	xxxxxxxx
	sagen	xxxxx
	sprechen	xxxxxxxxxxxx
Mother	fragen	
	antworten	x
	rufen	
	sagen	
	sprechen	x
Witch Figure	fragen	xxxx
	antworten	xxxx
	rufen	xxxxxxxxxxxx
	sagen	xxxxx
	sprechen	xxxxxxxxxxxxxxxxxxxxxxxxxxxxxxxx
Father	fragen	x
	antworten	x
	rufen	
	sagen	xxxxx
	sprechen	xxxx
Suitor	fragen	
	antworten	xx
	rufen	xxx
	sagen	xxxxxxx
	sprechen	xxxxxxxxxxxxxxxxxx

Note: The tales analyzed are "Rapunzel" (no. 12), "Hansel and Gretel" (no. 15), "Cinderella" (no. 21), "Little Briar-Rose" (no. 50), "Snow-White" (no. 53), and "Rumpelstiltskin" (no. 55).

Grimms' collection have a basic five-character cast: good daughter, dead mother, witch figure, father, and suitor.[2] Thus it is easy to compare these tales and to prepare a composite table that indicates the relative frequency of the five introductory verbs (table A.3). The proportions for these tales as a group echo those already discussed in the 1857 version of "Cinderella." The witch figure dominates conversation and questioning, while the prince enjoys a conversational edge—though not terribly pronounced—on the good daughter. Father and mother lag far behind, with the father dominating what chat there is, a pattern which continues in other categories.

In "Rapunzel" the heroine speaks twice, her mother (who does not die but disappears early along with her husband) once, Frau Gothel six times. (However, Frau Gothel uses *sagte* four times and *sprach* only twice, suggesting that she is less of a witch figure in Grimm's mind than the stepmother in "Cinderella." Indeed, these two characters have very different origins, Frau Gothel as a godmother and the stepmother from a long history of ill-tempered, mean-minded harridans.) Despite his early disappearance, the father speaks twice, like the prince.

"Hansel and Gretel" is a rather more verbose tale. Through her tears, Gretel has ten direct speeches. Of her three *sprach*s, two introduce questions. The children's natural mother never appears, and their stepmother's nine utterances (four of which are *sprach*) are not recorded here, despite the sometimes-cited theory that the stepmother and the witch are simply separate manifestations of different aspects of a single character.[3] The witch speaks nine times, the father six times, while Hansel carries the day with twelve utterances, five of which are *sprach*.

"Little Briar-Rose" is another tale in which remarkably little is said. The heroine speaks twice before she falls off to sleep, the wise woman once and the bad woman twice, the king not at all, and the prince only once.

Like "Cinderella," "Snow-White" is prototypical for patterns of speech in *Grimms' Tales*. Furthermore, its longer textual history offers us a closer look at the relationship between natural mothers and stepmothers, for in the Ölenberg MS, as well as in the first edition, a natural mother is transformed into the hideously jealous pursuer of her own daughter. Within the text of the 1812 edition, Wilhelm Grimm unwittingly offers the reader a glimpse of the relationship between the speech he allows his characters and their character as he perceives it, when the wicked queen loses her power and her speech at the very moment in which she hears that the prince has revived Snow-White: "When she heard that, she was terrified and she was so frightened that she couldn't express her fear" (Als sie das hörte, erschrak sie, und es war ihr so Angst, so Angst, daß sie es nicht sagen konnte).[4] It is only with the 1819 Second Edition that

2. Three other tales do not conform to this pattern (tables A.4–A.6): "The Frog-King" (no. 1), "Mother Holle" (no. 24), and "Jorinda and Joringel" (no. 69). "The Goose-Girl" is also not included here, because as a tale whose plot, motifs, and theme remained essentially unchanged over a long period, it is anomalous with respect to language use.

3. See Bettelheim, *The Uses of Enchantment*, 163.

4. Another, very different understanding of "Snow-White" is offered in Gilbert and Gubar, *The Madwoman in the Attic*, 36–42. They write that "the Grimm tale of 'Little Snow White' dramatizes the essential but equivocal relationship between the angel-woman and the monster-woman" (36), meaning not the two mothers but Snow-White and her stepmother. Given the results of my analysis, "equivocal" suggests an equality in speech which clearly does not obtain.

the two aspects of the mother's character are separated into two disparate personae, good biological mother and wicked stepmother. In 1810 Snow-White speaks once, her mother five times, the king and the prince not at all. In 1812 all speech is more or less tripled: Snow-White now speaks three times (*rief, sagte, sprach*) and her mother thirteen times, among which five are direct questions (*fragte*). The king and prince remain speechless. The 1819 Second Edition shows a radically different pattern. Cinderella speaks seven times, five of which are incantations introduced by *sprach;* her natural mother now dies soon after her birth, yielding place of pride to the paradox- ically beautiful stepmother who "asks" twice, "answers" once, "cries out" four times and "speaks" twelve times, for a total of nineteen direct speeches introduced by one of these five verbs. Outside the arena, the king, like Cinderella's father, says nothing, while the prince is allowed four direct speeches.

"Rumpelstiltskin" deviates slightly from the five-character pattern, in that no natural mother exists within the tale. Once again, the relative frequency of their direct speech produces a pattern that subordinates the good daughter to the witch figure, the dwarfish Rumpelstiltskin. The girl has six direct speeches, one of which is introduced by the usually fateful *fragte,* but which here allows her to actually ask if the dwarf's name might be Rumpelstiltskin. The girl does not "speak" but the king does (three times). Rumpelstiltskin has ten direct speeches, of which eight are introduced by *sprach.*

A certain ambiguity surrounds the tiny figure of the ill-used Rumpelstiltskin. He has kept his side of the bargain by saving the girl's life on three occasions, but she has refused to deliver up what she has promised, and so he strikes a second bargain involving guessing his outlandish name. His use of "speak" would appear to be licit because of his maleness, which corresponds to the fact that he is never once described as evil (bös)—but he suffers the sort of dreadful fate normally reserved for witch figures (see chapter 9). The analysis of these texts indicates that Grimm's assignment of a particular verb to introduce direct speech in the collection was part of a general pattern which can be corroborated collectively but not necessarily singly.

Several familiar tales do not conform to the five-character cast, but their patterns of speech consistently show the same constraints that render good girls silent, bad girls and women loquacious, and boys and men free to speak (tables A.4–A.7).

Christian Tales

The presence of Christian figures or institutions that determine the course of plot development define this group of tales: nos. 3, 31, 76, 87, 180, and the ten Children's Legends.[5] The Virgin Mary, Jesus, God, saints or angels, the devil, heaven or hell, biblical characters, and earthly preachers all qualify. As in the most popular tales, female earthlings define their character by the frequency of their utterances, and authority figures use *sprach.* This pattern reverses when a good male appears as the protagonist. Whether prince or peasant, he is free to speak, as in the legends "Poverty and Humility Lead to Heaven," "The Three Green Twigs," and "The Heavenly

5. Exclamations alone, such as the frequent "Oh, God" (Ach, Gott), have little to do with Christian values, as Rölleke points out in "Das Bild Gottes in den Märchen der Brüder Grimm," in "*Wo das wünschen noch geholfen hat.*"

Table A.4. "The Frog-King" (no. 1)

	fragen	
	antworten	x
Good Girl	rufen	
	sagen	xxx
	sprechen	
	fragen	
	antworten	
Father	rufen	
	sagen	x
	sprechen	xx
	fragen	
	antworten	xx
Suitor	rufen	xxxxxx
	sagen	
	sprechen	xxx

Table A.5. "Mother Holle" (no. 24)

	fragen	
	antworten	
Good Girl	rufen	
	sagen	x
	sprechen	
	fragen	
	antworten	
Mother (Holle)	rufen	x
	sagen	xx
	sprechen	x
	fragen	
	antworten	
Witch Figure	rufen	
	sagen	
	sprechen	x
	fragen	
	antworten	xx
Bad Daughter	rufen	
	sagen	
	sprechen	

Table A.6. "Jorinda and Joringel" (no. 69)

Good Girl	fragen	
	antworten	
	rufen	
	sagen	
	sprechen	
Witch Figure	fragen	
	antworten	
	rufen	
	sagen	x
	sprechen	
Suitor	fragen	
	antworten	
	rufen	x
	sagen	x
	sprechen	

Table A.7. "King Thrushbeard" (no. 52)

Good Girl	fragen	xxx:
	antworten	:
	rufen	x :x
	sagen	:x
	sprechen	xxx:
		A
Father	fragen	
	antworten	
	rufen	
	sagen	x
	sprechen	xxx
Suitor	fragen	:
	antworten	x:x
	rufen	:
	sagen	:
	sprechen	x:xxxxx
		A

A = point of chastisement

Wedding." Male figures may also out-talk divine authority figures, and they always exceed their wives in volubility. For instance, God out-talks Eve two to one in "Eve's Various Children," while both men in "The Poor Man and the Rich Man" out-talk their wives, and the rich man outstrips God two to one in the number of direct speeches. Grimm further counterbalances the verbal abuse (*Scheltworte*) of the rich couple with the pious silence of the poor (*still und fromm*). (See tables A.8–A.11.)

Further divisions appear when the tales are separated into those dealing primarily with women and those whose protagonists are male. In the female group, only one, "Our Lady's Child," arguably involves character change and development, while three concern the revelation of character ("The Girl without Hands," "The Pink," and "Saint Joseph in the Forest"). In contrast, the male tales seem to tap into the German *Bildungsroman* tradition, a genre devoted principally to male character development in the nineteenth century, for all three involve apparent development and change. In both groups *sprechen* is reserved principally for males, authority figures, and bad females. For example the Virgin Mary uses *sprach* eleven times to Marienkind's three. A typical distribution of these introductory verbs appears in the following exchange: "Then said [*sagte*] she: 'I am your wife, and that is your son, Sorrowful.' And he . . . said [*sprach*]: 'My wife had silver hands.' She answered [*antwortete*]: 'The good God has caused my natural hands to grow again.'" Exemplifying the fact that princes outspeak their—and other people's—fathers, the prince in "The Pink" "speaks" seven times and his father once, while both outtalk the queen 4.5:1 and 2:1 respectively. The male protagonists—prince, peasant, and even the hermit—all out-talk the other characters approximately 2:1, freely using *sprach*.

Table A.8. Christian Tales

Good Male	fragen	
	antworten	xx
	rufen	
	sagen	
	sprechen	xxxxxxxx
Bad Male	fragen	x
	antworten	
	rufen	x
	sagen	
	sprechen	x
Divine Figure	fragen	
	antworten	xxx
	rufen	
	sagen	
	sprechen	xxx

Note: The legends analyzed are "Poverty and Humility Lead to Heaven" (leg. 4), "The Three Green Twigs" (leg. 6), and "The Heavenly Wedding" (leg. 9).

Table A.9. Christian Family Drama

Good Girl/Queen	fragen	
	antworten	xxxxx
	rufen	
	sagen	xx
	sprechen	xx
Mother	fragen	
	antworten	
	rufen	
	sagen	x
	sprechen	xx
Witch Figure	fragen	
	antworten	
	rufen	
	sagen	xx
	sprechen	xxxxxxxx
King	fragen	
	antworten	xxxx
	rufen	
	sagen	xx
	sprechen	xx
Son	fragen	
	antworten	xx
	rufen	x
	sagen	x
	sprechen	xxxxxxxxxxxxx

Note: The tales analyzed are "The Girl without Hands" (no. 31) and "The Pink" (no. 76).

Table A.10. "Our Lady's Child" (no. 3)

	fragen	
	antworten	xx
Marienkind	rufen	x
	sagen	xx
	sprechen	xxx
Mother	(no direct speeches)	
	fragen	
	antworten	
Virgin Mary	rufen	
	sagen	
	sprechen	xxxxxxxxxx
Father	(no direct speeches)	
	fragen	
	antworten	
Suitor	rufen	
	sagen	
	sprechen	xx

Table A.11. "The Poor Man and the Rich Man" (no. 87)

Good Woman	fragen antworten rufen sagen sprechen		 x
Good Man	fragen antworten rufen sagen sprechen	 x xxx 	
Bad Woman	fragen antworten rufen sagen sprechen		 xx
Bad Man	fragen antworten rufen sagen sprechen	 xx x 	 xxxxxxx
God	fragen antworten rufen sagen sprechen	 x 	 xxxx

Animal Tales

These tales (nos. 2, 5, 48, and 132) break down roughly into a three-part dramatis personae: victim, despoiler and helper. The helper often appears in an ambiguous light in the world of animal tales, for his insinuating intelligence, used to assist the victim, undermines the figure who functions as the threatening despoiler (nos. 48, 132) under other circumstances. The threatening figures have more utterances than any other single character and their direct speech is introduced by *sprach* (nos. 2, 5, 132), thus demonstrating a link between language and power even in the animal world (table A.12).

Table A.12. Animal Tales

	fragen	xx
	antworten	xxxx
Victim	rufen	xxxxxxx
	sagen	xxx
	sprechen	x
	fragen	
	antworten	xxx
Despoiler	rufen	xxxx
	sagen	xxxxxxx
	sprechen	xxxxxxxxxxx
	fragen	x
	antworten	
Helper	rufen	
	sagen	xxx
	sprechen	xxxxxx

Note: Tales analyzed are "Cat and Mouse in Partnership" (no. 2), "The Wolf and the Seven Little Kids" (no. 5), "The Old Sultan" (no. 48), and "The Fox and the Horse" (no. 132).

Less Frequently Published Tales

As a group these tales are not uniform five-character family dramas.[6] Some of the tales' characters fit awkwardly—or not at all—into the slots that comfortably accommodate the characters in the most frequently published tales. Nonetheless they invite some interesting comparisons with familiar tales (table A.3).

The heroine in "The Three Spinners" (no. 14) occupies the position of "good girl" in the narrative by virtue of her initially being at risk and finally winning the prince. Her behavior, however, is far from exemplary, no demonstrations of nineteenth-century goodness leading to the happy ending. One might be able to classify her helpers as a collective maternal helper, but unlike other mothers in *Grimms' Tales* in human shape, the three ugly spinners remain very much alive. The speech of the lone male in this tale, despite his late appearance, outweighs that of each of the women.

In his predominantly male world Brother Lustig's (no. 81) unimpeded verbosity can

6. I use the term "family drama" in Derek Brewer's sense. See *Symbolic Stories*. The five-character designation is mine.

hardly be encompassed by a table like others in this appendix. In volubility he far outstrips St. Peter and all the other characters put together. The tale's sheer length may account for his forty-three speeches—but this leads the cautious reader to ask why tales about males are regularly longer than those about females.

The Faustian pact struck by Bearskin (no. 101) with the devil provides the frame for much conversation between the two. Among the three sisters whom he woos, the textual pattern of taunting loquacity for the two older sisters and meek silence for the youngest, so familiar from "Cinderella," persists, together with explicit narrative statements about her silence, i.e., "the bride was silent" (Die Braut schwieg still) and "the bride . . . never . . . spoke a word" (Die Braut . . . sprach kein Wort).

"The Old Woman in the Wood" (no. 123) offers a familiar paradigm with four of the five characters of the five-character family drama: maternal assisting figure (dove), good girl, witch, suitor—but no father. This tale engenders the good girl's wordlessness by making it part of the scheme by which she can overcome the evil witch's power, for her suitor tells her, "but on your life give her no answer" (Aber gib ihr beileibe keine Antwort), an injunction that the text clearly tells us she has complied with.

"The Hut in the Forest" (no. 169) offers an enigmatic portrayal of the prince figure. He first appears as a witchlike elder who dumps through a trapdoor the first two sisters who come to his house, sequestering them in the dangerous forest, an imprisonment their youngest sister saves them from when she, too, enters the forest. Thus the witch slot is not formally occupied, although her characteristics have to a certain extent been amalgamated with the prince's. Otherwise the tale fits into the five-character family drama with speaking father, silent mother, good and bad sisters, and suitor.

Within this group of tales, categories become fuzzy, and it is impossible to tally their speech acts on a single table. Nonetheless, individually the tales confirm the results rendered on other tables: men speak frequently and at length, their wives remain silent. Bad girls talk and good girls generally keep their tongues still. And witches, divine figures, and suitors suffer no particular constraint on their ability to speak.

Jests

Only a few reliable patterns emerge in this loud and disorderly lower-class world (nos. 34, 61, 104, 128, 164, 168). Tales about men tend to be longer than those about women, and the tales show a bipolar tension based solely on gender (tables A.13–A.15). As far as vocabulary is concerned, *sprach* is the preferred introductory verb. Characteristically, women's encounters with their environment are briefer and tend to establish the extraordinary stupidity of the titular heroines, while in jests about men much more talk emerges from their extensive and extensible adventures. And in a final denial of speech to female characters, Wilhelm Grimm—who clearly does not admire a woman who uses her language to fool her husband (no. 128)—speaks to the reader from the podium with his assay of the garrulous and lazy spinner's character:

But you yourself must own she was an odious woman!

Aber das mußt du selber sagen, es war eine garstige Frau.

Table A.13. About Married Couples

Wife	fragen	
	antworten	xxxxx
	rufen	xxxxx
	sagen	xxx
	sprechen	xxxxxxxxx
Husband	fragen	xx
	antworten	xxxxxx
	rufen	x
	sagen	xxxxxxxxxxx
	sprechen	xxxxxxxxxxx

Note: The tales analyzed are "Wise Folks" (no. 104), "The Lazy Spinner" (no. 128), "Lazy Harry" (no. 164), and "Lean Lisa" (no. 168).

Table A.14. About a Woman: "Clever Elsie" (no. 34)

Elsie	fragen	
	antworten	x
	rufen	x
	sagen	
	sprechen	xxxxxx
Mother	fragen	
	antworten	
	rufen	
	sagen	xx
	sprechen	xxx
Father	fragen	
	antworten	
	rufen	x
	sagen	
	sprechen	xxxxx
Suitor	fragen	x
	antworten	x
	rufen	
	sagen	
	sprechen	xxxx

Table A.15. About a Man: "The Little Peasant" (no. 61)

Peasant's Wife	(no direct speeches)	
Miller's Wife	fragen	
	antworten	
	rufen	
	sagen	xx
	sprechen	xxxx
Miller	fragen	xxx
	antworten	x
	rufen	xxxxx
	sagen	
	sprechen	xxxxxxx
Shepherd	fragen	
	antworten	x
	rufen	
	sagen	x
	sprechen	xxx
Peasant	fragen	
	antworten	xxxxxx
	rufen	
	sagen	xx
	sprechen	xxxxxxxxxx

Bibliography

Primary Sources

Afanasyev, Alexander. *The Bawdy Peasant*. London: Odyssey Press, 1925.
Apuleius. *The Golden Ass*. Trans. Robert Graves. New York: Farrar Straus Giroux, 1951.
Asbjørnsen, Peter Christian and Jørgen Moe. *Norske Folkeeventyr*. Christiana: Johan Dahls Vorlag, 1852. *East o' the Sun and West o' the Moon*. Trans. George Webbe Dasent. 1859; New York: Dover, 1970.
Ayrer, Jakob. *Ein Faßnachtspil von Fritz Dölla mit seiner gewünschten Geigen*. Stuttgart: Bibliothek des Litterarischen Vereins, 1865. 79:2829–48.
Basile, Giambattista. *The Pentamerone*. Ed. N. M. Penzer. 2 vols. 1932; Westport, Conn.: Greenwood Press, 1979.
Bechstein, Ludwig. *Sämtliche Märchen*. Munich: Winkler, 1983.
Boccaccio, Giovanni. *The Decameron*. Baltimore: Penguin Classics, 1972.
———. *Boccaccio on Poetry, Being the Preface and the Fourteenth and Fifteenth Books of Boccaccio's "Geneologia Deorum Gentilium."* Trans. Charles G. Osgood. Indianapolis: Bobbs-Merrill, 1978.
Chaucer, Geoffrey. *Canterbury Tales*. Trans. Neville Coghill. Baltimore: Penguin Classics, 1972.
Cinderella, or The Little Glass Slipper. Cooperstown: H. and E. Phinney, 1829, 1830, 1834.
"Der bösen weiber Zuchtschul Ein schöner Dialogue odder gesprech von Zweyen schwestern. Die Erste einn from unnd züchtig witfraw aus Meis sen. Die ander ein bös storrig unnd zornig weib vom gebirg. Zu lob unnd Eeren allen fromment Zur straff uñ underweisung den zornigen Frauwenn." *Flugschriften des frühen 16. Jahrhunderts*. Ed. H. J. Köhler, H. Hebenstreit, Chr. Weismann. Zug, Switzerland: 1980. Fiche 361, Nr. 2414.
Grimm, Jakob. *Circular wegen Aufsammlung der deutschen Poesie*. 1815; Ed. Ludwig Denecke. Cassel: Brüder Grimm Gesellschaft, 1968.
———. *Deutsche Mythologie*. 1835; Graz: Akademische Druck- und Verlagsanstalt, 1953.
———. *Deutsche Rechtsalterthümer*. 2 vols. 1828; Darmstadt: Wissenschaftliche Buchgesellschaft, 1965.
———. *Kleinere Schriften*. 8 vols. 1882–90; Hildesheim: Georg Olms, 1966.

Grimm, Jacob and Wilhelm. *Altdeutsche Wälder.* 3 vols. 1813–16; Darmstadt: Wissenschaftliche Buchgesellschaft, 1966.

———. *Deutsche Sagen.* 2 vols. 1816–18; Philadelphia: Institute for the Study of Human Issues, 1981. Trans. Donald Ward. *German Legends.* 2 vols. Philadelphia: Institute for the Study of Human Issues, 1981.

———. *Deutsches Wörterbuch.* 33 vols. Leipzig: S. Hirzel, 1852–1960.

———. *Sechs Märchen aus dem Nachlaß.* Ed. Johannes Bolte. Berlin: Brandus, 1918.

———. *German Popular Stories.* Trans. Edgar Taylor. London: John Camden Hotten, 1969.

———. *Grimms' Fairy Tales.* Trans. Margaret Hunt and James Stern. New York: Pantheon, 1944, 1972.

———. *Kinder- und Hausmärchen.* Large Editions: 1812–15; 1819; 1837; 1840; 1843; 1850; 1857. Small Editions: 1825, 1833, 1836, 1839, 1844, 1847, 1850, 1853, 1858.

Grimm, Wilhelm. *Altdänische Heldenlieder, Balladen, und Märchen.* Heidelberg: Mohr und Zimmer, 1811.

———. Marginalia in *Die gute Frau.* Ed. Emil Sommer. *Zeitschrift für deutsches Altertum* (1842).

———. *Kleinere Schriften.* 4 vols. 1881–87.

Haiding, Karl. *Märchen und Schwänke aus Oberösterreich.* Berlin: de Gruyter, 1969.

Kryptádia: Recueil de documents pour servir à l'étude des traditions populaires. 4 vols. Heilbronn: Henninger, 1883–88.

Lovechild, Lawrence. *Cinderella.* Philadelphia: George B. Zieber, 1847.

Lukacs, Josef, ed. *Die goldene Spindel: Spinnstuben- und Webermärchen aus vielen Jahrhunderten.* Münsingen: Fischer, 1981.

———. *Der silberne Faden: Erzählungen aus dem Sagenschatz der Spinnerinnen und Weber.* Münsingen: Fischer, 1980.

Mieder, Wolfgang. *Grimms Märchen—Modern: Prosa, Gedichte, Karikaturen.* Stuttgart: Philipp Reclam, 1979.

Neujahrsgeschenk für Kinder von einem Kinderfreunde. Frankfurt: 1783.

Ovid. *Metamorphoses.* Trans. Mary Innes. Baltimore: Penguin, 1955.

Perrault, Charles. *Contes de ma mère l'Oye.* The Hague: Jean Neaulme, 1745.

———. *Contes de Perrault.* 1697; Geneva: Slatkine, 1980.

———. *Perrault's Fairy Tales.* Trans. A. E. Johnson. New York: Dover, 1969.

Simrock, Karl. *Die deutschen Volksbücher.* 13 vols. 1892; Hildesheim/New York: Georg Olms, 1974.

Spiegel der regiersichtigen bösen Weibern. 1733; Frankfurt: Ullstein, 1982.

Straparola, Giovanni Francesco. *The Most Delectable Nights of Straparola of Caravaggio.* 2 vols. Paris: Charles Carrington, 1906.

"Wie in Eesachen unnd den fellen so sich derhalben zutra gennach götlichem billichem rechte(n) Christe(n)lich zu handelen sey." *Flugschriften des frühen 16. Jahrhunderts.* Ed. H. J. Köhler, H. Hebenstreit, Chr. Weismann. Zug Switzerland, n.d. Fiche 361, Nr. 1015.

Wolf, J. W. *Deutsche Hausmärchen.* 1851; Hildesheim/New York: Georg Olms, 1972.

Secondary Works

Aarne, Antti and Stith Thompson. *The Types of the Folktale.* Trans. Stith Thompson. FFC 184. Helsinki: Suomalainen Tiedeakatemia, 1964.

Adler, Max. *Sex Differences in Human Speech.* Hamburg: Helmut Buske, 1978.

Apo, Satu. "The Structural Analysis of Marina Takalo's Fairy Tales Using Propp's Model." *Genre, Structure and Reproduction in Oral Literature.* Ed. Lauri Honko and Vilmos Voigt. Budapest: Akademiai Kiado, 1980.

Ardener, Shirley, ed. *Defining Females: The Nature of Women in Society.* New York: John Wiley, 1978.

———. *Perceiving Women.* New York: John Wiley, 1975.

———. *Women and Space: Ground Rules and Social Maps.* London: Croom Helm, 1981.

Ariès, Philippe. *Centuries of Childhood.* Trans. Robert Baldick. New York: Vintage, 1962.

Armstrong, Robert Plant. "Content Analysis in Folkloristics." *Trends in Content Analysis.* Urbana: University of Illinois Press, 1959. 151–70.

Auden, W. H. "In Praise of the Brothers Grimm." Review of *Grimm's Fairy Tales. New York Times Book Review.* 12 November 1944: 1.

Austin, John L. *How To Do Things with Words.* The 1955 William James Lectures. Cambridge: Harvard University Press, 1962.

Bachofen, J. J. *Myth, Religion and Mother Right.* Trans. Ralph Manheim. Princeton: Princeton University Press, 1967.

Bange, Pierre. "Comment on devient homme: Analyse sémiotique d'un conte de Grimm: 'Les Douze Freres.'" *Etudes allemandes: Recueil dédié à Jean-Jacques Anstett.* Ed. G. Brunet. Lyon: Presses Universitaires de Lyon, 1979. 93–138.

Bastian, Ulrike. *Die Kinder- und Hausmärchen der Brüder Grimm in der literatur-pädagogischen Diskussion des 19. und 20. Jahrhunderts.* Frankfurt: Haag und Herelsen, 1981.

Bausinger, Hermann. *Formen der "Volkspoesie."* 2d ed. Berlin: Erich Schmidt, 1980.

———. "Schwank und Witz." *Studium Generale* 11 (1958): 699–711.

Bausinger, Hermann and Kurt Ranke. "Archäische Züge im Märchen." *Enzyklopädie des Märchens,* 1:733–43.

Bechstein, Ludwig. *Über den ethischen Wert der deutschen Volkssagen.* N.p., 1837.

Beit, Hedwig von. *Symbolik des Märchens.* 3 vols. Bern: Francke Verlag, 1956–57.

Belgrader, Michael. "Fluch, Fluchen, Flucher." *Enzyklopädie des Märchens* 4:1315–28.

———. *Das Märchen von dem Machandelboom.* Bern: Lang, 1980.

Ben-Amos, Dan, ed. *Folklore Genres.* Austin: University of Texas Press, 1976.

Berendsohn, Walter A. *Grundformen volkstümlicher Erzählerkunst in den Kinder- und Hausmärchen der Brüder Grimm.* Wiesbaden: M. Sändig, 1921.

Bettelheim, Bruno. *Symbolic Wounds: Puberty Rites and the Envious Male.* New York: Collier, 1962.

———. *The Uses of Enchantment.* New York: Vintage, 1977.

Bolte, Johannes. *Zeugnisse zur Geschichte des Märchens.* FFC 39. Helsinki: Suomalainen Tiedeakatemia, 1921.

Bolte, Johannes and George Polívka. *Anmerkungen zu den "Kinder- und Hausmärchen."* 5 vols. 1913–32; Hildesheim: Georg Olms, 1963.

Bottigheimer, Ruth B., ed. *Fairy Tales and Society: Illusion, Allusion and Paradigm.* Philadelphia: University of Pennsylvania Press, 1986.

———. "Iconographic Continuity in Illustrations of 'The Goosegirl' (KHM 89)." *Children's Literature* 13. Ed. Margaret R. Higonnet and Francelia Butler. New Haven: Yale University Press, 1985. 49–71.

———. "Tale Spinners: Submerged Voices in Grimms' 'Fairy Tales.'" *New German Critique* 27 (1982): 141–50.

———. "The Transformed Queen: A Search for the Origins of Negative Female Archetypes in Grimms' 'Fairy Tales.'" *Amsterdamer Beiträge* 10 (1980): 1–12.

Bovenschen, Silvia. "The Contemporary Witch, the Historical Witch, and the Witch Myth: The Witch, Subject of the Appropriation of Nature and Object of the Domination of Nature." *New German Critique* 15 (1978): 83–110.

Bramsted, Ernest K. *Aristocracy and the Middle Classes in Germany: Social Types in German Literature, 1830–1900.* 1939; Chicago: University of Chicago Press, 1964.

Brewer, Derek. *Symbolic Stories: Traditional Narratives of the Family Drama in English Literature.* Totowa, N.J.: Brewer/Rowman and Littlefield, 1980.

Bühler, Charlotte. *Das Märchen und die Phantasie des Kindes.* Leipzig: J. A. Barth, 1918.

Calame-Griaule, Geneviève. *Permanence et metamorphoses du conte populaire: La mère traîtresse et le tueur de dragons.* Paris: L'Institut National des Langues et Civilisations Orientales, 1975.

Calame-Griaule, Geneviève, Veronika Görög-Karady, and Michele Chiche, eds. *Le conte: pourquoi? comment?* Paris: Editions du CNRS, 1984.

Campbell, Joseph. *The Hero with a Thousand Faces.* Bollingen Series 17. New York: Pantheon, 1949.

Cerda, Hugo. *Literatura Infantil y Clases Sociales.* Madrid: Akal Bolsillo, 1978.

Christiansen, A. *The Norwegian Fairytales: A Short Summary.* FFC 46. Helsinki: Suomalainen Tiedeakatemia, 1922.

"Christliche Motive." *Handwörterbuch des deutschen Märchens.*

Cosentino, Donald. *Defiant Maids and Stubborn Farmers.* Cambridge: Cambridge University Press, 1982.

Cott, Jonathan. *Pipers at the Gates of Dawn.* New York: Random House, 1983.

Cox, Marian E. Roalfe. *Cinderella: Three Hundred and Forty-Five Variants of Cinderella, Catskin, and Cap O'Rushes.* London: Folklore Society, 1893.

Dahrendorf, Malte. *Das Mädchenbuch und seine Leserin: Jugendlektüre als Instrument der Sozialisation.* Weinheim: Beltz, 1970.

———. *Kinder- und Jugendliteratur im bürgerlichen Zeitalter: Beiträge zu ihrer Geschichte, Kritik und Didaktik.* Königstein/Taunus: Scriptor, 1980.

Darnton, Robert. "Peasants Tell Tales." *The Great Cat Massacre and Other Episodes in French History.* New York: Basic Books, 1984.

David, Alfred and Mary E. David. "A Literary Approach to the Brothers Grimm." *Journal of the Folklore Institute* 1 (1963): 181ff.

Dégh, Linda. "Folk Narrative." *Folklore and Folklife: An Introduction.* Ed. Richard M. Dorson. Chicago: University of Chicago Press, 1972.

————. *Folktales and Society: Storytelling in a Hungarian Peasant Community*. Trans. Emily M. Schlossberg. Bloomington: University of Indiana Press, 1969.

————. "Grimm's *Household Tales* and Its Place in the Household: The Social Relevance of a Controversial Classic." *Western Folklore* 38 (1979): 83–103.

————. "The Magic Tale and Its Magic." *Fairy Tales as Ways of Knowing*. Ed. M. Metzger and K. Mommsen. Bern: P. Lang, 1981.

Dégh, Linda and Andrew Vazsonyi. "The Dialectics of the Legend." *Folklore Preprint Series* 1, no. 6 (1973).

Denecke, Ludwig. *Jacob Grimm und sein Bruder Wilhelm*. Stuttgart: Metzler, 1971.

————, ed. *Brüder Grimm Gedenken*. Marburg: Elwert, 1963–.

Dielmann, Karl. "Märchenillustrationen von Ludwig Emil Grimm." *Hanauer Geschichtsblätter* 18 (1962): 281–306.

Doderer, Klaus, ed. *Über Märchen für Kinder von heute*. Weinheim: Beltz, 1983.

Dundes, Alan, ed. *Cinderella: A Folklore Casebook*. New York: Garland Press, 1982.

————. "From Etic to Emic Units in the Structural Study of Folktales." *Journal of American Folklore* 75 (1962): 95–105.

————. *Life is like a Chicken Coop Ladder: A Portrait of German Culture through Folklore*. New York: Columbia University Press, 1984.

————. "The Symbolic Equivalence of Allomotifs: Towards a Method of Analyzing Folktales." Geneviève Calame-Griaule, Veronika Görög-Karady, Michele Chiche, eds., *Le conte: pourquoi? comment?* Paris: Centre Nationale de la Recherche Scientifique, 1984. 187–99.

————. *Varia Folklorica*. Paris/The Hague: Mouton, 1978.

Eliade, Mircea. *Images and Symbols: Studies in Religious Symbolism*. Trans. Philip Mairet. Kansas City: Sheed Andrews and McMeel, 1961.

Ellis, John M. *One Fairy Story Too Many*. Chicago: University of Chicago Press, 1983.

Ellmann, Mary. *Thinking about Women*. 1968; London: Virago Press, 1979.

Elshtain, Jean Bethke. "Feminist Discourse and Its Discontents: Language, Power and Meaning." *Signs* (1982): 603–21.

Endrai, Walter. *L'évolution des techniques du filage et du tissage du moyen âge à la révolution industrielle*. Paris/The Hague: Mouton, 1968.

Enzyklopädie des Märchens. Berlin: de Gruyter, 1975– .

Ewers, Hans-Heino, ed. *Kinder- und Jugendliteratur der Romantik*. Stuttgart: Philipp Reclam, 1984.

Farrer, Claire R. *Women and Folklore*. Austin: University of Texas Press, 1975.

Fehling, Detlev. *Amor und Psyche: Die Schöpfung des Apuleius und ihre Einwirkung auf das Märchen. Eine Kritik der romantischen Märchentheorie*. Mainz: Akademie der Wissenschaften und der Literatur, 1977.

Fetscher, Iring. *Wer hat Dornröschen wachgeküßt?* Frankfurt: Fischer, 1975.

Fine, Elizabeth C. *The Folklore Text: From Performance to Print*. Bloomington: University of Indiana Press, 1984.

Fink, Gonthier-Louis. *Naissance et apogée du conte merveilleux en Allemagne 1740–1800*. Paris: Belles Lettres, 1966.

Fischer, John L. "The Sociopsychological Analysis of Folktales." *Current Anthropology* 4 (1963): 235–95.

Foucault, Michel. *The History of Sexuality*. Trans. Robert Hurley. New York: Vintage Books, 1978.

Fout, John, ed. *German Women in the Nineteenth Century*. New York: Holmes and Meier, 1984.

Franke, Carl. *Die Brüder Grimm: Ihr Leben und Wirken*. Dresden/Leipzig, 1899.

Franz, Marie-Louise von. *An Introduction to the Interpretation of Fairy Tales*. New York: Spring, 1970.

———. *Problems of the Feminine in Fairy Tales*. New York: Spring, 1972.

Freeman, Michelle A. "Marie de France's Poetics of Silence: The Implications for a Feminine *Translatio*." *PMLA* 99 (1984): 860–83.

Freitag, Elisabeth. "Die Kinder- und Hausmärchen der Brüder Grimm im ersten Stadium ihrer stilgeschichtlichen Entwicklung: Vergleich der Urform (Ölenberger Handschrift) mit dem Erstdruck (1. Band) von 1812." Diss., Frankfurt, 1929.

Geiger, Rudolf. *Mit Märchen im Gespräch*. Stuttgart: Urachhaus, 1972.

Gerstl, Quirin. "Der erzieherische Gehalt der Grimmschen Kinder- und Hausmärchen." Diss., Munich, 1963.

Gerstner, Hermann. *Die Brüder Grimm*. 1970; Hamburg: Rowohlt, 1973.

Gilbert, Sandra and Susan Gubar. *The Madwoman in the Attic: The Woman Writer and the Nineteenth-Century Literary Imagination*. New Haven: Yale University Press, 1979.

Gilligan, Carol. *In a Different Voice*. Cambridge: Harvard University Press, 1982.

Ginschel, Gunhild. "Der Märchenstil Jacob Grimms." *Deutsches Jahrbuch für Volkskunde* 9 (1963): 131–68.

Gmelin, Otto. *Böses kommt aus Kinderbüchern: Die verpaßten Möglichkeiten kindlicher Bewußtseinsbildung*. Munich: Kindler, 1972.

Göttner-Abendroth, Heide. *Die Göttin und ihr Heros*. Munich: Frauenoffensive, 1980.

Gomme, George Lawrence. *Folklore as an Historical Science*. London: Methuen, 1908.

Grätz, Manfred. "Das Märchen in der deutschen Aufklärung. Vom Feenmärchen zum Volksmärchen." Diss., Göttingen, 1984.

Grenz, Dagmar. *Mädchenliteratur: Von den moralisch-belehrenden Schriften im 18. Jahrhundert bis zur Herstellung der Backfischliteratur im 19. Jahrhundert*. Stuttgart: Metzler, 1981.

Hamann, Hermann. *Die literarischen Vorlagen der "Kinder- und Hausmärchen" und ihre Bearbeitung durch dir Brüder Grimm*. Berlin: Mayer und Müller, 1906.

Hand, Wayland D. "Status of European and American Legend Study." *Current Anthropology* 6 (1965): 439–46.

Handwörterbuch des deutschen Märchens. Ed. Lutz Mackensen. Berlin: de Gruyter, 1930–40.

Harder, Hans Bernd and Ekkehard Kaufmann, eds. *Die Brüder Grimm in ihrer amtlichen und politischen Tätigkeit*. Cassel: Weber and Weidemeyer, 1985. (Vol. 3 of exhibit catalog for "200 Jahre Brüder Grimm," 1985–86, Cassel.)

Harkort, Fritz, Karel C. Peeters, and Robert Wildhaber, eds. *Volksüberlieferung*. Göttingen: Otto Schwartz, 1968.

Hazard, Paul. *Books, Children and Men*. Trans. Marguerite Mitchell. Boston: Horn Book, 1984.

Hennig, Dieter and Bernhard Lauer, eds. *Die Brüder Grimm. Dokumente ihres Lebens und*

Wirkens. Cassel: Weber and Weidemeyer, 1985 (Vol. I of exhibit catalog for "200 Jahre Brüder Grimm," 1985–86, Cassel.)

Herder, Johann Gottfried. *Werke.* 10 vols. Frankfurt: Deutsche Klassiker, 1985.

Heuscher, Julius. *A Psychiatric Study of Fairy Tales.* Springfield, Ill.: Thomas, 1963.

History of Technology. 8 vols. Ed. C. Singer, E. J. Holmyard, A. Rittell. Oxford: Clarendon, 1954–84.

Höck, Alfred. *Die Brüder Grimm als Studenten in Marburg.* Marburg: Elwert, 1978.

Horn, Katalin. *Der aktive und der passive Märchenheld.* Basel: Schweizerische Gesellschaft für Volkskunde, 1983.

———. "Fleiß und Faulheit." *Enzyklopädie des Märchens* 4: 1262–76.

———. "Motivationen und Funktionen der tödlichen Bedrohung in den KHM der Brüder Grimm." *Schweizer Archiv für Volkskunde* 74 (1978): 20–40.

Husson, H. *La chaîne traditionelle.* Paris, 1874.

Jackson, Anthony. "The Science of Fairy Tales?" *Folklore* 84 (1973): 120–41.

Jacoby, M., V. Kast, and I. Riedel. *Das Böse im Märchen.* Fellbach: A. Bonz, 1978.

Jason, Heda, and Dimitri Segal, eds. *Patterns in Oral Literature.* Paris/The Hague: Mouton, 1977.

Jessen, Jens Christian. "Das Recht in den 'Kinder- und Hausmärchen' der Brüder Grimm.'" Diss., Kiel, 1979.

Joeres, Ruth-Ellen B. and Mary Jo Maynes, eds. *German Women in the Eighteenth and Nineteenth Centuries: A Social and Literary History.* Bloomington: University of Indiana Press, 1986.

Johnson, Barbara. *The Critical Difference.* Baltimore: Johns Hopkins University Press, 1980.

Jolles, André. *Einfache Formen.* 5th ed. Tübingen: Niemeyer, 1972.

Jung, Jochen, ed. *Märchen, Sagen und Abenteuergeschichten auf alten Bilderbogen neu erzählt.* München: Heinz Moos, 1974.

Kaiser, Erich and Georg Pilz. *Erzähl mir doch /k/ein Märchen!* Frankfurt: Diesterweg, 1981.

Kamenetsky, Christa. "Folktale and Ideology in the Third Reich." *Journal of American Folklore* 90 (1977): 1968–78.

———. *Children's Literature in Hitler's Germany.* Athens: Ohio University Press, 1984.

Kamuf, Peggy. *Fictions of Feminine Desire.* Lincoln: University of Nebraska Press, 1982.

Karlinger, Felix. *Grundzüge einer Geschichte des Märchens im deutschen Sprachraum.* Darmstadt: Wissenschaftliche Buchgesellschaft, 1983.

Katz, Jacob. *From Prejudice to Destruction: Anti-Semitism, 1700–1933.* Cambridge: Harvard University Press, 1980.

Kemminghausen, Karl S. and Georg Hüllen, eds. *Märchen der europäischen Völker.* Münster: Aschendorff, 1961.

Kiefer, Emily. *Albert Wesselski and Recent Folktale Theories.* Bloomington: University of Indiana Press, 1947.

Klíma, Josef R. "Arbeit." *Enzyklopädie des Märchens* 1:723–33.

Knüsel, Käthi. "Reden und Schweigen im Märchen." Diss., Göttingen, 1980.

Köhler, Ines. "Die geschwätzige Frau." *Enzyklopädie des Märchens* 5:148–59.

Könneker, Marie-Luise, ed. *Kinderschaukel: Ein Lesebuch zur Geschichte der Kindheit.* Darmstadt: H. Luchterhand, 1976.

Koszinowski, Ingrid and Vera Leuschner, eds. *Ludwig Emil Grimm 1790–1863 Maler, Zeichner, Radierer.* Cassel: Weber and Weidemeyer, 1985 (Vol. 2 of exhibit catalog for "200 Jahre Brüder Grimm," 1985–86, Cassel.)

Kramarae, Cheris. *Women and Men Speaking: Frameworks for Analysis.* Rowley, Mass.: Newbury House, 1981.

Kramarae, Cheris, Muriel Schulz, and William M. O'Barr, eds. *Language and Power.* London: Sage, 1984.

Krippendorf, Klaus. *Content Analysis: An Introduction to Its Methodology.* Beverly Hills: Sage, 1980.

Krohn, Kaarle. *Übersicht über einige Resultate der Märchenforschung.* FFC 96. Helsinki: Suomalainen Tiedeakatemia, 1931–32.

Künneman, Horst. *Märchen—Wozu?* Hamburg/Munich: LESEN Verlag, 1978.

Labes, Eugen. *Die bleibende Bedeutung der Brüder Grimm für die Bildung der deutschen Jugend.* Rostock: Adler, 1887.

Landy, Marcia. "The Silent Woman." *The Authority of Experience: Essays in Feminist Criticism.* Ed. Arlyn Diamond and Lee R. Edwards. Amherst: University of Massachusetts Press, 1977.

Lanser, Susan Sniader. *The Narrative Act: Point of View in Prose Fiction.* Princeton: Princeton University Press, 1981.

Lenz, Friedel. *Bildsprache der Märchen.* Stuttgart: Urachhaus, 1980.

Le Roy Ladurie, Emmanuel. *Love, Death and Money in the Pays d'Oc.* New York: Braziller, 1982.

Levin, Isidor. "Das russische Grimmbild." *Brüder Grimm Gedenken* (1963): 375–403.

Leyen, Friedrich von der. *Das deutsche Märchen und die Brüder Grimm.* Düsseldorf: Diederichs, 1964.

Linke, Werner. *Das Stiefmuttermotiv im Märchen der germanischen Völker.* Berlin: Ebering, 1933.

Linnig, F. *Deutsche Mythen-Märchen: Beitrag zur Erklärung der Grimmschen Kinder- und Hausmärchen.* Paderborn: Ferdinand Schöningh, 1883.

Lüthi, Max. "Belohnung, Lohn." *Enzyklopädie des Märchens,* 2:92–99.

———. "Dialog." *Enzyklopädie des Märchens* 3:585–601.

———. *Es war einmal: Vom Wesen des Volksmärchens.* Göttingen: Vandenhoeck und Ruprecht, 1962.

———. "Ethik." *Enzyklopädie des Märchens,* 4:499–508.

———. *The Fairy Tale as Art Form and Portrait of Man.* Trans. Jon Erickson. Bloomington: University of Indiana Press, 1985.

———. *Märchen.* 7th ed. Stuttgart: Metzler, 1979.

———. *So leben sie noch heute.* Göttingen: Vandenhoeck und Ruprecht, 1969.

———. *The European Folktale: Form and Nature.* Trans. John D. Niles. Philadelphia: Institute for the Study of Human Issues, 1982.

———. "Über den Ursprung des Rapunzelmärchens (AaTh 310)." *Fabula* (3) (1960): 95–110.

———. *Volksliteratur und Hochliteratur: Menschenbild—Thematik—Formstreben.* Bern: Francke, 1970.

————. *Volksmärchen und Volkssage*. Bern: Francke, 1961.

Mandrou, Robert. *De la culture populaire aux XVIIe et XVIIIe siècles: la Bibliothèque bleue de Troyes*. Paris: Stock, 1964.

Mayer, Anton. "Erdmutter und Hexe: Eine Untersuchung zur Geschichte des Hexenglaubens und zur Vorgeschichte der Hexenprozesse." *Historische Forschungen und Quellen* 12 (1936): 1–66.

McConnell-Ginet, Sally, Ruth Borker, and Nelly Furman. *Women and Language in Literature and Society*. New York: Praeger, 1980.

Medick, Hans and David W. Sabean, eds. *Interest and Emotion: Essays on the Study of Family and Kinship*. Cambridge: Cambridge University Press, 1984.

Meletinsky, E., et al. "Problems of the Structural Analysis of Fairytales." *Soviet Structural Folkloristics*. Ed. Pierre Maranda. Paris/The Hague: Mouton, 1974. 73–139.

Merkel, Johannes and Dieter Richter. *Märchen, Phantasie und soziales Lernen*. Berlin: Basis, 1974.

Miller, Nancy K. *The Heroine's Text*. New York: Columbia University Press, 1980.

Mönckeberg, Vilma. *Das Märchen und unsere Welt: Erfahrungen und Einsichten*. Cologne: Diederichs, 1972.

Moser, Dietz-Rüdiger. "Altersbestimmung des Märchens." *Enzyklopädie des Märchens*, 1:407–19.

————. "Christliche Erzählstoffe." *Enzyklopädie des Märchens*, 2:1385–1400.

————. *Die Tannhaüser-Legende*. Berlin: de Gruyter, 1977.

————. "Theorie- und Methodenprobleme der Märchenforschung: Zugleich der Versuch einer Definition des "Märchens." *Jahrbuch für Volkskunde* 3 (1980): 47–64.

Moser-Rath, Elfriede. "Frau." *Enzyklopädie des Märchens* 5:100–37.

————. *"Lustige Gesellschaft": Schwank und Witz des 17. und 18. Jahrhunderts in kultur- und sozialgeschichtlichem Kontext*. Stuttgart: Metzler, 1984.

Müller, Elisabeth. *Das Bild der Frau im Märchen: Analysen und erzieherische Betrachtungen*. Munich: Profil, 1986.

Müller, Wilhelm. "Die Sage vom Schwanenritter." *Germania* 1 (1856): 418–40.

Nathhorst, Bertel. *Formal or Structural Studies of Traditional Tales*. Stockholm: Kungl. Boktryckeriet P. A. Norstedt, 1969.

Neumann, Erich. *The Great Mother: An Analysis of the Archetype*. Bollingen Series 47. Trans. Ralph Manheim. Princeton: Princeton University Press, 1955.

Newall, Venetia. "Antisemitismus." *Enzyklopädie des Märchens*, 1:611–18.

Nisard, Charles. *Histoire des livres populaires ou de la littérature du colportage*. Paris: Maisonneuve et Larose, 1968.

Nitschke, August. *Soziale Ordnungen im Spiegel der Märchen*. Stuttgart: Frommann, 1976.

Obenauer, Karl Justus. *Das Märchen: Dichtung und Deutung*. Frankfurt: Klostermann, 1959.

Ostriker, Alicia. "The Thieves of Language: Women Poets and Revisionist Mythmaking." *Signs* 8 (1982): 68–90.

Panzer, Friedrich. *Märchen, Sage und Dichtung*. Munich: Beck, 1905.

Peju, Pierre. *La petite fille dans la forêt des contes*. Paris: R. Laffont, 1981.

Peschel, Dietmar. "Märchenüberlieferung: Fundsachen und Einfälle zur literarischen

Vorlage des Grimmschen Märchens 'Der gläserne Sarg.'" *Germanistik in Erlangen: Hundert Jahre nach der Gründung des Deutschen Seminars.* Ed. Dietmar Peschel. Erlangen: Universitätsbund Erlangen-Nürnberg, 1983.

Petsch, Robert. *Formelhafte Schlüsse im Volksmärchen.* Berlin: Weidmannsche Buchhandlung, 1900.

Peuckert, Will-Erich. *Deutsches Volkstum in Märchen und Sage, Schwank und Rätsel.* 1938; Berlin: de Gruyter, 1984 (microfilm).

———. "Märchen." *Deutsche Philologie im Aufriß.* 3 vols. Ed. Wolfgang Stammler. Berlin: Schmidt, 1957. 3:2677–2726.

Pool, Ithiel de Sola, ed. *Trends in Content Analysis.* Urbana: University of Illinois Press, 1959.

Prandi, Julie. *Spirited Women Heroes.* New York: Peter Lang, 1983.

Prestel, J. *Märchen als Lebensdichtung. Das Werk der Brüder Grimm.* Munich: Max Hueber, 1938.

Propp, Vladimir. *Morphology of the Folktale.* Trans. Laurence Scott. Austin: University of Texas Press, 1968.

———. *Theory and History of Folklore.* Trans. Ariadna Y. Martin and Richard P. Martin. Ed. Anatoly Liberman. Minneapolis: University of Minnesota Press, 1984.

Psaar, Werner and Manfred Klein. *Wer hat Angst vor dem bösen Geiß? Zur Märchendidaktik und Märchenrezeption.* Braunschweig: Westermann, 1976.

Ranke, Kurt. "Betrachtungen zum Wesen und zur Funktion des Märchens." *Studium Generale* 11 (1958): 647–64.

———. "Charaktereigenschaften und -proben." *Enzyklopädie des Märchens,* 2: 1240–48.

———. "Der Einfluß der Grimmschen 'Kinder- und Hausmärchen' auf das volkstümliche deutsche Erzählgut." *Papers of the International Congress of European and Western Ethnology.* Ed. Sigurd Erixon. Stockholm, International Commission on Folk Arts and Folklore, 1951.

———, ed. *Internationaler Kongress der Volkserzählungsforscher in Kiel und Kopenhagen: Vorträge und Referate.* Berlin: de Gruyter, 1961.

———. "Kategorienprobleme der Volkspoesie." *Fabula* 9 (1967): 4–12.

———. *Die Welt der einfachen Formen: Studien zur Motiv-, Wort-, und Quellenkunde.* Berlin/New York: de Gruyter, 1978.

Rebel, Hermann and Peter Taylor. "Hessian Peasant Women, Their Families and the Draft." *Journal of Family History* 6 (1981): 347–78.

Reiher, Ruth. "Die Brüder Grimm in ihrem Verhältnis zur nationalen Tradition." *Wissenschaftliche Zeitschrift der Humboldt-Universität zu Berlin* 5 (1984): 515–17.

Richter, Dieter, ed. *Das politische Kinderbuch: Eine aktuelle historische Dokumentation.* Darmstadt: Luchterhand, 1973.

Richter, Dieter and Jochen Vogt, eds. *Die heimlichen Erzieher: Kinderbücher und politisches Lernen.* Reinbek bei Hamburg: Rowohlt, 1974.

Robertson, Priscilla. *An Experience of Women: Pattern and Change in Nineteenth-Century Europe.* Philadelphia: Temple University Press, 1982.

Röhrich, Lutz. *Erzählungen des späten Mittelalters.* Bern: Francke, 1962.

———. "Märchen und Psychiatrie." *Märchenforschung und Tiefenpsychologie.* Ed. Wilhelm Laiblin. Darmstadt: Wissenschaftliche Buchgesellschaft, 1975.

————. *Märchen und Wirklichkeit: Eine volkskundliche Untersuchung.* 1956; Wiesbaden: Franz Steiner, 1974.

————. *Sage und Märchen: Erzählforschung heute.* Freiburg: Herder, 1976.

Rölleke, Heinz. "Alte Marie." *Enzyklopädie des Märchens* 1:380–82.

————. *Die älteste Märchensammlung der Brüder Grimm.* Cologny-Genève: Fondation Martin Bodmer, 1975.

————. *Kinder- und Hausmärchen: Nach der zweiten vermehrten und verbesserten Auflage von 1819, textkritisch revidiert und mit einer Biographie der Grimmschen Märchen versehen.* 2 vols. Cologne: Diederichs, 1982.

————, ed. *Kinder- und Hausmärchen.* 3 vols. Final Authorized Edition. Stuttgart: Philipp Reclam, 1980.

————. *Die Märchen der Brüder Grimm. Eine Einführung.* Munich: Artemis, 1985.

————. "The 'utterly Hessian' Fairy Tales by 'Old Marie': The End of a Myth about the Earliest Fairy Tale Notes of the Brothers Grimm." Trans. Ruth B. Bottigheimer. *Fairy Tales and Society: Illusion, Allusion and Paradigm.* Philadelphia: University of Pennsylvania Press, 1986.

————. *"Wo das Wünschen noch geholfen hat."* Bonn: Bouvier, 1985.

Rollka, Bodo. "Kinderarbeit, Öffentlichkeit und Gesetzgebung im 19. Jahrhundert in Preußen." *Die gesellschaftliche Wirklichkeit der Kinder in der bildenden Kunst.* Exhibit catalogue. Berlin: Elefanten Press, 1979.

Roloff, Volker. *Reden und Schweigen: Zur Tradition und Gestaltung eines mittelalterlichen Themas in der französischen Literatur.* Munich: W. Fink, 1973.

Rooth, Birgitta. *The Cinderella Cycle.* Lund: Gleerup, 1951.

Rosengren, Karl Erik, ed. *Advances in Content Analysis.* London: Sage, 1981.

Rötzer, Hans-Gerd. *Märchen.* Bamberg: C. C. Büchner, 1981.

Ruberg, Uwe. *Beredtes Schweigen in lehrhafter und erzählender deutscher Literatur des Mittelalters.* Munich: W. Fink, 1978.

Rumpf, Marianne. "Spinnstubenfrauen, Kinderschreckgestalten und Frau Perchta." *Fabula* 17 (1976): 215–42.

————. *Ursprung und Entstehung von Warn- und Schreckmärchen.* FFC 160. Helsinki: Suomalainen Tiedeakatemia, 1955.

Sahr, Michael. "Zur Wirkung von Märchen." *Kinderliteratur und Rezeption.* Ed. Bettina Hurrelmann. Series of the German Academy for Children's Literature. Battmannsweiler: Burgbücherei Wm. Schneider, 1980.

Sale, Roger. *Fairy Tales and After.* Cambridge: Harvard University Press, 1978.

Schenda, Rudolf. *Die Lesestoffe der kleinen Leute: Studien zur populären Literatur im 19. und 20. Jahrhundert.* Munich: C. H. Beck, 1976.

————. "Prinzipien einer sozialgeschichtlichen Einordnung von Volkserzählungen." *Studia Fennica* 20 (1976): 185–91.

————. *Volk ohne Buch: Studien zur Sozialgeschichte der populären Lesestoffe 1779–1910.* Frankfurt: Klostermann, 1970.

Scherf, Walter. *Lexikon der Zaubermärchen.* Stuttgart: Alfred Kröner, 1982.

Schittar, Domenico Carponi, ed. *Cappucetto Rosso ed il "suo" Lupo: Un Proceso a Venezia.* Marghera: Pistellato, 1985.

Schmidt, Kurt. *Die Entwicklung der Grimmschen "Kinder- und Hausmärchen."* Halle: Niemeyer, 1932.

Schoof, Wilhelm. *Zur Entstehungsgeschichte der Grimmschen Märchen.* Hamburg: Hauswedell, 1959.

Schott, Georg. *Weissagung und Erfüllung im deutschen Volksmärchen.* Munich: Deutsche Erzieherakademie, 1936.

Schupp, Volker. "'Wollzeilergesellschaft' und 'Kette': Impulse der frühen Volkskunde und Germanistik." Marburg: Elwert, 1983.

Schwarz, Paul. "Eva: Die neue Eva." *Enzyklopädie des Märchens,* 4:563–69.

Scott, Joan. *Women, Work and Family.* New York: Praeger, 1978.

Scribner, Robert W. "Cosmic Order and Daily Life: Sacred and Secular in Pre-Industrial German Society." *Religion and Society in Early Modern Europe, 1500–1800.* Ed. Kaspar von Greyerz. London: George Allen and Unwin, 1984. 17–32.

———. *For the Sake of Simple Folk.* Cambridge: Cambridge University Press, 1981.

Searle, John. "A Classification of Illocutionary Acts." *Language in Society* 5 (1976): 1–23.

Seitz, Gabriele. *Die Brüder Grimm: Leben, Werk, Zeit.* Munich: Winkler, 1984.

Sexton, Anne, *Transformations.* Boston: Houghton Mifflin, 1971.

Showalter, Elaine. "Towards a Feminist Poetics." *Women Writing about Women.* Ed. Mary Jacobus. New York: Barnes and Noble, 1979.

Siecke, Ernst. "Über die Bedeutung der Grimmschen Märchen für unser Volksthum." *Sammlung wissenschaftlicher Vorträge* 11. Hamburg, 1896.

Siegmund, Wolfdietrich. *Antiker Mythos in unseren Märchen.* Kassel: Erich Röth, 1984.

Smith, Philip M. *Language, the Sexes and Society.* Oxford: Basil Blackwell, 1985.

Snyder, Louis. "Cultural Nationalism: The Grimm Brothers' Fairy Tales." *Roots of German Nationalism:* Bloomington: University of Indiana Press, 1978. 35–54.

Sokolov, Y. M. *Russian Folklore.* New York: Macmillan, 1950.

Sparing, Margarethe Wilma. *The Perception of Reality in the Volksmärchen of Schleswig-Holstein: A Study in Interpersonal Relationships and World View.* New York: University Press of America, 1984.

Spender, C. "Grimm's Fairy Tales." *Contemporary Review* 102 (1912): 673–79.

Spörk, Ingrid. *Studien zu ausgewählten Märchen der Brüder Grimm: Frauenproblematik—Struktur—Rollentheorien—Psychoanalyse—Überlieferung—Rezeption.* Königstein/Taunus: Hain, 1985.

Stedje, Astrid, ed. *Die Brüder Grimm—Erbe und Rezeption.* Stockholmer Germanische Forschungen 32 (1985).

Steig, Reinhold. *Clemens Brentano und die Brüder Grimm.* Stuttgart: Cotta, 1914.

Stone, Kay. "Things Walt Disney Never Told Us." *Journal of American Folklore* 88 (special issue: *Women and Folklore*) (1975): 42–50.

Strutynski, Udo. "The Survival of Indo-European Mythology in Germanic Legendry: Toward an Interdisciplinary Nexus." *Journal of American Folklore* 97 (1984): 42–56.

Sydow, Carl Wilhelm von. "Märchenforschung und Philologie." *Arsbok* (1932): 5–21.

Tal, Uriel. *Christians and Jews in Germany.* Ithaca: Cornell University Press, 1975.

Tatar, Maria. *The Hard Facts of the Grimms' Fairy Tales.* Princeton: Princeton University Press, forthcoming.

Textor, Georg. "Die Ahnen der Märchenfrau." *Heimatbrief* 9 (1965): 4–15.

Thelander, Dorothy R. "Mother Goose and Her Goslings: The France of Louis XIV as Seen through the Fairy Tale." *The Journal of Modern History* 54 (1982): 467–96.

Thiselton-Dyer, T. F. *Folk-Lore of Women*. 1906; Detroit: Singing Tree Press, 1968.

Thompson, Stith. *Motif Index of Folk-Literature*. 1932–36; 6 vols. Bloomington: University of Indiana Press, 1955.

———. *The Folktale*. 1946; Berkeley: University of California Press, 1977.

Thorne, Barrie, Cheris Kramarae, and Nancy Henley, eds. *Language, Gender and Society*. Rowley, Mass.: Newbury House, 1983.

Todorov, Tzvetan. *Einführung in die fantastische Literatur*. Munich: Carl Hanser, 1972.

Travers, P. L. "Grimm's Women." *The New York Times Book Review*. 16 November 1975.

Traxler, Hans. *Die Wahrheit über Hänsel und Gretel: Die Dokumentation des Märchens der Brüder Grimm*. Frankfurt: Bärmeier und Nikel, 1963.

Troll, Max. *Der Märchenunterricht in der Elementarklasse*. Langensalze, 1911.

d'Unrug, Marie-Christine. *Analyse de contenu et acte de parole*. Paris: Editions Universitaires, 1974.

Uther, Hans-Jörg. "Brunnen." *Enzyklopädie des Märchens*, 2:941–50.

———. "Schönheit im Märchen: Zur Ästhetik von Volkserzählungen." *Lares* 8 (1986): 2–12.

Waelti-Walters, Jennifer. *Fairy Tales and the Female Imagination*. Montreal: Eden Press, 1982.

Walker, Barbara. *The Crone: Women of Age, Wisdom and Power*. New York: Harper and Row, 1984.

Ward, Donald. "Baum." *Enzyklopädie des Märchens*, 1:1366–74.

Weber, Eugen. "Fairies and Hard Facts: The Reality of Folktales." *Journal of the History of Ideas* 42 (1981): 93–113.

Weber-Kellermann, Ingeborg. *Die deutsche Familie: Versuch einer Sozialgeschichte*. Frankfurt: Suhrkamp, 1977.

———. *Frauenleben im 19. Jahrhundert: Empire und Romantik, Biedermeier, Gründerzeit*. Munich: Beck, 1983.

———. "Interethnische Gedanken beim Lesen der Grimmschen Märchen." *Acta Ethnographica Academiae Scientiarum Hungaricae* 19 (1970): 425–34.

Wehse, Rainer and Sigrid Früh, eds. *Die Frau im Märchen*. Kassel: Erich Röth, 1985.

Welsford, Enid. *The Fool: His Social and Literary History*. Gloucester, Mass.: P. Smith, 1966.

Wesselski, Albert. *Deutsche Märchen vor Grimm*. Vienna: Rudolf M. Rohrer, 1938.

———. *Märchen des Mittelalters*. Berlin: V. Stubenrauch, 1925.

Woeller, Waltraud. "Der soziale Gehalt und die soziale Funktion der deutschen Volksmärchen." *Wissenschaftliche Zeitschrift der Humboldt-Universität zu Berlin* (Gesellschafts- und Sprachwissenschaftliche Reihe) 11, no. 2 (1962): 281–305.

Zipes, Jack. *Breaking the Magic Spell: Radical Theories of Folk and Fairy Tales*. Austin: University of Texas, 1979.

———. *Fairy Tales and the Art of Subversion: The Classical Genre for Children and the Process of Civilization*. New York: Wildmann, 1983.

———. "Grimms in Farbe, Bild und Ton: Der deutsche Märchenfilm für Kinder im Zeitalter der Kulturindustrie." *Aufbruch zum neuen bundesdeutschen Kinderfilm*. Ed. Wolfgang Schneider. Hardeck: Eulenhof, 1982. 212–24.

Index